Ben Cousins played 270 Austr⋯⋯⋯⋯⋯⋯⋯⋯⋯⋯⋯rom 1996 to 2010. The son of forⱭⱭⱭⱭⱭⱭⱭⱭⱭⱭ Ɑins, Ben grew up in Perth, where hⱭⱭⱭⱭⱭⱭⱭⱭⱭⱭⱭⱭⱭⱭⱭ was captain of the West Coast Eagles from 2001 to 2006. He won the Brownlow Medal in 2005 and played in the Eagles' AFL premiership side in 2006. He was the AFL's Rookie of the Year in 1996 and was selected in the All-Australian team six times. After his off-field problems brought his 238-game West Coast career to an end in 2007, he returned to the AFL in 2009 to play two seasons for the Richmond Tigers. Ben lives in Melbourne.

BEN COUSINS

my life story

MACMILLAN

Pan Macmillan Australia

First published 2010 in Macmillan by Pan Macmillan Australia Pty Limited
1 Market Street, Sydney

Reprinted 2010 (three times), 2011 (four times)

National Library of Australia
Cataloguing-in-Publication data:

Cousins, Ben.

Ben Cousins: my life story / Ben Cousins with Malcolm Knox.

9781405040006 (pbk.)

Cousins, Ben.
Football players–Australia–Biography.
Australian football players–Australia–Biography.
Australian football–Biography.

Knox, Malcolm.

796.336092

Typeset in 12/16 pt Sabon by Midland Typesetters, Australia
Printed by McPherson's Printing Group

Papers used by Pan Macmillan Australia Pty Ltd are natural, recyclable products made
from wood grown in sustainable forests. The manufacturing processes conform to the
environmental regulations of the country of origin.

TO ALL THOSE WHO SUFFER
FROM ADDICTION

*It is my great hope and wish that you receive the
same support from your family, friends and
counsellors/carers that I have*

CONTENTS

Spring 2005

HEAVEN

Once, I walked for a week without my feet touching the ground.

Since I was a kid I'd dreamt of this: grand final week in the Australian Football League. It was the week when I would discover the truth about myself.

In seven of my ten seasons as an AFL player, I'd played in teams that had made the finals, but were knocked out early. Each September I'd watched the grand final teams and wondered what I'd feel in their place. Every moment from Sunday to Saturday, I wondered how I would react. How would I sleep? How would I stop myself thinking about the game every minute of every day? How would I avoid burning myself up with nerves? Grand final week: the total sum of all you've done in your career, everything culminating then and there. It was a big thing to get your head around.

When it finally happened, it went so fast.

On the preceding Friday night the Sydney Swans had qualified for the grand final, beating St Kilda after a lucky escape against Geelong. On the Saturday we had to play Adelaide, who had tipped us out of the minor premiership on percentages and been our bogey team for many of those early finals exits. We held them off by 16 points at home. We'd beaten the bogey, and now it was just us and the Swans. We'd edged them in the first week of the finals. We were confident. This was our year.

The AFL had talked about flying me to Melbourne on the Monday of grand final week for the presentation of the Brownlow Medal, for which I was a favourite. They offered me a private jet, but I said no. I didn't like the look of flying in like some kind of rock star, and didn't want the distraction. This week was all about Saturday, not Monday. There were guys in football who were desperate to win a Brownlow – I wasn't one of them. I'd finished close before, and been a favourite before. When I won it that night, watching on television from Perth, I accepted it, then forgot about it. It was surprisingly easy. I really did believe this week was about Saturday, not Monday: another thing I learnt about myself.

EVERY SEPTEMBER you had ailments. You were drawing deep from your reserves for each game, and you knew there were only so many times you could go back to the well. But in grand final week 2005, my body felt *amazing*. At training in Perth I was running well, without any tendonitis or tightness in my hammies. I wasn't rubbing any sore spots. I said to one of my teammates, 'There's not a chance in the world I'll ever feel as good as I do right now.'

I had a big-game routine, which I followed to the nth degree. I'd learnt it through hard experience. As a kid, especially in a big game like the western derby, West Coast against Fremantle, I'd fallen into the habit of playing the game in my head during the week. If I heard a song on my car radio that got me going, I'd visualise the whole game in the three minutes of that song. I'd be dying to play it right then and there. But I wanted to play it too much. My nerves would go through the game numerous times during the week, and then, by the time the actual game came around, I'd be spent. I rarely played my best in the derby.

Eventually I figured out that I had to use the week to get away from the game: I had to put myself to sleep. The bigger the game coming up, the more I had to forget it. In grand final week 2005, if I heard one of those inspirational songs, I turned it off. I didn't read the papers or watch the news; they'd be all about the footy. No phone calls. I had to stop my adrenaline making me manic. At training, I did some chores to soak up the energy. Concentrate on anything but the game.

Over the years, even what I did after each game was part of my preparation for the next. When a game was over, I'd needed somewhere to escape. The havoc I put myself through ensured that I wouldn't think about game day until Wednesday or Thursday. I only needed thirty minutes to think about a game, not a whole week. I justified my secret double life because of the help I thought it was giving my football.

That lifestyle was the furthest thing from my mind this week. It had been a month since I'd been high on anything other than football. I had made arrangements for after the grand final, but that was still over the horizon; after the grand final, I would be a different person.

WE FLEW to Melbourne on the Thursday, moved into our hotel, and I stuck to my routines. The phone was ringing all week and I didn't pick it up. I didn't read the papers or watch the news or get caught up in footy talk. I didn't listen to music. I shut down in my room, watched *The Sopranos* on DVD and read *Shantaram*, the novel by Gregory David Roberts. I really loved that book. Chris Judd lent it to me. When I was looking for a book, Juddy was always good for a tip. He'd put me on to *The Sopranos* as well. Tools to help me survive.

Even though I was captain of our team, I was thinking it'd be nice to get out of the grand final parade, stay in my hotel room instead. I was getting antsy about keeping a lid on things. If any of our guys were laughing too hard, acting too happy with the situation, saying, 'How good's grand final week!' I'd get snappy. Who wanted to enjoy the week, then play poorly on the day? Not me. I was on constant lookout for things I might regret for the rest of my life. This could be the only time I'd get here. The *only* time. Look at where we'd come from, how long since we'd won anything. I couldn't relax and enjoy it. Not me.

The Friday night, we had our team meeting at the hotel. John Worsfold led it: once my captain, now my coach. The only West Coast captain to win an AFL premiership. Tomorrow I could become the second.

At the team meeting, nothing earth-shattering was said. Worsfold had a quiet businesslike air, reinforcing his usual messages: Be unfazed by external factors. We prepare each game the same way, whether it's 90,000 at the MCG or in Canberra against North Melbourne. Turn up for every game.

We watched some videos with music which the staff had put together to celebrate the things that were important to us, highlights from the season and themes we wanted to pursue against the Swans. As I looked around the room, I was overwhelmed by love for these guys. Juddy, Dean Cox, Adam Hunter, Drew Banfield, who'd been there the last time West Coast won, in 1994. Everyone had their job. David Wirrpanda, who had started at the club with me. My oldest and best mates in football, Michael Gardiner and Daniel Chick. There were so many: every single bloke had a role, and I appreciated every one. I fell in love with the strengths each bloke brought to that side. They came from all walks of life. No matter whether they were eighteen years old or thirty, educated or not, religious or not, city or country, on the next day all of our strengths were going to come together.

I looked at Travis Gaspar. He always came to mind when I was thinking about the character in that group. He didn't play a hell of a lot for the Eagles, because he had stress fractures in his feet and that season had rolled both his ankles badly. But he never whinged once. He took his setbacks like a man, and then some. He set a new bar for a bloke's commitment to getting himself right. For treating ankles, you had to do a forty-minute session, dipping them in hot and cold water. Two minutes hot, one minute cold. I'd do it for forty minutes and that was it. Well, Travis Gaspar did it seven times a day. Seven forty-minute sessions. Five hours dipping your feet in water, day after day.

Even when he was injured, Travis made us stronger. Sometimes if you got dropped, or missed a game with an injury, the temptation was to think how unlucky you were. *Poor me.* But you couldn't do that in front of a bloke like Travis.

In 2005, after yet more setbacks, he'd come into our side for the semifinal and the grand final. We'd win it for him. We'd win it for all of us.

The coaching staff handed us material on the Swans: how they wanted to play, how we wanted to play, who were their key players, what was our focus. As was my habit, I barely gave it a glance.

I'd thought grand final week would change my world, and everything would be new. But Worsfold made clear that we were going to stick to what we always did. It was just another week when my mates and I turned up to play football.

When the meeting was over, I had dinner with the boys but didn't hang around afterwards. I went to my room, watched TV, read *Shantaram* for an hour and a half, and had a couple of sleeping pills. All week, down to the finest detail, I was obsessed with monitoring and totally controlling my mood. Control the anxiety, control the fear. Sleeping tablets were my way of controlling sleep. I loved my sleep, and had no intention of lying awake worrying about whether I could drop off or not.

SATURDAY MORNING, finally! I threw the curtains open on Melbourne: what a beautiful day to play footy. I'd never felt this good for a finals match. How good was this? I couldn't believe it – I'd had eight hours of beautiful sleep. That's not the way it's meant to be, is it? I'd have got by on two hours' sleep!

More control, more routines: I guzzled a litre of water to hydrate myself for the day. I wouldn't need breakfast straight-away after that, so I went for the morning walk-stretch with the team, had a bit of a kick, and we went back to the hotel. Most of the guys had already eaten breakfast. I went to the restaurant and had my normal four Weet-Bix with a sprinkle of Just Right, then a few pieces of toast. Grabbing a couple of bananas, I went back up to my room for a shower: a hot shower, then a cold shower. There's nothing like cold showers in Melbourne. The air rushed into my lungs. I'm alive! I'm awake!

On the bus, I ate two bananas and finally allowed myself to listen to some music. I didn't like tough-guy music, the AC/DC or Prodigy or Metallica that a lot of players got into. It was never my go. Not that I'd necessarily listen to what I liked, either. Instead I'd listen to a love song, picturing going back with the flight of the ball to take a mark. Normally I hate Crowded House, but a couple of songs, like 'Private Universe', soft songs, were what I listened to. The softer songs from the Hunters and Collectors album, *Cut*. Softly.

HEAVEN

Now was when I studied my handout on the Swans, on our tactics. This was when I wanted my focus to tighten.

Then into the rooms, and a massage while listening to the headphones. It was all about controlling each step.

Mood control.

When we ran through the banner onto the MCG, my feet weren't touching the ground. The air felt so filled with electricity my skin was crackling. Ninety-two thousand people, all there for the biggest reason. Among them Mum and Dad, my brother and sisters, my girlfriend, my mates, everyone who was important to me.

In three hours, I would be holding up the AFL premiership cup.

In four hours, I'd be flying.

Only one of those was in my control.

Winter 2008

HELL

My father has been a lot of things to me. As a footballer for the Geelong and Perth clubs, Bryan Cousins was my first hero. He was my role model, and I imitated him in everything from how I ran to how I dressed at school. I'd wear shorts every day of the year, because Dad said that's what he'd done when he was a kid. He was the best coach I had, both one-on-one and in teams. He was my mentor, my confidant and my manager. He was, and still is, my closest mate.

But for a while, I turned him into something else: my victim. He suffered horribly from the things I did, and when I reflect on it now it thumps me in the gut. Remorse? That doesn't even begin to describe it.

There was this night in 2008, in the dead of winter in the worst year of my life. I was a drug addict, publicly disgraced, without a job, and living with my parents in southern Perth. I'd fallen a long way, but I still clung to the convenient belief that the only person I was harming was myself.

Home rehab was a stage in my recovery, but every minute of every day was a battle I lost as often as I won. Even though I was surrounded by people who loved me I felt sick and hunted and angry, and lived in a reality where all my parameters of what was normal would have been unrecognisable to anyone who had not been there themselves. My skin itched. I couldn't sleep. Thoughts chased each other around in my head. I was a wreck.

Although I was mostly clean during home rehab, every minute I thought about drugs. One thought led to a hundred more, and I wasn't strong enough for that. I was totally scattered, lost inside my disorganised mind. I lived in my bedroom, reviewing interviews from a documentary that was being made about me, facing up to the shame of seeing on film what my family thought of me; but there was only one firm anchor for my racing mind, one idea that could keep me on track: where I could get more gear. Just thinking about how I would go about scoring, who I would visit, how I would get there, how much I'd get, and how I'd use it, gave me a merciful distraction from the loneliness, the regret, the anger, and the four walls closing in around me.

Dad, Mum and my sisters Melanie and Sophie were my keepers. They were in tears a lot of the time, seeing me battling this thing that we all knew was ruining me. Through the night, they had a roster of guard duty outside my bedroom door. Two-hour watches, from ten to midnight, midnight to two, two to four, and so on. I was still using, not a lot but just enough – I wasn't ready yet for abstinence. At this stage I was smoking ice and cocaine, whichever I could get. It helped me focus on the small tasks and routines that got me from one hour to the next, and gave me fleeting moments of escape from myself.

It was about three in the morning when I began to obsess about running out of gear. I wasn't quite out yet, but was nearly hysterical at the prospect of not having any to hand. I was that far gone, I didn't need to run out before I started panicking.

Having worked out a plan, I took a shower. Now that I knew where I was going and why, I was all business. I began to get dressed: jeans, a T-shirt and a jumper.

Mum, who was on shift, heard me moving around in my room.

'What are you doing up?'

'Nothing,' I said.

From my earliest childhood, I can only ever remember loving my mum. I thought she was the most beautiful lady in the world, as much an idol, in her way, as Dad was in his. But the thing with Mum was, I'd always been able to work her. Dad says my three siblings and I had Mum well trained. But it wasn't manipulation. We just loved to charm her.

When she saw I was dressed, she got me to sit down and talk with her. I imagined I was drawing on all those lifelong tricks to persuade her to let me go.

'I've got to go, Mum.'

'Where?'

Beyond the odd harmless fib, I don't believe lying had been part of my repertoire in getting my way with Mum in the past. But I was a different person now, a stranger to both of us.

'I've got to go and see Rani,' I said. The widow of one of my best mates, Chris Mainwaring, Rani was close to our whole family. We'd been to hell with her. 'I'm going to help her get the kids ready for school.'

It was three o'clock in the morning. The thing about the lies, in this state, is that you don't know how ridiculous they sound. I really thought Mum would believe anything I said.

Instead, shaky and weepy, she said she was going to get Dad.

'Don't tell him – he's not going to understand,' I burst out. 'I don't want a huge blue over this. I'm going. I've done the right thing, I've told you I'm going, I'm not sneaking out, I've given you a heads-up, so just let me go.'

Mum ran up the stairs and got Dad, who appeared at my bedroom door in tracksuit pants and a singlet. I'd say he was half-asleep, except that Dad was never really sleeping those nights. He looked shocking.

'I'm off,' I said.

Dad shook his head. 'You've come too far to do this.'

'I need to go and get something. Don't ask me to explain. I've been upfront, I'm not just leaving, but I'm telling you that this is what I need to do.'

Dad braced himself across the doorway. As tired and stressed as he was, he still had his fit, compact footballer's body: the body his genes had given me.

'You're not going anywhere.'

We'd had our blues from time to time, but it had never come to this. I was ready to charge him.

'Don't try and stop me,' I said, 'because you know you can't.'

He met my stare. 'I know you're going to get some stuff, I know what you're doing.'

'I just need to get out,' I said, becoming frantic. 'I can't handle this anymore.'

In that moment, something passed over Dad's face. He'd known I was using at home, and while he and Mum didn't condone it – far from it – they took some comfort from at least knowing where I was.

'Okay,' he said. 'If it's that fucken important to you and you're going anyway, I'll drive you. You can get it and bring it back here.'

Dad went out and got into the car. Once I was sitting beside him and we were moving, he noticed the difference in me.

'Now you know you're getting your stuff, you're okay.'

'No,' I lied.

'I can see it. A few minutes ago you were going to belt me, and now you're relaxed.'

I told him the address, in a semi-industrial area in the back of Canning Vale, and said: 'You can't come all the way. If I rock up to these people's place with you in the car they'll pull a gun out. They'll think you're a cop.'

When we were a few blocks short of the place, I told Dad to stop and get out, and I'd take the car the rest of the way.

It was pouring with rain, pitch-black and cold.

'What am I going to do here?' Dad said. 'It's pissing down.'

I didn't see any of this as a problem. I was on my own mission. Dad was a means to the end I was seeking. I told him to wait under a lamppost, and that was where I left him, in the dark, in the rain, in nothing but his trackie daks and a singlet, no phone, not even a pair of shoes.

Memory is an incredible thing. I went to my dealer's, woke him up and got what I wanted, but I only have a hazy recall of that meeting. It was, as with a lot of my drug-using life, a mundane occurrence just like any other. What I have a much clearer vision of is where I wasn't. What I can see is Dad. As the rain got heavier, he found a bus shelter and curled up on the bench. A man came up and asked him if he was all right. Dad said yes, he was okay, he wasn't waiting for a bus. Dad was wondering what he'd do if the cops came past and asked him what he was doing, without shoes or a phone, hanging around a bus stop at this hour. He worried that he'd be recognised, and that more bad headlines and public embarrassment would follow.

He worried that I wouldn't turn up.

I did come back, and Dad got into the car.

'Did you get something?' he said.

HELL

I was still feeling stubborn, not wanting to give an inch. He was only trying to understand me and take the journey with me, but I wasn't ready to let him on board.

'Yeah, not much,' I grunted.

'Is it going to make life any easier?'

I said nothing. I'd left my hero out in the rain, half-dressed, on a winter's night, and all I could think about was what I'd do when I got home.

We stopped at a service station and bought the newspaper as well as a pie and a chocolate milk for me. It was days since I'd eaten. At home, Dad changed into work clothes and started his day, again. And I went to my bedroom and got on.

There have been any number of incidents that brought me public shame. But none of those has any weight compared with my private shame once I came to grips with what I'd done to the people who loved me and whom I loved. The only person I was harming was myself? What a load of crap. That day, I wasn't up to making amends. But it wasn't long before I'd start.

1

NAMES FROM THE BIBLE

When Dad was growing up in the 1960s in Armadale, which was still a rural town south-east of Perth, one of his biggest influences was his gran, Jessie Thatcher. She was an English lady, years ahead of her time, a businesswoman and a member of the boards of hospitals and other institutions. She and her husband had hand-cleared a farm down at Byford, further south, when they'd arrived from England, but when she got older she lived next door to her daughter Jan, who was married to my grandfather Fred Cousins.

Fred Cousins worked seven days, driving a machine at a brickworks during the week and as a powder monkey blasting and splitting shale in a quarry on weekends. Dad used to go and watch him work. It was a rare chance to spend time with his father, because the only day off Fred took all year was Christmas.

It's something I think about a lot: how much harder each generation of our family has worked than the one that followed. Dad's father worked like a Trojan, and Dad would have it easier than him. But Dad's had to work a lot harder than I have, too. It's humbling when you think about it.

Dad was the second of Fred and Jan's four children. A sister came before him, and twins after. They all went to school locally, but Dad was so fond of his gran, Jessie, that after he'd done his chores each afternoon and kicked a football around, he'd go to her place to have a cup of tea. When he had to do his TEE, or school leaving certificate, Dad moved in with his gran so that he could have his own room to sleep and study in. She'd impressed on him the importance of going to church. Dad went to Sunday school and became an altar boy at his gran's insistence. Through their long chats, Dad got it into his head that names in the Bible, from either the Old Testament or the New, were somehow stronger than other names. He liked Benjamin, the youngest brother of Joseph of the coat with many colours. He also liked the gospel according to Luke.

WHILE HE was still at school, Dad stood out as a sporting talent. He played cricket and ran and tried his hand at everything going, but in his late teens it was clear that he had a big future in Australian Rules football. He was not tall, but he was fast and skilful and tough, and he had a big tank.

City clubs spotted him, and as a schoolboy he was playing first grade for the Perth Football Club, based at Lathlain Park, just north of the Swan River. In his last year, he played in the grand final of the West Australian Football League, about as high as you could go as a Perth footballer unless you were taken to the sport's top level, the Victorian Football League in Melbourne.

Being a professional footballer was still no more than a dream in the early 1970s, especially for a kid on the wrong side of the Nullarbor. Dad enrolled in a course to become a physical education teacher at the University of Western Australia. He only lasted a few months. He couldn't sit still, hated studying. To this day he can't sit through a movie, not even in the comfort of his own home, and friends won't invite him out on boat trips because he'd be wanting to dive overboard. Among the many things he'd pass on to me was his low tolerance for being parked at a desk.

But one good thing – the best thing – came out of his stint at teachers' college. He met Stephanie Hales, a fellow student. She had long wavy brown hair, olive skin and the most beautiful smile. I've always thought of her, without any shadow of a doubt, as the most beautiful woman on earth, and I can only imagine what Dad was thinking.

They went out a couple of times, but after that whenever he asked her she said she was busy. He didn't know what he'd done wrong, but he got the message. He dropped out of university, thinking only of football, but he had to do something on weekdays so he re-enrolled in an accountancy course at the WA Institute of Technology. He hated that as much as teachers' college, but to drop out of two courses in one year was unthinkable. He stuck with the accountancy full time for one year, then got a job with an accountant while finishing his degree part-time.

About a year after he'd last gone out with her, he came across Stephanie Hales again and asked her out for a coffee. To his great surprise, she said yes. He didn't know what he'd done right.

Her father, Steve Hales, was well-known as a regional manager for the Commonwealth Development Bank and as a sportsman. He had played first-grade cricket and football in the WAFL, so he and Dad connected over sports. Like Dad, Steve Hales had a hard core of beliefs that he would never compromise. More than any other quality, he valued loyalty: to your friends and to your family. Once you were on Steve Hales's side, he'd make your enemies his enemies. If anyone crossed him or his family, Steve was onto them like a ton of Fred Cousins' bricks.

It wasn't long before the two families merged. Dad's twenty-first birthday party was at his uncle Fred Thatcher's, and when he got up to make his speech Dad said: 'It's a double celebration: Steph and I are going to get married.'

They were young, but there was a reason for taking the plunge: Dad had been invited to Melbourne to play in the big league for Geelong, the Cats, who had made him one of their two young players each VFL club was allowed to sign up per year. The great West Australian Graham 'Polly' Farmer had trodden that same path, and Dad jumped at the opportunity. Stephanie had already agreed to go with him, but they thought it was a good idea to get married first.

Steve and Judy Hales were happy to see their daughter go off interstate with a footballer. It wasn't just that Bryan Cousins impressed them with his honesty and integrity. When he came home with a new car for Steph, the first thing she did was back it out of the driveway with the door still open and rip it right off its hinges. Instead of blowing up at her, as most young blokes would, Dad just shrugged and said it was no big deal, he'd get it fixed. When they saw this side of him, Steph's parents liked him even more.

So they drove off across the country to Geelong in 1975, renting a house in the neighbouring suburb of Belmont. It was their honeymoon; it would last an eventful five years. On 29 June 1978, at the Baxter House maternity home in Geelong, Stephanie went into labour with their first child. He was a big one, and her labour lasted twenty-seven hours. On 30 June, the chubby baby finally made his appearance. When they sat down and talked about names, Dad remembered his gran Jessie, and the strength of those names from the Bible. That's how I came to be called Benjamin Luke Cousins.

2

A CHILDHOOD PARADISE

I always like to have a football in my hands. This may seem obvious, but even in a club of professional footballers blokes often notice my special relationship with the Sherrin. When I go to the football club, I carry one in my bag. When I leave, I've got it. I sit in meetings with it. I run with it. When I do weights, I have a football by my side.

For as long as I can remember, people have made jokes about how I've got my hands on the best footy in the club. At the end of a week's training, when it's been raining and all the footballs are muddy and bruised and cut up, I'm still carrying one in pristine condition, that I've been treating with love and respect and care and tenderness. At the end of every training session, I bring out my treasured footy and have an extra touch.

I wouldn't go so far as to say a football in my hands is a lucky charm, but it does give me a kind of mystical good feeling. Like if I have a footy, I'm safe. And it gives my hands, which tend to fidget or get up to mischief, something to do.

From when I was in the cot, footballs were nearby. Our life was saturated with the game. I was a fat baby, my cheeks so chubby that they pushed my eyes into slits. I was born with a lopsided smirk, which I began deploying to my advantage within weeks. Before I knew anything, people were saying I had a cheeky grin. Dad says I looked like a smirking Sumo wrestler. One of his teammates at Geelong, Mick Turner, would drop over and ask, 'Where's the Incredible Hulk?' Mum wasn't thrilled with the nickname, but beauty's in the eye of the beholder and facts were facts: I was known for my size and appetite. From when I could eat solids, I'd be downing two, four, six milk-soaked Weet-Bix for breakfast.

Mum and Dad left Geelong at the end of 1979. He wasn't sure about leaving at age twenty-six because, after a couple of quiet years to start with, he'd steadily improved there until his last year was his best, in a team boasting Sam Newman, Bruce and Ian Nankervis, John Scarlett, Gary Malarkey, Mick Turner and Terry Bright. After seventy-two VFL games, he was on the crest of a big career in the biggest league in the country, but he and Mum had always intended to return to Perth and in 1979 an opportunity arose. Dad's uncle, Fred Thatcher, had left his farm south of Perth to become a partner in a real estate agency in the city. An opening had come up, and he'd invited Dad to join the firm. The security of a career after football, and a return to the warm weather and family ties in Western Australia, were too much for Mum and Dad to resist.

Back in Perth, they rented a place in Thornlie, then built a house in the new suburb of Leeming. It was a fast-growing planned suburb for young families, full of cul-de-sacs and palm trees and parks and schools. If you could afford something slightly better than the norm, Leeming, just ten minutes south of the city on the Kwinana Freeway, was the type of place you headed for.

The house my parents built in Reilly Court, Leeming was single storey with dark-brown bricks and a tan tiled roof at the top of a cul-de-sac that only had sixteen houses. It had tree ferns and palms in the front yard, a good-sized yard at the back, and a driveway that wound from the carport down to the road.

Leeming was a kind of paradise to grow up in, though it wasn't completely without its dangers. One day when I was about five, my parents found me sitting in the back garden holding a red-back spider. I didn't look fazed by it, but there was a mark on my hand that looked like a bite. Dad rushed me to Fremantle Hospital, about fifteen minutes to the west, where I was given antivenene and put under observation. Knowing I was a very active young bloke, Dad told the staff that I might be a bit of a handful so he didn't mind staying at the hospital to help look after me.

'No, no,' they said, 'he'll be fine. You can go home.'

Dad went home, but in the middle of the night there was a call from the hospital: 'Mr Cousins, would you mind coming down?'

Dad didn't know what mayhem I'd been causing. When he got there I was rampaging around the ward, picking up toys and medical equipment. I wasn't causing trouble, the nurses said, 'but he does need a lot of attention and we don't have the time to look after him'.

There was no doubt I was a jack-in-the-box, so the best thing Mum and Dad could do was give me a playmate. Matthew came along two years after me, and by the time he could walk he was already my partner in crime. For most of our childhood we shared a bedroom, me on the top bunk, him on the bottom, and we had as close and fiery a friendship as any two brothers.

When I look back, I realise what an idyllic childhood I had. There was bush everywhere that we could explore on our own, and every second lot seemed to have a building site with a new house going up. Matthew and I were intrigued by building sites, and loved wandering through the wooden frames, fiddling with the materials and climbing up onto the half-finished roofs. Nowadays kids can't get into building sites, which I reckon is a real shame.

Everything was contained within a short walk; our house felt like the centre of a universe bounded by Karel Avenue to the east, Farrington Road to the south, the Kwinana Freeway to the west and South Street to the north. A few minutes' walk away was Leeming Primary School, a bushy, spread-out campus of low yellow-brick buildings with khaki corrugated-iron roofs. Our school was cut into the bush itself, with banksias, grass trees, burnt-out stumps and gum trees throughout the school grounds. The football field was roughly marked, with rusty goalposts painted red and white. The school's colours were red and blue, our emblem a banksia. I enjoyed primary school, but when the air-raid siren went off to signal the end of the last class, that was when my day really started.

In Reilly Court we arranged street games with the neighbours' kids. We'd play cricket on our drive, and the outfield would be the paved roadway. There were kids everywhere, and it was easy to roust up a few mates for a game. Other kids were always at our house, staying for lunch or dinner, and Mum became one of those mothers who was constantly preparing meals for kids besides her own.

When I was seven, I got a new bike for Christmas. It was my first one with hand-operated brakes, but nobody had told me that. I jumped straight on it and set off down the hill of Reilly Court. I was halfway down when I realised I had no idea how the brakes worked, and my panicky back-pedalling did nothing. I turned the handles and sailed straight over the kerb, onto someone's front lawn, over the handlebars and into a rose bush. Needless to say, if you went to Reilly Court now you'd find the slope isn't all that steep, but at the time it seemed like coming down Mount Everest.

I wasn't alone in my taste for danger. One school holidays, three or four of the neighbours' kids were at our place, and Mum had to duck off to the shops for fifteen minutes. When she came back, her heart leapt into her throat: there was an ambulance backed into our drive with the doors open.

One of my visitors, Damian Cook, happened to be the son of an engineer. Naturally he had a lot of good ideas. That day, the game was to climb a tree and rig a rope in such a way that if one of the other kids pulled it, they'd yank the kid from the fork of the tree up into the air. When one of us landed hard on his arm and broke it, it was Damian, the instigator, which was probably lucky for the rest of us.

Since I had so much energy to burn off, it was only natural that Mum and Dad saw sports as a necessary outlet. I was involved in cricket, Little Athletics and swimming, but football was always my first sporting love. My earliest memories involve kicking a ball with Dad in our front or back yard, learning how to kick with both feet and watching the ball all the way into my hands; Dad would also take us to the Perth Football Club at Lathlain Park, now Eftel Stadium, over the other side of the Swan River, where he was consolidating a top-line career in the WAFL, where he would win a Sandover Medal for best and fairest player in the competition. Sometimes Dad let Matthew and me go with him to training on Sunday mornings, and we'd be out of the car almost before he'd parked it. Blokes would be sitting in the changing rooms taping their ankles and lacing up their boots, amid the smell of Dencorub and the sounds of metal studs clicking on the floor. This was soon our natural habitat, and Matthew and I would be making conversation, picking our way among the gear, or finding footballs to take off with and kick around. The smell of the liniment, the men's talk, the importance of the game, the tight tension before a match and the exhaustion afterwards, these giants slumped against the wall with barely enough energy to peel their socks and boots off – all of it intoxicated us. We were privileged to be a part of it.

We didn't leave our cheek at home. One Sunday morning Dad and the Perth team were standing on the oval listening to their coach, when gradually the players' attention wandered to something up high. Dad was one of the last to look, but when he did his eyes nearly popped out of his head. There were Matthew and me, walking along the roof of the grandstand, risking life and limb, laughing away like it was a stroll in the park.

Looking back, I feel a little sorry for what Dad had to put up with. When we were seven or eight, we were badgering him to take us to World Championship Wrestling, which was big on TV at the time. Dad had no interest in it, so we set out to find another victim. Before long, a great big woolly-haired footballer called Mick 'Stinger' Ray went up to Dad and said, 'Bryan, since you won't take them, what about I take the boys to the wrestling?' Dad just looked at us as if to say, 'You're a pair of schemers, but if you can get away with it, good luck to you.' I reckon Stinger was the one who really wanted to go; he just needed us as an excuse.

By six, I was in a junior footy program, and by eight was playing for the local club, Bullcreek Leeming, at Beasley Park, about a five-minute walk from our house. We had an access path between us and the next house to make the walk quicker. Beasley Park was a typical southern Perth suburban ground, broad and open and ringed by eucalypts. The surface was well-grassed but hard, with half-size goalposts and floodlights for night practice. Down the north-west corner was a little scoreboard, and along the side was a flat red-brick dressing shed with seating for spectators. We were obsessive about the game. Matthew was not quite as mischievous or as much of a risk-taker as I was, but he had a bit of dash. He was strong, fit and athletic, and a really talented sportsman. He was more mellow than me, but he was one of those guys who, when pushed to his breaking point, would go so wild he was frightening. Being the type of kid I was, I loved pushing him, of course – but when he snapped, I'd back right off. There was one teenage fight when we both pulled out knives. We had no intention of using them – at least, I don't think we did! – but poor little Sophie, our youngest sister, wandered in and saw us waving the blades at each other. Terrified, she burst into tears and screamed off to tell Mum.

A typical Saturday for Matthew and me was to play junior footy for Bullcreek Leeming in the morning – our club colours were navy blue with a light-blue sash – then go and watch Dad play in the afternoon. Mum, being the most supportive sporting mother imaginable, would watch us and Dad equally avidly (and later, she'd watch every netball game our sisters played). At Dad's games, Matthew and I would stand behind the goalposts waiting for the footy. It was pretty brutal, with kids from six to eighteen years of age in open competition. There was always a dust-up as everyone went for the ball, and you had to learn the pecking order pretty smartly.

Mum gave us a long leash. When I was five, our sister Melanie was born, and Sophie came when I was eleven, so Mum had her hands full. But it was also her nature to let things slide. I reckon that's a beautiful attribute in a mother, but as a kid all it meant to me was: here's an opening. Put simply, Mum could see no bad in us, and our response was to make the most of her leniency. When a cheeky smart-arse like me sees that kind of leeway, he takes advantage of it. If I wanted a sick day off school, I could always con Mum into letting me take it. I was a little shit sometimes, and looking back I know that Mum deserved more respect. But part of being a little shit was being unable to see that.

It was different with Dad. From time to time when we got up to no good Mum would threaten to tell Dad when he got home, but we knew she wouldn't, because with Dad there were real consequences. He's one of those men who, the bigger the problem, the more calm he gets. In the crises in our lives, Dad has been as steady as a rock. But over small things, he can absolutely crack the shits. So when Melanie was once picked up by the cops the worse for drink, Dad was brilliant, only to go spare at her for something really small a week later. When I've been in trouble, he's been all cool authority; I've looked at him and thought, gratefully, he's a bigger man than anyone on this earth. But when, say, Matthew and I forgot to put out the rubbish bins, he'd get so mad he wouldn't speak to us for a fortnight.

I can remember some other examples. At one point, he came to notice the number of unreturned tapes we had from the local video store in our living room. Dad came home and gave us his routine:

'How do you reckon the video guy makes his money?'

Lying around in front of the TV – for some reason I always lay on my stomach, with a pillow or cushion on my backside – we looked up at him like he was thick and said, 'Rents out videos?'

We'd taken the bait. 'Right,' Dad said. 'And how do you reckon he can rent out these videos that you lot haven't returned for the last month?'

He got us back one night when, before he left work, we asked him if he could pick up a tape for us. When he got to the video store and picked out the tape, the bloke at the counter said: 'That'll be seventy-six dollars, thanks.'

Dad said: 'What?!'

'Four dollars for the tape rental and seventy-two dollars in late fees.'

Even as we'd asked him to get the tape, we'd known we were in trouble, so we made ourselves scarce when he got home. He finally rounded us up and told us that he'd got our video, but cancelled our membership and put us on the black list.

Another time he cracked it at us was one Sunday in the footy season. I can't remember what year it was, but we'd been in the car with Dad listening to the highlights on the radio from the previous day's games, and they said Gary Ablett had taken one of the marks of the century, against Essendon I think. Because Dad had played for them, Geelong was the VFL club we followed, and Ablett, aka God, was our hero. We rushed home to watch it on TV, and sure enough, Ablett had taken this screamer, made all the better because it had been a wet and boggy day in Melbourne.

It happened to be wet in Leeming too. We had a nice front lawn that Dad looked after well, but the next day someone got the idea that we could turn it into Kardinia Park and do the Ablett mark. We ran the hose onto the lawn for hours, until it was totally under water. You could have gone fishing on it. Then we rounded up six or eight kids from the neighbourhood, put goals at each end, and re-enacted the mark over and over. In the process, we turned Dad's pride and joy into an absolute bog, destroying it almost beyond repair. As this was only a small matter, nothing as bad as we got up to at other times, Dad totally lost it. We were beneath contempt, not even worth wasting his breath on for the next week.

CONVERSATIONS AROUND the dinner table often revolved around football. Mum must have been a bit of a frustrated gourmet chef, because she has since shown how adventurous she can be in her cooking, but back then Dad insisted on the basic meat and three veg. My tastes were pretty basic too. I was up to nine Weet-Bix for breakfast, and would take six or seven green apples to school. I was addicted to those foods and couldn't get enough of them. I might be wrong, but I don't reckon the Granny Smith apples they have today are anywhere near as green and shiny and tasty as they were then.

As we'd shovel in the food, we'd discuss our own games or Geelong's latest. Most West Australian kids would have a passing interest in the WAFL, but Victoria was where the real action was and Geelong were turning into one of the top VFL sides, studded with personalities such as Ablett, big blond Billy Brownless, the mulleted Gary 'Buddha' Hocking, Barry Stoneham and Mark Bairstow. My first jersey was a Cats one, with Ablett's number 5. He was also leaping in the biggest poster on my bedroom wall. When I was eleven, in 1989, they played an epic grand final against Hawthorn, who were premiers several times that decade. It was Geelong's first grand final appearance since 1960. Ablett kicked nine goals and won the Norm Smith Medal for the best on ground, but the Cats went down by a kick. Ablett threw his runners-up medal away. Dad remained staunchly loyal to his old club, and we were fanatical, shoulder to shoulder with him as they suffered the first of a string of September disappointments.

But we could still admire opponents. When Dermott Brereton got flattened by Mark Yeates at the opening bounce, Dad said, 'Now we'll see what Brereton's made of.' We were hoping he'd mince off to the bench, but instead he went forward, broken ribs and all, and kicked a bunch of goals. You had to respect that, even if you hated the end result.

Even while he was still playing for Perth, Dad got involved with the coaching of some of our sides at Bullcreek Leeming. Like Mum with her cooking and caring, Dad was more than a parent or a coach, he was a kind of tribal elder. He knew how to build a rapport, usually through football, with some of the toughest kids in the area. These were the kids who weren't loved by their teachers, but Dad would get them coming to training and wanting to work hard. They loved him, and if you have a beer with those guys now, they'll all speak fondly of those times and my old man.

From age ten, when people had first noticed that I was among the more talented kids in my age group, I'd been promoted to compete with boys a year older. I took my footy as seriously as any professional, and to play with these older blokes felt like a great honour as well as a challenge. One was Brett McDowell, who lived across the street. He had conservative parents and was a bit of an introvert, but he was a very good athlete and footballer, as we could see from games in the street. The problem was, his parents wouldn't let him play for the club. Dad went to work on them, and eventually persuaded them to let Brett play for our side, the Sharks. He was great, and we finished among the top sides that year. Acquiring Brett was seen, in our league, as a big-name signing that Dad had engineered.

Another of my mates in that group was Dan Hopkins, a tall guy who was a year older than me. At one point Dan got alopecia, a condition that caused his hair to fall out. Mum and Dad had put in a swimming pool at our place, which was extra-special because it had a waterfall and you could jump into the pool off the rocks. Dan was over, jumping into the pool, and his hair was falling out in clumps. It wasn't long before he lost all of it, and was looking like Peter Garrett, or the hard Carlton backman Mil Hanna. If you didn't know Dan you'd have sworn he was very dangerous; he was a rugged footy player, but also a top kid.

One of the tougher older boys I became good mates with was Rick Mulligan. He was up to more mischief than anyone, always getting into fights, and he became a sort of protector for me. He was a big guy, a strong footballer despite his pronounced pigeon toes, and the first to have a goatee and long hair. He was tough as nails and needed to be, as he copped heaps from older kids who were always after him for something or other. There were some real brutes among them, and if I had them after me I'd be shitting my pants. But Rick would just take it in his stride.

It was with Rick that I first got into a bit of shoplifting. For me it was less about stealing things than being initiated into the world of older, tougher boys. Rick was ahead of me, but I was soon catching up. We'd go to Myer and cruise around in rolled-up overalls, into which we'd stuff a Jag belt or some piece of trash. It wasn't about taking anything big. It was the adrenaline rush. I was finding that there was something in that rush that I wanted to go back for. Dad didn't know what I was getting up to, but he had an idea. He was fond of the rougher kids, but not to the point where he wanted me to become one of them. He took me aside at one point and said, 'Mate, you want to be careful who you're knocking around with.' He wouldn't stop me, he said, but he was warning me.

I got prickly and defensive. In all the movies I liked, there was a common theme: stand up for your mates when your loyalty's tested. Have a bit of dash by sticking up for them when the authorities want to break you up.

'All I'm saying is that if you don't apply yourself in school,' Dad said, 'you and your mates will end up on the bones of your arse.'

As well as loyalty, what was gluing me to those blokes was that they were where the fun was. It was slightly skewed, my social life, and I think it played havoc with the way I grew up. I had a group of school friends, but my 'real' friends were older and cooler than me, tougher, bigger risk-takers, and I was dying to do what they were doing. I played footy with them, and they were my crew. Eventually it kind of pulled me apart; I wasn't quite part of my school year, but I wasn't quite part of the older group either. Growing up with these divided loyalties, not really fitting in, was something I'd come to regret.

I made a pact with myself: I'd do what Dad said, and put my head down in school, but as a trade-off, I'd also do what I wanted, which was to hang out with those blokes. It was the first of a series of similar trade-offs, little deals with the devil. As the years went by, they'd become a lot less innocent.

3

TWO LIVES AT ONCE

Mum and Dad were a very harmonious couple, but if I've given the impression that this was because Mum gave ground on every contested point, that would be wrong. For example, she was adamant that us four kids would go to private secondary schools. Dad knew what a killer four sets of school fees could be, so he joked that he might be able to get us into the school at Armadale, the tough area where he'd grown up. Mum was having none of it, though, and as Dad saw the family in a traditional light – Mum had finished her career as a teacher around the time I was born – it meant he had to work his ring off.

At the time, I think I took for granted how hard the old man had to work for us. We had no scholarships, so it was full freight as far as the fees were concerned. I didn't necessarily make the connection between the horrendously long hours he worked and me going to a private school. But that's the way of childhood, I guess. To me, everything was going my way, so much so that I ended up taking a lot of my family's sacrifices for granted.

The school they chose for me and Matthew was Wesley College, in South Perth. Ten minutes up the freeway, on the bank of the Swan, Wesley was in a more affluent area than Leeming. I talked Mum into driving me there in her Tarago rather than leaving me to catch the train. We approached through tree-lined avenues of mansions and Perth institutions such as the zoo and the Royal Perth Golf Club. I'd believed Leeming was paradise on earth, but this was a different world.

My first day, I was a bit overwhelmed by the beautiful gabled old buildings, red brick with whitewash around the edges of the windows, and the lush fields for hockey, cricket and football. Each of the fields was manicured and bordered by a painted green fence. The perimeters of the school were hand-cut sandstone. After Leeming Primary, it was physically huge and impressively rich.

I was starting in year seven, which was the last year of prep school. I hadn't been too keen on staying at Leeming Primary for year seven, because my footy mates had gone on to high school. I was desperate to be a year older than I was. My entire focus was footy, so I framed every personal challenge as a football challenge: you have to keep working, push yourself beyond your limits, never rest on your laurels or believe you are as talented as people are telling you. I was obsessed, never satisfied with anything I'd achieved, and hyper-focused. So much of my childhood was normal, yet this drive came from somewhere else, was far from typical, and separated me from the kids whose maturity was at the same level as mine. Without knowing it, I was suffering a bit of a crisis.

That first day at Wesley, I was so overcome by nerves and the atmosphere that I started feeling ill. It was something like homesickness: I just wanted to go back to Reilly Court. I considered myself a tough kid, but the emotions started to well up; as well as feeling frightened, I was ashamed of my fear.

I reacted in what was becoming the usual way: I tried to hide it. I knew a couple of other blokes there, including Dan Hopkins and a guy called Aaron Hewitt who I'd been introduced to through family friends. Aaron would end up being my best mate through secondary school. I told him I was crook and had to go to the sick bay. He helped me find it, and I lay down, knowing I was not really sick, but unable to go to class. It must have been pretty obvious that I was only trying to save face, but Aaron, being a good mate, didn't say anything about it.

I was setting a pattern that would limit my school years. Whenever something came up that didn't fit in with my tough guy self-image, I'd avoid it. I could have done drama or dance or played a musical instrument, but did none of them, which was stupid. I regret not having the courage to stand up and do what I wanted, or try something new, but that's the way it was for us kids: image was everything.

There was something about school uniforms that triggered my rebellious streak. I just had to tamper with them in some way. If you asked anyone about my image at Leeming Primary, I reckon the first thing they'd say is that I was the bloke who wore footy shorts every day. Every day of the year – rain, hail or shine. Always shorts. Tight footy shorts, too, Aussie Rules shorts. It was ridiculous, but Dad had told me that when he was at school in Armadale he and a couple of mates had dared each other to wear shorts every day of the year. As with a lot of things involving the old man, once I heard this story, all I wanted to do was imitate him.

At Wesley, even I knew I couldn't go that far. It was strictly tie, jacket and the correct pants, long in winter, short in summer. Our colours were yellow and black. Failure to wear the correct uniform wouldn't endear me to some of the teachers at Wesley, which was a very proper, conservative old school, but I had to do something. I also had a bit of charm, and worked out which teachers I could win over and which ones I had to steer clear of. So I became known for wearing sneakers everywhere, like I was ready to run. Definitely not standard-issue black leather shoes for me. I guess it wasn't that important in itself, but I needed another boundary to test. I did it essentially because they were comfortable, and because nobody else seemed to be able to get away with it.

The reason I was allowed such liberties was, ultimately, football. I didn't think of myself as a gun player, because at Bullcreek Leeming I'd been in teams with guys a year older than me. There were parents who'd praise me, but Dad was the only one I really listened to, and his response to even my best games was to gently suggest some area in which I could improve. He didn't berate or belittle me – he wasn't that kind of footy father – but he saw that what I needed was someone to analyse my play and keep me grounded, not just join the cheer squad. I was far from the best player in the Bullcreek Sharks, and in our matches against our arch-rivals, the Bullcreek Leeming Bombers and the Karoonda team, I wasn't able to dominate by any means. We were in the strongest zone and I was playing a year up. I played well, but it was cut-throat. I felt I was only just making the grade, always thinking I was on the verge of being left out. It's frightening how much talent there was in the club, not just in my year but in others too. Simon Black was in the club, a year younger than me, and the Carr brothers, Josh and Matt, were Bullcreek boys, also a year younger. Jonathan Hay, who'd be an All-Australian at the Hawthorn club, was there, and I can think of a whole lot of blokes who had the potential to play AFL but for various reasons didn't.

It was a good environment to be in, not having things all on my own terms. I became so competitive because I had to be. Did

I have a nemesis during those years? There were too many to count! I took all my rivalries very seriously, I'm sure more seriously than my rivals took me.

Later, in the AFL, I'd come across young blokes who had been stars from the year dot, and they struggled to adapt to the inevitable adversity, whereas I'd learnt early on that there were a lot of bigger, harder, nastier and better players on the field than me. Observers may have seen me as a star, but in my own eyes I was an underdog, fighting to keep up.

I also had to fight a less obvious handicap, which was that I'd been diagnosed with asthma. I can't remember when it started, but sometimes after heavy exercise I got short of breath and wheezy, feeling like my lungs were closing up. It was quite distressing, though it never got so bad that I had to go to hospital. I was given a Ventolin spray to inhale whenever I felt it coming on, and that nipped it in the bud. Soon my Ventolin would be as essential as boots and a mouthguard in my footy kit; I never went to a match without it. When I was told that Paul Kelly, the Swans' famous super-fit workhorse, was asthmatic too, it was kind of inspiring. I don't want to overplay the issue; I never saw my asthma as a serious impediment. What strikes me more, looking back, is how very early in my football career I became habituated to medication, to the idea that whatever was wrong with me I could fix with chemicals.

While I was at Wesley, I continued to play for Bullcreek Leeming. I'd often play two or even three games a week, for the Bullcreek Sharks and for Wesley on weekends, and sometimes for rep teams midweek. At Wesley, playing with my own year group, I was standing out. As a kid, I kicked the footy better than I did at my peak as an adult in the AFL. Because I had the footy in hands all day, was constantly playing with it, I had good timing. I could kick it further than kids my age. We'd play school carnivals and I'd kick thirty goals in a day. I wasn't super-quick, but could read the play and get to where the ball was going. It would surprise anyone who saw my later years in the AFL, but as a kid I could kick goals from anywhere. Still, I never allowed myself to grow complacent and base my game on talent alone. I learnt early that serious footballers founded their careers on the thing they could control: their run. If you trained hard enough, you didn't need to rely on the ball bouncing your way. You could make yourself fitter than the next guy, you could train yourself to run harder right through the course of a game. In my pre-seasons, even at thirteen and fourteen, I'd go running at six in the morning, no matter how desperately I wanted to stay in bed. Even if it was raining and I wasn't in the mood, I never let myself off the hook. I developed a real masochistic streak. The fact that I was not a morning person – I've always loved my sleep – only made it more imperative that I get myself up for these sessions. Not only that, but the runs I did were far from easy. I'd flog myself. If I had anything left at the end, I'd finish with a hard sprint, just to make sure I'd worked myself to the limit.

I bought a yard clicker, to measure distance. On empty ovals I did solo skills and sprints work, even in the height of summer. There were blokes who were natural runners, who got up and went for a 10-kilometre jog without thinking about it. I was defi-nitely not one of them. For me, every time was hard, but I had this internal voice barking at me that the harder it was, the better. The more I hated it, the more I loved it, if that makes any sense: I loved it because I could use it as fuel later, when I was against an opponent on the football field, when I could think of how I'd punished myself to run harder than him, and how he had not suffered the same way. I built up my football self-esteem through suffering. 'Professional' before I was earning a cent, my obsessive approach to fitness was fundamental to my later success, but also a warning sign that I was incapable of seeing.

*

MY FIRST teacher at Wesley was Andrew Beloti. Once his students had assembled in his class on the first day of the school year, Andrew introduced himself to his new class and promptly told us we were the luckiest students in the school. Why? Because we had him as our teacher. He then went on and told us all about himself, his family, how much he loved his mum and dad and so on. I remember thinking: *This bloke's a bit strange.* Then he said we had to get up – one by one – and not only introduce ourselves, but also tell the rest of the class about ourselves. It was a bit of a shock to the system but, looking back now, it was a great way to start. By morning recess, I knew a little bit about everyone in the class.

Andrew is the most enthusiastic and positive teacher I have ever known. While sport was very much his passion, he showed great interest in and passion for whatever any of his students were doing. If it were art, music, debating or whatever, I am sure each of Andrew's students felt that he enjoyed what they were doing as much as they did.

The most important Wesley teacher for me was my year eight football coach and phys ed teacher, Glenn Stewart. He ended up being fitness coordinator at the West Coast Eagles for my entire time there, and has remained one of my biggest influences. I have to admit that I didn't really like him in class. I found him to be a bit of a wanker. He had no warmth and was probably over dealing with kids. But I saw him as a bloke I could learn from. He had this incredible knowledge of the science of physical training. When I was fifteen or sixteen, he wrote me out the equivalent of an AFL weights program, and allowed me into the gym during applied art classes. Applied art was an optional class, and I'd just walk out. The teacher, Mr Yakinthou, didn't really care when I played him like this, although I was a tiny bit scared of him. He spoke in broken English and was a karate instructor; a couple of times he'd give me this stare and I'd be shitting myself as I got out the door.

I'd complain about some teachers to Dad, and he translated his response into the language I best understood: footballese.

'Are you only going to play well for coaches you like? It doesn't matter if he's right or wrong. He's the coach!'

Dad knew how to get the message through. I did only study hard for teachers of classes I needed for my TEE, and tried not to take the disciplining from the others too personally.

So instead of applied art, I'd take a fitness run along the Swan or go to Wesley's beautiful gym to do a weights session. Blokes would see me cruising around during classes and some teachers were understandably hard on me. We had a few clashes. I'd come home saying how unfairly I was being treated, but Dad would just sit me down and say:

'Life isn't always fair, mate, you won't always get a fair deal. From what you're telling me, these teachers are giving you a hard time. I could probably go down and ask them to leave my son alone. But you're going to cop that all your life. You'll have footy coaches who won't pick you or will play you out of position. It happens all the time, and their parents come down and question the coach: "Why isn't my son getting a game? Why isn't he playing on the ball?" It may be what the parent wants to do, but it's not the best thing for the kid. So I'm not going to speak to those teachers. You're going to have to deal with it yourself.' I remember that vividly.

IN THE under-13s and under-15s, the Sharks won the local comp. Dad stepped aside from coaching us, and we had Gary Gibillini, another tough nut from the WAFL. Playing for East Fremantle, Gibber used to love belting Dad, but they had a lot of values in common. Dad talked Gibber into coaching us, and became our runner.

Gibber was the perfect bloke to instil a bit of hardness and discipline. He gave us some old-fashioned sprays. He could rev you up but he also knew how to play the game. You don't often find coaches like that, who are not only footy blokes but community mentors. What they instilled above all was the importance of competing as a team unit. It was impossible under Gibber to come off the ground feeling happy with your own game when the team hadn't done well. But the flipside was, if the team had got up and won, it didn't matter how many mistakes you'd made personally: if the team had played well, it had been a good day.

Our biggest rivals were Kurunda, coached by Greg Bennett, a former teammate of Dad's who had won a SAFL premiership under Neil Kerley in Adelaide. You can imagine how competitive those two were, and Kurunda had a very good side, led by a terrific player who would become a good mate of mine, a blond surfer named Blair Taylor. In the under-13s, -14s and -15s, Kurunda were undefeated in the home and away seasons. But Dad and Gibber said that going undefeated all year is the worst recipe going into a finals series. Kurunda had no experience of being ambushed. In the under-13s and -15s, that was how we won premierships – in the finals we moved some players around and tried other surprise tactics – and it shitted the Kurunda blokes no end.

As Dad said, you could tell your own kids something a thousand times, but they wouldn't listen until they were told by Gibber. One example was a pre-match spray he gave us after seeing some kids in another team smoking dope.

He went off his head. 'If I ever catch one of you kids smoking dope, I'll kick you in the arse!' He went on for ages. Simon Black's brother Ben was in the team, and Ben's dad Ray went up to Dad later and said, 'I've told Ben that twenty-five times and it never made a dent, but Gibber saying it, that was magnificent.'

When Gibber gave us this lecture, I kept my head down. I wasn't much of a dope smoker, but by the time I was thirteen I was already living a double life.

I'd be at Wesley during the week, but on weekends I was one of the knockabouts, in flannelette shirts, black jeans and Doc Martens, carrying on like a bunch of cut-price hoons at the Leeming rec centre.

The rec centre was a giant cement hangar at the edge of the Leeming shopping centre. Inside it had basketball and squash courts, indoor cricket pitches, gym equipment and a café. Outside was a car park full of paperbark trees, a big oval, a graffitied skateboard park, cricket nets, a long-jump pit and eight tennis courts. The local high school was right next door. It was where all the hoods had their cars, these guys five years older than us doing burnouts and getting into blues, setting fires and tagging walls with their spray cans.

Rick Mulligan was at the forefront of everything. It was a complex kind of friendship, because although in some ways I looked up to him, because of his age and experience, in other ways I felt sorry for him. He was a regular target for beatings from older blokes, being a bit different, and it sometimes seemed that he needed a mate. Everyone around there had a self-destructive side, but Rick was mad. Mad on motorbikes. Mad on fighting. Mad on drinking piss and annihilating himself. Rick loved explosives, and knew how to weld, so he could make stuff. When it was hot he wouldn't wear long sleeves or long pants, so after he'd been welding for a while he'd emerge with these huge burns. I'd say, 'I know it's hot, Rick, but look at you.' He had calluses and busted knuckles and all the marks of manhood that I coveted and admired.

It was at the rec centre that blokes hung out with the local girls. Being younger than my mates, I was very much an apprentice in all this. There was a girl called Katie Priest. I thought she and her sister Christie were amazing; they were my ideals. Only problem was, Katie was a year older than me and Christie three or four years older: they were way out of my league, and I was just dreaming. They were cousins of Blair Taylor, who was also a year older than me. If girls like that knew of me at all, it was as some squirt tagging along with the older boys.

The Priest sisters were the benchmarks, so if Dan Hopkins or Rick Mulligan had been down at the rec centre and seen a new girl around, they'd say, 'She's better than Katie Priest,' or 'She's up there with Christie Priest.' I'd nod along as if I was part of it all. But I wasn't. I was just a wannabe.

I remember Katie having a party, inviting Blair Taylor and all his mob, my sworn football opponents. Christie was orchestrating things, trying to get things moving for boys and girls who liked each other. Somehow I found myself down the back of the rec centre tennis courts with a girl. Christie was standing there saying to her, 'Do you want to kiss him or not?' I have a vivid memory of this girl – and other girls too – shaking their heads and saying no. I would have kissed just about anyone, I was that desperate to get involved. Being rejected by one girl after the other only made me burn all the more to hurry, to catch up with what everyone else was doing.

Although my parents were worried that the rec centre scene would lead me astray, the true situation was a bit different. In my early teens I was under no peer pressure to drink alcohol or smoke pot. My older mates knew me as the young kid in the footy side; they knew how dead-serious I was about my football, and saw the work I put in, so they took care, if anything, to keep drink and drugs away from me. The leaders of that group – Rick Mulligan, Michael 'Spud' Spitalis and Dan Hopkins – gave me a bit of leeway. I could have been picked on and excluded, or teased until I joined in. I knew when they were drinking or smoking pot, and it ate me up, but I wasn't involved. I can't remember much about the first time I smoked pot, but it was a one-off. It would have been with Rick and

Spud and a bloke called Bogger. I didn't particularly like it. It was never my drug. Years later, I would grow to like smoking pot at the end of a bender, but that was during a period when I went as close as I ever went to totally losing my mind. Now, if I even smell marijuana, it makes me feel funny in the head. Other drugs I could plough through for days, but I never really liked pot.

I do remember the first time I drank alcohol. I was in year eight. I did it with Brett McDowell, from Reilly Court, and Peter Waite, a top cricketer who'd come from North Narrabeen in Sydney and was a good mate of mine. They'd both been pissed before, and I was revved up from hearing their stories. One weekend we got an older guy to buy us a bottle of Southern Comfort and a two-litre cask of cheap wine. There was a Moscow circus or something in the city, on the other side of the river, and we had some kind of plan to go and see it. We started drinking at Peter's place in South Perth. Then we set off walking towards the city with the intent of going to the circus. We opened the bottle of Southern Comfort. None of us knew what we were doing. We were passing it around, no-one wanting to miss out, and we went through it in about two minutes. Then we got on the goon. Within a very short time the three of us were lying unconscious on the river bank. Eventually we woke up feeling so crook that we never wanted to touch alcohol again. (This was another first: that total abhorrence of what you've done, which in a miraculously short period flips over into a desire to go back and do it again. I would become well acquainted with that cycle.)

Brett, a bit older and heavier, was the first to come good. The circus long forgotten, we had to get back to Peter's house. He was the only one who knew the way back, but it was a few kilometres away – a marathon when you're thirteen and blind drunk. Peter was walking along with his eyes shut. Every now and then we'd come to a corner and say, 'Pete, where are we?' He'd open his eyes, point left or right or straight, then shut them again and keep walking.

Eventually we crashed at his place. The next morning at seven-thirty, his old man made the biggest plate of bacon and eggs you've ever seen. As a hangover cure it sounds good, but we were still too crook to think about eating. I remember sitting there, green around the gills, looking at this food and thinking, 'This is totally beyond us.' Peter's old man must have known, but nothing was said.

4

MY SANCTUARY

Until my middle years at Wesley, I was still playing sports other than football. Dad encouraged us to have a go at anything – Matthew played water polo and hockey at school, and I played tennis – but in summer it was all about cricket. Wesley was renowned for its cricket. Ben Holioake, who would play international cricket for England before dying in a car accident, was a close mate of mine, and we had some others who represented the state. I was not destined to be one of them. Cricket only brought out my trouble-making side.

While I loved mucking around with a bat and ball in street games, my hyperactive personality wasn't a good fit for organised cricket. In years eight and nine, I played cricket for Wesley and am still dirty about the hours I spent waiting to bat and bowl. I was an enthusiastic fast bowler: I could come off a long run-up and fling it down reasonably quick. But all I wanted to do was bat, for which I had little talent and absolutely the wrong temperament.

At nets practice, I was all bravado but no bravery. I hated facing fast bowling that was aimed at my body. My so-called mates would steam in and hurl bumpers from 16 yards, pissing themselves as I'd jump around trying not to get hit.

In a typical school match I'd have a bowl, then hang around in the sun fielding, waiting for another go, growing bored as the game dragged on. I'd wander from position to position, talking to everyone else. It usually took me about an over of this before I'd start scheming about how I could get someone else to come on and substitute for me while I went off to get a milkshake or fish and chips. Then, when it was our turn to bat, I'd be down at number seven or eight and dying to get out there. I'd pace around talking and pestering the others, becoming more and more wound-up as the wickets fell. When it was finally my turn, I'd be so excited that I'd go for a huge slog and get out cheaply. I'd come off the field and throw my bat on the ground and rant and rave about how I'd never play this stupid game again.

In year ten I wasn't good enough to play in the firsts. I was in the seconds until I got dropped for sending the twelfth man in to field while I went off to take a swim in the school pool. It was hot, wasn't it? But I probably shouldn't have left the game for three hours.

They made me captain of the thirds, who had this bloke Nathan Thompson, a fanatical cricketer if not overly blessed with coordination. Nathan had never made a half-century in his life, but that day he dug in. While he was batting on and on, I was going out of my brain. He was batting so long it looked like I wasn't going to get a turn. So when he got to forty-eight, I declared. What an ordinary thing to do. I thought it was funny at the time, but I'll never forget the distraught look on his face when he came in. Years later, I'd see him in Perth, where he worked in the city, and we'd stop and have a yarn. I never got to explain to him that I only did what I did because I hated cricket so much, it was nothing personal. Luckily, he didn't hold a grudge. It was better than I deserved.

In the end I quit cricket. I played a bit of tennis and still trained with the athletics team, but by then I was doing weights programs and my real focus was football. The only other sport I stuck with was surfing. I started when I was about thirteen. Blair Taylor was a surfer, and I'd join in with a group of guys going to one of the city beaches, Trigg or Leighton or Scarborough. One of the dads, Bill Mitchell – who was a founding director of the West Coast Eagles Football Club – drove us down to the beach first thing in the morning. We'd surf, come in, set a fire, cook a tin of baked beans, eat them and then go back out. It was average surf, but great for kids.

The family spent the odd holiday at Smiths Beach, in the Yallingup area down near Margaret River, and this was where I really got into my surfing. I remember as a fourteen-year-old being down there with a good mate of mine, Simon Cugley. In Cowaramup Bay, there were two heavy waves, called South Point and North Point, but in the middle of the bay was a break called Huzzas. It was a forgiving place to learn how to surf larger waves. I remember one quiet, magic Sunday afternoon outside peak season. The size was overhead and a half, and I was surfing with Simon. That moment gave me as much inner joy and peace as I can recall in my entire life. The old man had been nagging us to start the three-hour drive home, but I'd begged him to let us stay longer. It was such a magical day. I'd do anything to have those couple of hours again.

As WESLEY was a boys' school, my first experiences with girls were part of my 'second' life. Since those cruel rejections from the likes of

Katie Priest and her crew, I'd felt awkward and inadequate around girls, and wanted desperately to disguise that inadequacy. I knew of boys, and girls, who would wait until they were in love before they'd start experimenting sexually, but I wasn't one of them. I just wanted to get it out of the way and say that I'd done it. So my early sexual experiences weren't particularly memorable for me, and I can't imagine they'd have stuck in the memories of the girls either.

When I was fourteen, Katie Priest wasn't my ideal anymore. That mantle had passed to Samantha Druce, far and away the most beautiful girl in that neighbourhood group. She had long brown hair, was very trim, and had exquisitely fine bone structure, with wrists like china. She was not only beautiful but a little bit wild. Her parents were from South Africa and had settled in Perth. I built her up into this idea of perfection and asked her out a few times, but I don't think I covered myself with glory and we soon went our separate ways.

Looking back, I regret that I was in so much of a hurry. Some blokes hadn't been with a girl simply because they weren't ready, and I wish I understood that it wasn't anything to be ashamed of. I wish I'd had faith that things would work out all right for me. But I was insecure. I thought that if I didn't rack up a certain number of experiences, everyone would see me as a loser. After our brief romance at fourteen, Sam realised that a lot of the older guys were showing an interest in her, so she could easily upgrade from me. She started going out with my mate Dan Hopkins. I spent the next three years longing for her but feeling that any girl I really liked was, like Sam, bound to be way out of my league.

WHEN I look back, it's crystal clear. I spent a lot of my teenage years feeling inadequate. I couldn't put my finger on it at the time – it was just this general sense that I didn't do things very well,

I didn't function as a normal human should. In school, I couldn't sit still, I had to fight my urge to get up and *do something* all the time, and the result was that I didn't do as well academically as I could have.

But more importantly, as a teenager, I had a deep sense of inadequacy about my body. When I looked in the mirror, I saw someone who was chubby and plain. I was probably a healthy kid, but I didn't see that in the mirror. Girls were not interested in me, and I knew why. It wasn't just that they were older, and going out with older blokes. It was because I was not appealing. I never really outgrew that, so that when girls did eventually show some interest, most of the time I didn't trust them. I thought they were only interested in the famous footballer, not the inadequate Ben Cousins I saw myself to be.

Overcompensating, I put on an act of being the suave cool guy, a bit of a ladies' man, a bloke who knew what was what. But it wasn't me. I wasn't suave or cool. I was just scared. The one place where I wasn't scared, where I was in control and adequate and coordinated and at home, was that oval inside the white line.

Football was my refuge from all that insecurity. I threw myself into it so methodically that even if I didn't have any natural talent I would have been a good player anyway, through sheer willpower and fitness. I had a footy in my hand and was playing so much, I only needed a little bit of talent to be a better than average player. But although footy was my place where I could be a properly functioning person, it tended to feed the inadequacy I felt at other times. I didn't feel comfortable in my skin *unless* I was playing footy. I *only* felt comfortable on the field.

TRADITIONALLY, THE Perth private school system produced more than its share of top footballers. Schools like Hale, Scotch,

Guildford and the powerhouse of the time, Aquinas, were production lines for WAFL and VFL/AFL stars.

Not so Wesley. For years they'd been the also-rans, sometimes going through the whole ten-match Alcock Cup season without winning a game. By the time I got to year eleven, the last time Wesley had won the cup was fifteen years earlier, when George Spalding was the coach and his son Earl, destined to become one of Melbourne and Carlton's best, was in the team. They'd won the premiership, but hadn't achieved the prize of going through undefeated.

In the summer before I started year eleven, a group of parents decided they'd had enough of it. Bill Mitchell was one. Bill's son David, who I'd surfed with, was in our Wesley First XVIII. So was Alex James, whose dad was Ken James, one of the owners of the Brand advertising agency. The boarding master, Nigel Fairbairn, a history teacher, was rallying the whole school to get behind us. Our captain was Blair Taylor, once my rival but now a good mate at Wesley and in the surf.

These parents were disappointed in the lackadaisical attitude of some of the teachers, who were happy just to turn up and send teams out. It wasn't that these dads were fixated on winning; they just wanted the boys to be doing their best. Their stroke of genius was the appointment of my old man as coach. When he'd finished his WAFL career a few years earlier, Dad had wanted to be a league coach. He'd coached WAFL reserves, but not first grade, and hadn't wanted to be hanging around the Perth club all his life, so he'd struck out on a new path. He'd had a passion for horses for as long as he could remember. If Dad was driving in the country and there were horses in a paddock, he'd pull over just to watch them running around. Other families he'd known in Armadale were in the trotting industry, and as a teenager he'd spend any of his spare time on weekends with them and more importantly their horses.

When I was about eleven, one of Dad's cousins, Ian Gossage, who had some pacers at Byford, had asked him if he wanted to help out with their preparation. Three times a week – two weekdays and every Saturday – Dad would haul himself out of bed at 3.30 am and drive down there for a 4.15 am start. After a couple of years he started training his own pacers and driving them in races. We were all supportive but wondered if he was on a trip to nowhere. He was so fired up about the whole thing, believing he had champions, then he'd take them to race and they'd come last. When he stopped driving them and gave that job to the experts, he began to train some winners.

He'd supplemented this with helping Gary Gibillini as our runner at Bullcreek Leeming. By my late Wesley years, when the influential parents were rounding up a team of some promise, they approached Dad and asked him to coach. He appeared at a meeting in the school auditorium in front of about 150 kids, and gave them his pitch.

'Put up your hand if you've ever beaten Aquinas,' he said.

Hardly anyone did. The previous year, the firsts had lost to Aquinas 36.19 to 0.1. It was beyond a joke.

'How does that make you feel?' Dad asked, to general silence. 'I tell you what, if it was me it'd drive me nuts. And there is nothing I wouldn't do to prepare myself to compete against them – just to give them a real contest.'

There were kids looking at each other like this bloke didn't have a clue, but Dad went on, talking about how they'd improve, bit by bit, a step at a time. 'It's only about doing your best,' he said. 'Anything less is disrespectful to yourselves, your team-mates, your opponents, and the game itself.'

Nobody really believed we could beat Aquinas, but this Cousins fellow was clearly passionate and knowledgeable, if a tiny bit mad.

He got the pre-season going like we were preparing for the

AFL. Having prepared like this throughout my teens, I was loving it. At the end of a rugged summer of training, the parents organised a professional jumper-presentation event. Ken James set up some big screens with footage of us in games and pre-season training, backed by the West Coast Eagles theme song. The parents had raised money for us to go on a trip to Melbourne to play Geelong Grammar and Geelong College. And Bill Mitchell invited Mick Malthouse to come and address us.

I had mixed feelings about this. The Eagles, having only entered the AFL in 1987, made the grand final in 1991 and won it in 1992 and 1994. A lot of Perth got behind them, but I hated them. They were arrogant and slick, and had beaten my idols, Geelong, in those two grand finals.

But Malthouse, the former Richmond Tiger and St Kilda Saint who'd come across to coach West Coast to their two premierships, was a revered person in the sporting world, looked up to by Dad and therefore by me. He was calm and centred, with an almost visible aura: he walked into the room and everyone took a breath. His speech wasn't fanatical about footy. Instead he spoke about the balance between football and study, which resonated with what Dad had been saying to us.

'There are three areas in your life,' Mick said. 'Sport, study and your social life. A healthy life has all three in balance. What I say to you is, keep them going but don't mix them up with each other. When you're doing your sport, focus entirely on that. When you're doing study, focus entirely on that. And then you're allowed your social time. Allocate time to each and give them your full attention.'

Mick inspired awe in all of us, but at heart I was still a ratbag. I could focus on footy sure enough, but school, for me, was part of my social life. We had a competition where we dared each other to climb out of the classroom window, sprint a lap of the quadrangle, then climb back in and be in your seat before the teacher noticed you were missing. I was the champion at this one – helped, no doubt, by wearing runners. Some teachers I could wrap around my finger. With one, five minutes before lunchtime I'd pack up, stand and make for the door.

He'd say: 'Where are you going, Ben?'

'I want to get in the canteen queue before the rush,' I said.

While other teachers might have made me sit back down or sent me to the headmaster's office, this one sighed, handed me some money, and said: 'You might as well get something for me while you're there.'

But they weren't all like that. Early in year eleven, just before we were due to take the trip to Geelong, I was in the science lab. I wondered what would happen if you turned on the gas taps and put a lit match to them. Experimentation, right? Wasn't that what science was about?

I lit up, and an almighty whoosh roared through the room, nearly setting me, my desk and some of the other boys on fire.

For once, one of my pranks had serious consequences. I was sent to the office of the headmaster, Rod Kefford, and carpeted. That was okay. What wasn't okay was that he suspended me for a week, meaning I'd miss the footy tour to Melbourne. I couldn't believe it. I went home and raged to Dad, but he just said: 'You might not think it's fair, but it wouldn't have happened if you hadn't done what you did.'

I was absolutely devastated. The build-up to that season meant everything to me: the focus, my dad coaching, the fundraising, the incredible jersey presentation with Malthouse. And I'd fucked up. Not only for me but for Dad, who'd be taking the team, not just to Melbourne but to Geelong, without his own son. I guess if he'd wanted to, he could have tried to get me on the tour. As coach, he might have been able to swing it. But instead, he said I needed to learn my lesson. It was about Dad's integrity, too. He wasn't a parent to undermine the school's authority.

Besides, Dad had had enough of my stupidity. There was the time I'd gone to a party at Cottesloe with Rick Mulligan and another mate called Nathan Mayz. I'd given the old man some alibi about where I was going that night. I had a few drinks and found myself in a dust-up with some bloke. It was not over anything important, or anything I can remember, but it ended up with him king-hitting me. I was in such a bad way that they had to call Dad. He came and picked me up from the party and drove me halfway home. Talking to me in the car, he realised I wasn't making much sense. I thought I was all right, but clearly I wasn't, so he took me to Fremantle Hospital, where I had to stay overnight for observation. I was concussed, and had a fat lip among other superficial wounds: a bit of a sight in black jeans, black Bundaberg Rum singlet, and a blood-spattered shirt. The next morning, I was waiting to be picked up . . . and Dad didn't show. He refused to come and get me. When Mum eventually arrived, she let me know that what had hurt Dad wasn't the fight, or the injuries, but that I'd lied to him about where I was going that night. This was the thing with my old man: honour was the overriding value. If you behaved dishonourably, you deserved whatever punishment you got.

So off the team went to Geelong, and I stayed at home. They played their games and went down to Torquay for a night out. Graham 'Bomber' Bomford, the school's guidance officer, briefed them on their big night with the words: 'Don't fuck up, or I'll fuck *you* up.' It worked. They were a great bunch, and being left at home only sharpened my appetite to rejoin them and not let them down again.

Blair Taylor was the leader in every way. For the Sharks against Kurunda, I'd played on Blair and he gave me a couple of good touch-ups. Finally being on the same team as him was a real buzz. Dad pushed for him to be captain of the Wesley firsts even though he was a bit of a larrikin. In the pre-season Quit Cup, a round robin played among private and public schools, we played a curtain-raiser for an Eagles match at Subiaco Oval. It was amazing playing on the big ground in front of massive, if still half-empty, grandstands, and we won. Afterwards, we were sitting up the back of the grandstand for the Eagles game. Blair thought he'd go down to the bar and buy us all a beer – it wasn't a bad time to celebrate. We were in our school tracksuits, though, and none of us was bright enough to realise that breaking school rules wasn't the best idea. Blair got busted by the school, of course, and was told he wasn't allowed to captain the team. But Dad was adamant that he was the right man for the job, so he went to Rod Kefford. Dad managed to get that one through, and it was a good thing for our side. Blair was fearless in his attack on the footy, a great bloke to marshal the troops, and I learnt a lot from him about the art of captaincy.

OUR FIRST game was against Aquinas. Their coach was Peter Spencer, a Sandover medallist and 300-game player in the WAFL. Given the previous year's result, most people expected our season to be over as soon as it started. In the week leading up to the game, it was pissing down with rain. Dad, as usual, was the first to arrive at training, straight from work. Some of the blokes dribbled into the sheds and asked him if we were going to go ahead with it.

'These are the nights you live for,' Dad said, bouncing around. 'This rain is beautiful. It gives us an opportunity to practise our skills in the wet. Over at Aquinas, what do you reckon they're doing? They're sitting inside nice and dry. When you run out on Saturday, you'll know that they've been squibbing it all week while you've been training in it.'

Against all expectations we beat Aquinas, which set our season going. Not too many people came to watch, but week by week the crowds built up, from just the parents, to a few dozen, up into the hundreds. In game after game we were behind at half-time, but came back to win. There's nothing for morale and confidence like a come-from-behind victory. In one game, we were three or four goals behind at the break. As we went into the changing rooms, the boys were talking about the opposition's full-forward, who'd already kicked six goals on our fullback, Johnny Ferguson.

Dad hit us with a surprise question: 'How does anyone reckon Johnny Ferguson's playing?'

There was an awkward silence. Everyone knew the answer, but no-one knew what we were meant to say.

'He's getting his arse kicked,' Dad said, glaring at all of us. 'Anyone know why? Because you blokes aren't giving him a hand.'

He proceeded to give us a valuable tactical lesson. 'There's eighteen of you and you can all do something. Backmen, play 10 metres inside your opponent. If that full-forward leads, I want you taking his line. I want the ruckmen to play centre back. Midfielders, you have to be putting more tackling pressure on, to stop those pinpoint passes to him.'

What he was telling us was, Johnny Ferguson wasn't alone in a one-on-one match with the other team's full-forward. Defence was for all of us. The full-forward didn't kick another goal, and we won the game. When we came in, Dad said, 'That's how you help your mates. Johnny Ferguson beat that full-forward today because of his mates looking after him.'

THE OLD man left no stone unturned. Most nights at dinner, we'd sit talking about how we were going to play and train, what kid we'd recruit from other sports. Drew Bartram, a Wesley boarder, was a really good hockey player. Dad staged a big coup by getting him to play footy, and he was one of our best players. We had no true ruckman that year. A couple of guys tried, but they were struggling, so Dad got Percy Johnson down. A well-known player, and ruck coach at various times for Perth, Fremantle, and West Coast, Johnson had been everywhere. My dad respected Percy as much as anyone in footy. I often heard him say that Percy would help out any team, any footy player, because he loved the game so much. We'd do match simulations with Percy jogging around telling the ruckmen where to run, how to read the play. I appreciated a refresher on the fundamentals I'd been taught by the old man. Footy was about channelling the ball through centre half-forward, getting front and square, knowing how to read it off the pack, being good with your hands, using your opportunities up forward. If you could understand and anticipate those patterns, you were halfway there.

I was playing midfield and half-forward in that team. Today's exceptional schoolboy footballers would have more natural stamina than I had. I became a hard runner, but I had to work at it. I was obsessed with the working side of it, which meant more to me than the thrill of playing in front of a crowd. Thanks to the work ethic Dad instilled in us, that was how the whole team applied itself. We had some talent, but our foundation was work, running hard, putting your head over the footy. We weren't blessed with more natural ability than anyone else, but we and the parents were part of a school that had been belted around for so long, we just wanted to make something of our chance.

No successful season is without humour, though. Every training session Dad would focus on some fundamental 'one per cent-er', like smothering or shepherding or spoiling. He'd say, 'I can cop you losing, but I won't cop you taking short cuts.' One night, he wanted us to do a spoiling drill. He was in a bit of a bad mood, and the blokes were fart-arsing about. So as he was demonstrating this drill, the first thing Dad did was miss the ball and slip over. The kids burst out laughing.

Dad got up, fuming.

'That's fucking typical of this school! You've never won a thing in your life, you're playing the bottom team this weekend and you'll get your arses kicked because you're all clowning around, and something you've worked for all year won't happen.'

He went berserk. Not one of us was moving.

'Just get out there and run some laps,' Dad said in disgust. As we filed out, one of the staff, John Caulfield, went up to Dad.

'That was a brilliant spray! Did you plan that?'

'No,' Dad said, 'they were laughing, they were giving me the shits. I lost my temper.'

John didn't believe him. 'Brilliant, brilliant,' he said, walking off and shaking his head at Dad's psychological genius.

WE BEAT Hale, Scotch and then Trinity, who were coached by Gary Malarkey. He'd been fullback at Geelong with Dad, and they were close mates, so that game really meant something. After nine games, we were undefeated. The last match was against Guildford Grammar, and we had to win it to be guaranteed outright premiers. Guildford was half an hour east of town, a semi-rural area, and their ground was a bit of a cow paddock. They weren't in the top echelon of teams that year, but those big, well-developed farmers' kids always gave you a hard match.

By this stage there were upwards of a thousand people coming to our games, including scouts from the WAFL clubs. Their presence didn't really figure in my thinking – they were off in the background while I was focused on the job.

We were always ahead in that game, and when the siren finally went, all the blokes converged. I was off to the side, and was suddenly overcome by tears. I didn't jump around with the others. I felt strangely distant from it, watching everyone else jumping over the top of each other in pure elation. It almost meant too much to me. The entire season flashed before me.

I thought of how Dad had engineered it with the other parents, seeing us build something from the ground up. There was the pre-season hell, the jersey presentation with Malthouse, me missing the Melbourne trip, our struggles to find a ruckman, the rainy winter nights and afternoons, the tense games when we'd come from behind. Everyone had played their role, and I felt a deep love for each and every bloke in that team. When you're part of the development of a side, looking back at where you've come from and where you've got to, looking over your shoulder as you're running out and seeing these guys, you feel the blood running like mercury in your veins. When you go on and win a premiership, and see how much it means to everyone, it's magic. It's the best feeling there is.

But I was still off to the side, until Dad came over to bring me into things. There's a look he and I have given each other at certain times, whether they're good or bad. If something good has happened, that look between us is almost a smirk, to say, 'What have we got away with here?' We exchanged that look at Guildford. It meant so much to him. He'd had a great playing career, but he was really into this team.

I had no idea how rare those moments would be. Winning premierships in the under-13s and -15s for the Sharks, and now for the Wesley firsts, would mean as much to me as anything since. In fact, I'd only taste that satisfaction once more: for West Coast in 2006, another time we'd built a team from the ground up. This is how fleeting success can be. Sometimes even the greatest players in the game never win a flag, at any level.

Even in 2006, I was still remembering that day when Wesley beat Guildford Grammar. Ever since, I'd been wishing I hadn't been so detached and quiet and overwhelmed. I wished I could have jumped around and celebrated the way you're meant to when you win. In 2006, when we eventually won the AFL premiership, I was criticised for going over the top with my celebrations. After all, I was never one to carry on after kicking goals. It's one of my pet hates, blokes who over-celebrate instead of acknowledging the blokes who have done the work for them up the ground. But when we won that AFL premiership, that was the one time in my life I was going to let my hair down. Because the moment passed me by when I'd been playing for Wesley, I felt I was entitled to it now. I did go overboard – but what nobody knew was, it was linked directly to that moment twelve years earlier on the cow paddock at Guildford Grammar.

5

INITIATIONS

After our premiership in my second-last school year, the 1995 season was a bit of an anticlimax. Despite my mischief-making at school, I was made a prefect in year twelve. The boarding master, Nigel Fairbairn, told Dad that I should have been school captain. 'Ben's the one the kids follow,' he said. 'They'll make some other bloke school captain and try to turn him into a leader, but the best way of selecting your captain is to find the natural leader and knock the rough edges off him.'

Be that as it may, I wasn't really the right type. Leeming was a great place to come from, but there was a clear class difference between Leeming and South Perth. If I hadn't made my rough edges visible enough with my various transgressions, I did it one day in a practice footy match when I went down after a hard knock. In front of all the Wesley parents and teachers, I screamed out, 'Mum, I've broken me fucken arm!'

INITIATIONS

I did get injured a lot in my teens, due to the amount of footy I was playing. Looking back, it was probably unwise to be playing hard games on Saturday for Wesley, on Sunday for my club, and midweek for a rep team. But I couldn't be stopped – until my body sent out signals that couldn't be ignored.

IN THE summer of 1994–95, I went down to the East Fremantle WAFL club to do the pre-season. Bullcreek Leeming was in their catchment area, and East Freo was where a lot of my mates moved on to play. Training and playing with grown men introduced me to a new level of intensity. The East Fremantle coach was Tony Micale and the captain was Steve Malaxos, who'd been captain of West Coast – both of them, in my eyes, giants of the game.

On 8 April 1995, I made my WAFL debut – at sixteen, the same age Dad had first played for Perth – against Claremont at East Fremantle Oval. I did all right, and played another seven games before the Wesley season was due to start. The school rule was that you had to represent Wesley first, so the plan was that I'd sit out the rest of the WAFL season.

Going into the Alcock Cup season, Dad knew we weren't going to be as strong as the previous year. Blair Taylor and the older blokes had left. Dad tried to talk the school into giving out football scholarships, and some of the other parents were happy to chip in, but Rod Kefford wouldn't have it; it was a point of pride that we were a school that wouldn't 'cheat' by bringing in gun players on scholarships.

In any case, I ended up missing the majority of the season. A lot of my injuries were due to playing too much footy while I was growing, and I'd been suffering from osteoarthritis in the front of my knees and in my heels. In year twelve I also developed a growth plate in my hip, where the bone was growing abnormally. I'd miss ten weeks of football.

While this was disappointing for Wesley and me, it created an opportunity for the old man. He and Mum had often been sitting me down and warning me not to fritter away my chances in life. 'Enjoy your mates and have fun,' they said, 'but you're too smart to chuck away your education.'

Being very happily married, they were able to present me with a united front. There was no gap for me to work my way through. With Mum, I'd been able to get away with murder, talking her into driving me in the Tarago to Wesley every day, or copping a sick day from school – the types of things I'd never get past Dad. But when it came to seriously attacking my TEE in year twelve, Mum and Dad were equally strict.

For all his dedication to football, Dad was adamant about me studying hard. I'd exceeded his expectations as a junior footballer, but he also knew that you could be the best kid in the country at sixteen and never play an AFL game. It happens a lot more than it doesn't, and it happened more back then. I just wanted to play footy, whether I got paid or not, and Dad reminded me that my football career may well be like his: going to training three nights a week after work. So I needed to prepare to get a job.

My injury did the rest, and I knuckled down. I did English, maths, human biology, geography and history, and my last report card was straight As. But I wasn't your typical straight-A student; when it happened, nobody believed me. There was a mixture of charm and bluff in with the hard work. Every other year I'd been mucking around, getting Bs and Cs, just enough to pass. Matthew and I were the kind of students who thought the ideal mark was 55 per cent: a pass, but any more time spent on it would be wasted. Surprisingly, in year twelve I actually enjoyed studying hard. I didn't relish the sitting down, but loved the feeling of accomplishment from getting a good mark. And having a rounded education stood me in better stead going into professional sport, whether I used it directly or not.

*

INITIATIONS

WHILE I was doing rehab that winter, Glenn Stewart arranged for me to go to the West Coast Eagles club to get used to how the football club worked. Being a Geelong supporter, I loathed West Coast; but that visit from Mick Malthouse had begun to turn me around. Plus, this was an opportunity to suck in knowledge that I couldn't let go to waste.

West Coast's talent scout was Mick Moylan, whom Dad knew since his footy days, and the chief executive Trevor Nisbett invited me to come down on Monday nights to do a bit in the gym and some recovery and swimming sessions. This was at the old Subiaco Oval, with a gym in the bowels of the grandstand. Mum would drop me off, and I'd limp in. The Eagles would be having a meeting to dissect the weekend's game. I'd go to the gym and then to the physio and recovery, using their pool, and doing Pilates-style exercises. On Monday nights they'd have a barbecue and some steaks, the full club with some of the directors and ex-players.

I knew Jarrad Schofield, a Wesley boy a few years older than me, but otherwise it was pretty daunting. It sounds exciting, but it's not exactly enjoyable for a young kid. These guys were larger than life: the soft-spoken but rock-hard captain John Worsfold leading a roster of household names such as Guy McKenna, Peter Matera, Peter Sumich, Ashley McIntosh, Dean Kemp, Glen Jakovich, Chris Lewis, and the popular hero Chris Mainwaring. Even the fringe players were Perth heroes.

I was mingling only as much as you can when you're sixteen. The first-team players would say, 'G'day, mate. How ya going, young fella?' but I didn't feel like I was part of it. I was just looking. They were friendly enough, but there was not a lot they could say to make me feel I belonged. It's a rite of passage you have to go through, facing your fears and putting yourself out there. It's what all kids have to do in their lives, and not just kids: a decade and a half later, I would have to go through the same kind of nervous settling-in process as a thirty-year-old at Richmond.

It was an experience I had to survive rather than enjoy. I was so anxious, even getting involved in drills was nerve-racking. *What if I fuck up a kick, or drop a simple pass?* For some kids it takes three or four years to get a sense of belonging. Every minute you feel like everything's on the line, the tiniest mistake can be catastrophic, you're analysing every word you're saying. I was so nervous I hated it, like almost anyone would.

I WAS never part of the AFL's draft system until I was thirty years old – and thank God for that, I thought. When I was a seventeen-year-old, I was lucky enough to qualify for three AFL clubs outside the draft system. The Eagles were one, because the father–son rule applied to fathers who'd played in the WAFL, and West Coast got access to sons of WAFL players. The Fremantle Dockers, who'd come into the AFL in 1994, were in some ways the most natural fit because I'd already played for East Freo, I was in their catchment, and so many of my mates and teammates in state junior teams had gone on to the club. Phil Smart, their recruiting manager, was a really good bloke, and Dad had a lot of time for their coach, Gerard Neesham.

The third club was my beloved Geelong, for whom I also qualified under the traditional father–son rule. I was flown over to spend a weekend in Melbourne, staying with Stephen Wells, the Geelong recruiting manager. If I'd been nervous at Subiaco, that was nothing compared with my weekend in Geelong. For a start, I had to play golf with Malcolm Blight. Once a full-forward with North Melbourne, Blighty was a charismatic and intimidating personality. He was massively keen on his golf, and I was told that if I wanted a good chat with him I needed to go out with him on the golf course. Problem was, I'd never played. Golf is hard at the best of times, but I was utterly hopeless. I couldn't get the ball off the ground. It was the longest four hours of my life and by the end of it I was just happy to get out of there. I had no idea what Blighty thought of me.

Compared with the golf course, Kardinia Park was a comfort zone. In the day I trained with the seconds, and at night with the firsts, and watched them play on the Saturday. I remember having a kick with Buddha Hocking in the change rooms, aware of Gary Ablett lurking in the shadows. I was such a big Cats fan, I felt like I'd been taken up to some kind of Mount Olympus with my gods.

LATE IN the Wesley season, I was ready to play again. During my break, there was a minor drug issue involving the school. Rod Kefford told Dad that a couple of players in the First XVIII had been caught smoking pot. They were suspended from school, and missed the next game, a decision which Dad supported. Wesley lost, and at the next training session Dad addressed the players.

'The consequences of your actions matter,' he said, looking at the two blokes. 'This footy side got beaten because of what you two did. But this is just a footy game. One day you'll do drugs and it'll cost you your job or your relationship.'

Then he got emotional. He grabbed a kid and said to the others, 'You won't ever see this kid touching that shit, and you won't ever get that shit off this quality of kid.'

Unbeknown to any of us, including Dad, the headmaster was watching. He rang Dad the next day to tell him what a good speech it was. I was never in any doubt about Dad's attitude to drugs, and at that point in my life I would have backed him up 100 per cent.

When I was back on the field, East Fremantle wanted me to play again, as they were heading into a finals campaign. One of their staff came to Wesley training and asked Dad if I could play in their first final, on a Sunday, against their traditional rivals South Fremantle. But Wesley were playing Guildford Grammar on the Saturday.

Dad called Steve Malaxos at East Freo and said he'd sort it out. Wesley were down the ladder that year, so there wasn't as much at stake as the year before. Against Guildford, he put me in the forward pocket and gave me rests during the game. I played okay, kicking a few goals, but was out of the engine room. And when we won and had a big end-of-season celebration night, I was at home, freshening up for the match among the men. We won, but lost the next week against Subiaco, and that was it for a short and frustrating 1995 season.

ALTHOUGH HE was a couple of years older than me, Daniel Chick and I had developed a close friendship. He was from Geraldton, and when I was in year eleven he came down to Perth to board with the Thompsons, friends of ours whose son was our ruckman at Wesley. Chicky was cutting his teeth in the seniors at East Fremantle, and we'd become good mates since I'd started training and playing there.

At the end of year twelve, the big leavers' week was at Rottnest Island. There were 20,000 kids there, and it was mayhem. Chicky came over with me for a weekend, and we hung out together. There was a house that the Wesley boys had rented, and that Saturday night it was carnage, kids coming in and out getting totally trashed. Then, out of nowhere, this group of older blokes came in and occupied the living room. They wouldn't leave. They were tough guys with facial hair, metal piercings through the eyelids and so on. The Wesley boys couldn't get them out of the house.

Chicky and I looked at each other and said, 'Let's do it.'

We walked into the living room and said, 'Boys, you've got to get out.' I half helped them up to usher them towards the door. I had this hairy guy by the elbow, and as we got near the door he stopped and dropped his beer on the floor. With that, I cracked him, punched him straight in the face. Before he hit the ground Chicky had put a knee into him. We tore into them like madmen, and they scuttled out of the place. It felt like David and Goliath. We were a pair of Davids and we'd conquered these monsters. It sealed our friendship and would be an event we'd refer back to years later, when we became the closest of mates. As with a lot of the things we got involved in together, that night ended up in chaos. Luckily for us, we had the type of friendship that thrived on adversity.

I'D HAD a couple of girlfriends in the meantime, but since our brief fling at fourteen I'd been pining for Sam Druce. She and Dan Hopkins had been apart for about a year when I saw her again in year twelve.

She was training to be a beautician, and I was at Wesley. Unable to skip applied art to go for a run by the river, I'd used the class to develop my skills in manufacturing fake IDs. That's what applied art is, isn't it? With some friends I was going to the Metropolis nightclub in the old part of Fremantle, across the street from Gino's restaurant. One night I saw Sam there, and she offered me a lift home. We walked along, and got in the car, and had a kiss. That was how it started.

Sam had two older brothers who I got along well with. I spent a lot of time with the younger of the two, Wayne, who was a bit of a tripper, a really cool guy in an offbeat way. He was an eccentric, but he had his own style. A raver, he loved his music, his tatts and his piercings, and kicked a hacky sack. Unlike a lot of the blokes I knew, he preferred laughing to fighting. I looked up to him, and his friendship was part of the appeal of knocking around with Sam.

It's funny – my transformation from a bloke dead against drugs into someone who was extremely interested seemed to pass in a blur. It happened really quickly. Something inside me changed. To that point, I'd been drunk only on rare teenage binges, and had smoked dope just enough to know I didn't like it. But trying out some new drug experiences was what everyone in the older group was getting up to. As always, I wanted to catch up.

One night in the summer of 1995–96, there was a party in Leeming, at the place of a girl whose parents were out of town. The weekend party scene was quite wild. A small group of us would walk and ride bikes from party to party in Bullcreek and Leeming. If necessary, we'd gatecrash. Then there'd be blues, and it'd suddenly be a melee of 300 kids, back fences knocked down, and paddy wagons parked out front.

One Saturday night when there was a big party coming up, just on an impulse I said to Sam, 'Let's have a night, eh?' She knew what I meant.

I remember the night vividly, and I'm not going to pretend it wasn't fun. Nobody can understand the dangers of drugs unless they also understand the great thrills that come along with them.

I was seventeen years old. I had been given one yellow and one green pill and I decided to try it. It was amazing. Being the elite athlete, I didn't want anyone knowing, so only Sam knew, cloak and dagger. We were in the party when this warm, euphoric feeling started to kick in for me. I wandered up the street with Sam and we sat on the kerb. I had my hand on Sam's leg and we lay back on the grass and talked to each other, gazing up at the stars, sighing with pure bliss. I can't describe how beautiful that feeling was, my heart rate slowing, my eyes feeling open for the first time.

The yellow pill was ecstasy. I felt for the first time in my life that I'd taken something that resonated with me personally.

INITIATIONS

Alcohol hadn't done it for me. I'd get pissed for the sake of doing it and then feel crook as a dog. When I got stoned it rocked me and I couldn't move.

Then I had the green one. It wasn't the same but it was still a good pill. We talked, walked down to the park, went back to the party for a few drinks, and I had the night of my life.

I felt I had got lucky – or perhaps unlucky. I guess it was like those people who walk into a casino and win. Is it good luck or bad? I don't know, but from that very night my obsession with a particular kind of drug began. Over the years I would have a lot of pills, and they varied a lot, good and bad, but nothing was as pure or euphoric as that first time, warm and calm, feeling great about my football, school behind me, and talking peacefully with the girl of my dreams.

6

THE BABY EAGLE

This was a golden time in my life. Three AFL clubs wanted me, I was with Sam, and my eyes had just been opened to something totally unexpected. But as much as I'd loved that night, I wouldn't take drugs again for the best part of a year. Football was too important.

As far as the AFL was concerned, there was no such thing as a bad choice. Fremantle was where a lot of my mates played, West Coast was the richest and most professional club in the league, and Geelong was where my heart was. It was funny how my emotions came to affect my choice. I grew up barracking for Geelong and whoever West Coast were playing. I hated West Coast. Everything that made them great irritated me. They were that good, it gave me the shits. But when it came to what sort of footy club I wanted to be part of, it was those qualities that swayed me. Although part of my thinking was that I didn't want to leave my family and friends and go to Geelong, backing myself to join the Eagles seemed like the most daring option. It was no fait accompli that I'd make the grade, not by any stretch. Some friends said, 'You're going to West Coast? You're not going to get a game!' My response was to think, if I'm good enough to make it into seniors, I want to make it in the best side.

And just like choosing to take a particularly hard run, or singling out the toughest opponent to prove myself against, it was now part of my nature to gravitate towards the most difficult challenge. Where did it come from, this need to prove myself? I can't say, and no amount of amateur psychoanalysis is going to convince me it was in my relationship with my dad or anyone else from early on. It was just me. So this was another reason the West Coast Eagles were my choice: precisely because it was where I felt least comfortable going.

Until I made the final decision, Dad had never told me which club he thought I should join. Acting as my manager, he came to some of the meetings. He said, 'I have a personal preference but they're all good clubs. You make your decision and I might tell you after you've made it.' The only personal note he added was to remind me of my feelings for Matthew, Melanie and Sophie, who were all very young, and ask whether I wanted to miss seeing them grow up.

When I decided on the Eagles, Dad said he was pleased, because that was the club he'd hoped I would choose. But there was an awkward moment. I didn't want to make the calls to Freo and Geelong, but the old man said, 'These are things you have to do.'

I felt I was letting both clubs down. I made the calls, and they were both good about it. I was just a kid, carrying more weight on my shoulders than I needed to. I was nothing if not serious about this.

*

AFTER MY school exams, I enrolled in a commerce course at the University of Western Australia. In a way I was only paying lip-service to a career, because in my mind I was throwing everything at being a professional footballer. But who knew what the future held? My brother Matthew, who was a hugely talented foot-baller, suffered a series of injuries in his late teens from which he was never able to recover, and whatever senior footy career he'd planned was a might-have-been. I couldn't assume that the same wouldn't happen to me. And my parents were very keen for me to go to uni. So I chose commerce, in full knowledge that the course had pretty flexible hours and a light schedule that wouldn't get too much in the way of my main priority.

Dad negotiated me a two-year contract for about $30,000 base salary, plus $2000 a game. In the second year my base would rise to $35,000. It doesn't sound like a lot, but for an eighteen-year-old it was like I'd won the lottery. They were *paying* me to play footy. I had to pinch myself.

But although it seems a golden time in retrospect, I never sat back and thought, 'Hey, this is amazing, look where I am.' I didn't allow myself to be satisfied. Just being an Eagle wasn't enough. It might have been for some other kids, but it wasn't for me. Always, *always*, I had to search for something extra. It felt like complacency was the enemy, even though complacency was never a trap I'd fallen into.

The Eagles' process of easing me into the club, through my months in rehab, had done its job. I felt as comfortable as a seven-teen-year-old could feel when he's going into pre-season training alongside John Worsfold, Glen Jakovich, Peter Matera, Chris Mainwaring, Chris Lewis, Peter Sumich, Dean Kemp and the rest. I was shitting myself actually, but all the routines of the football club were helping to push my fear down beneath the surface.

THE BABY EAGLE

We'd meet at Perry Lakes, several hectares of parklands between Perth city and the ocean-side suburbs, for our training. It was midsummer, and the trees and lakes weren't providing much relief. We had to run around an undulating track twice for a 2-kilometre time trial, and I'd give it everything. Then we'd break up into groups to do specialised training – this was in the early days of refining pre-season work to suit each player's body type and maturity, and the needs of the position they'd be playing. As it was envisaged that I'd be playing in the forward pocket, I was in a sprints group. Fortunately, since Glenn Stewart had written me his training programs back when I was at school, I'd been exposed to the Eagles' methods for a long time. Mark Neates, the sprints coach, had been working with me too. And unlike some of the other teenage recruits, I'd finished growing. I was the same height (179 centimetres) and weight (80 kilograms) as I was for my entire career. Not as developed, but the same height and weight.

By late January I thought the pre-season was going well, but little did I know that my attitude was raising alarms. Dad was very close with Ian Miller, one of the coaching staff at the Eagles, and they'd chat on the phone every week. Ian told Dad that Mick Malthouse wanted to speak to him. Dad's initial reaction was, 'Oh no, what the hell has Ben done now?'

He called Mick, who said: 'We're a bit concerned about Ben.'

Dad asked what I'd done wrong.

'It's not anything he's done wrong,' Mick told him. 'We're concerned that he's so full-bore at training. We're still in pre-season, and Ben's ready for the comp to start next week.'

Mick asked Dad to have a word with me, and tell me to simmer down. I was too obsessive. It had never struck me that you could be *too* keen. Dad spoke to me, and I reined it in – a little. But for me, there were no half-measures. I couldn't help it, and if it was another warning sign, I was more than happy to brush it off.

I wasn't in the Eagles seniors from the start, of course. Although Carlton had beaten Geelong in the previous year's AFL grand final, the Eagles, premiers in 1992 and 1994, were still widely recognised as the benchmark for the competition. Their 1995 season could be written off due to a heavy injury toll. In Perth, even though the Fremantle Dockers were newly in the AFL, the Eagles were *the* team. No way was I going to walk into the seniors. I just wanted to improve the basics in my game and finish the year a better player than when I started. I'd be stoked if I got one senior game. That's all my expectations ran to: one game. I thought that if I went really well, really outdid myself, I might jag four or five games as a replacement.

After a couple of runs for the Eagles in the pre-season Ansett Cup, I played on the ball for East Fremantle in the first two WAFL rounds of 1996. The second round was the big derby against South Freo, on Foundation Day, and in the lead-up I'd rolled my ankle quite badly. I taped it up and took painkillers and got myself up for the game. The ache quickly went away as I got into the rhythm of the match, and I ended up having a good day, kicking the goal that got us across the line. Dad was watching on TV at home, and one of the commentators, the former WAFL player Trevor Sprigg, said of me, 'The disappointing thing for East Fremantle supporters is that this is going to be the last game he'll play for them. He'll be playing for the Eagles next week.'

THE EAGLES hadn't started the season well, losing in rounds two and three. Malthouse was moving around training with more than his usual thoughtful frown. He had an amazing aura, he really did. For me, as a seventeen-year-old, it was all-consuming; I felt like I knew where he was at every minute. Sometimes coaches can blur the line of familiarity with the players, but there was no question of that with Malthouse. No question about who was boss.

At training one night early in the week, the butterflies started in my stomach as he walked my way. There was no fanfare; he just said quietly, 'Ben, we're going to play you this week. Congratulations.'

I felt like throwing a backflip – except for one big problem. I was trying to conceal my rolled ankle that was still sore from the week before and very tender from the weekend's Foundation Day game.

This was more than just another rolled ankle, because I already knew Malthouse had some real bugbears. One was moulds, or boots with moulded studs. Most players prefer wearing moulds to boots with long-stops, or metal studs, because they're easier on the soles of your feet. But what you're gaining in comfort, you're losing in traction. Malthouse let players make their own choices on moulds, he wouldn't order them to wear long-stops, but if you wore moulds and you slipped over in a game he would go absolutely wild at you. You were fine in moulds – as long as you didn't fall over.

A similar bugbear was taping your ankles before training or a match. You do it to stabilise your ankles against rolling, but it's a drag, you have to wait in line to have it done, and a lot of players would just as soon do without it. Again, Malthouse would leave the decision on taping up to the players, but watch out. If you decided not to tape your ankles, and you then rolled one, he'd crack it.

You were petrified of slipping over, or rolling your ankle, because you knew what Malthouse's reaction would be. But nothing riled him more than concealing an injury. If you declared yourself fit for a match, when you crossed the white line you were a 100 per cent fit player. He was the same as on the boots or the taping: it was your decision, but if you were exposed as not fully fit, he would be absolutely savage on you.

And so here I was, picked in my first AFL game, but breaking two of Malthouse's three golden rules. No way was I not going to play, injury or no injury. But at the same time, I was shitting myself all week because I didn't know if my ankle was going to be right, and was hiding the fact from my coach.

The week was nerve-racking, even without my ankle. The opponent, on top of everything else, was Geelong – my heroes. Ablett was out injured, but Billy Brownless, Barry Stoneham, Peter Riccardi, John Barnes and all their other stars were in.

We had a jersey presentation, and I was given number 35. Being a young player you were given a 'heavy' jumper, or one with a high number. Also making his debut that week was Phil Matera, who'd been one of my opponents at South Fremantle. Phil and I were the fourth and fifth debutants Malthouse would be blooding in the first four rounds as he sought to regenerate a team that had been 'up' for six years. We'd both be playing in the forward line, supporting Mitchell White, and the ruckman Malthouse was going to try moving up front. I wasn't yet strong or fit enough to play on the ball at senior level.

Through the week, the senior guys didn't make a big deal of things. They were very experienced, and looking for a win against the team that had become their arch-rivals. Geelong had been in three of the previous four grand finals, in two of which West Coast had beaten them. Premiership players like Chris Lewis, John Worsfold, Chris Waterman, Don Pyke, Chris Mainwaring, Guy McKenna – I felt that I walked taller with those blokes beside me, no question. They'd give me an encouraging slap and say things like, 'You deserve to be here,' and 'Play your own game.'

Thrown in at the deep end, it was a situation I thrived on. I pictured myself as a guy who ate up pressure, the more pressure the better. But a good deal of this was pure bravado.

It was a good and bad thing that Malthouse had informed me

of my selection early in the week. It beat wondering for five days if I was going to play. But on the other hand, it gave me a lot of time to get stirred up thinking about it, and worrying about my ankle. I just tried to stay calm and follow the same preparation regime I'd undertaken for big games in the past. I'd played a lot of games that I took very seriously – for Wesley, for Bullcreek Leeming, for junior rep teams, for East Fremantle – so I could fall back on big-game routines. Dad and I had always taken preparing for footy very seriously. For example, I never stayed overnight at a mate's place the night before a game. I was allowed to, but I chose not to. Dad was the antithesis of the parent who would control what you did. He left it to me, and I did the best thing for my footy. I loved my eight hours, and would get to bed early and have a good night's sleep. So when it came to the biggest game of my life, I had enough of a grounding to relax and not be up all night worrying.

ON THE morning of Saturday 21 April 1996, I got up around eight o'clock. It was a beautiful sunny morning, warm for late April, the kind of day I loved. Winter was coming, but you could still get sunburnt on a day like this. A couple of years earlier we'd moved to a bigger house in Leeming, in another cul-de-sac, Oakland Heights. Only a few minutes away from Reilly Court, the new place was double-storey, sandstock bricks with a corrugated-iron roof, with a more established garden and a garage. It was in a slightly better part of Leeming, I guess.

It also had a public oval down the bottom of the road, and as soon as I got out of bed I picked up a football and walked down the hill. The oval was a rough one, sandy soil ringed by native bush, with no marked boundaries and the goalposts just low junior-size rusty metal ones. I jogged a couple of laps, bouncing the ball, and did some stretching, testing my ankle and thinking about the game.

Then I went home and had some breakfast, tinned spaghetti on toast. It was what I'd always eaten on match days. It was what the old man ate! But I never really liked it. I hated it, actually. It took me a few years to work out that I could eat something on match morning that *I* liked, not just what Dad liked.

After breakfast, I had a shower and stuffed around the house. There was a bit of a buzz in the place, with Mum and Dad and my siblings all trying not to show too much excitement. At that stage, as Dad sometimes said, they were all my servants, the whole family geared towards the pursuit of my football career. I don't know if that was quite true in general, but certainly that day nobody was unaware of the importance of what was happening.

Late morning I put on my team-issue suit and tie, with elastic-sided boots, and packed my footy kit. I had to be at Subiaco Oval by noon for a 2.10 pm game. The whole family came along, of course.

When I got there, everything happening in the changing rooms was crisp and professional. The colours, the smells, the sounds, were all vivid to me. I was in some kind of sharpened, heightened reality. The ground was filling up. The biggest crowds I'd played in front of were maybe 8000 in the WAFL, but this was going to be several times that.

We got into our footy gear and went out for warm-ups. It was a fast deck, good for clean football. I was in my element. And at 17 years, 295 days, I was the youngest-ever debutant for the Eagles, passing the mark Chris Lewis had set back in their first year in the league.

But the ankle wasn't right. I could feel it aching, and in the warm-ups I couldn't run at full pace. I steered clear of where Malthouse might take too close a look at me. I remember thinking, 'I'm playing with fire here.' I was just hoping that the amount of adrenaline rushing through my system would anaesthetise me.

THE BABY EAGLE

There were 30,000 in the ground when we ran on, among them Mum and Dad. Mum tended to get pretty nervous about me hurting myself, and I imagine she was terrified watching her boy on the field with all those grown AFL players. Dad, on the other hand, said he was calm. He wasn't expecting me to achieve a great deal that year, so it was just a matter of learning something from this game and hoping I might get another.

As we ran through the banner, I assume there was a huge roar from the high banked stands, but I was both aware of it and numb to it. Nerves can do funny things to you, and it was almost like an out-of-body experience.

What my nerves also did was distort any normal sense of time. I started in the forward pocket, and once the game began everything was flying by. The pace was phenomenal, like nothing I'd ever experienced. Geelong's defender Martin McKinnon was on me, but in the first quarter I didn't see much of the ball: Geelong kicked eight goals to our two, and were threatening to give us a towelling.

I can't say I really 'felt' the game. It was just a test of instinct. Some kids adapt to the pace of AFL quicker than others, and thankfully for me, I gradually found that pace and caught up with it. Down by thirty-five points at half-time, we kicked six goals in the third quarter to bring it back to thirteen. In a blur of action I kicked a goal, then another at the start of the fourth quarter. That took us to within seven points, but it was as close as we got. In the end, Geelong beat us by three goals.

Part of me was elated – two goals and a good game – but the rooms weren't the happiest place in the world. We'd just lost our third game in a row, the first time the Eagles had done this since Malthouse became coach in 1990. For the second time in a row we'd lost to Geelong, sacrificing some of the psychological edge we'd got through two grand final wins. But the balancing act between your own feelings and your team's is one of the biggest challenges in sport. As I looked around at the drained faces of the best players in the AFL, everyone slumped against the walls, sitting on the floor or getting treatment from the physios, I knew one thing for sure. As relieved and even happy as I felt about my debut, now was not the time to flash a cheeky grin or crack a joke.

7

RISING STARS

A week later, we made it four losses in a row, losing to the premiers, Carlton, at Optus Oval in Melbourne – by one point. My record as the youngest West Coast player lasted exactly seven days. One of my teammates against Carlton was ten months younger than me, David Wirrpanda from Healesville in Victoria.

Wirrpanda was a sixteen-year-old boy wonder, a real good bloke and as clever as they get. He was an amazing talent, with true charisma. When he was selected, there was a huge press contingent at training to watch him. He was the best trainer on the track, lightning-quick, and he'd glide over the ground, picking the ball up and disposing it so cleanly that the rest of us players would stop and say, 'Fuck, how did he do that?' He had a ponytail, too, and a bit of mystique about him. But that was as far as the 'black magic' thing went. Wirrpanda would take the piss out of the 'magical powers' stereotype that people like to impose on any gifted Aboriginal player. When he came to Perth, he was a long way from home, which was hard for him but he had the courage to be independent. He was a clever guy and a great storyteller. I called him 'Nelson', after Nelson Mandela, for his ability to stand up and spin a yarn.

Wirrpanda was one of a bunch of young guys I became close to immediately. Right from the outset I was friends with Chad Morrison, who had made his debut a few weeks before me. Brayden Lyle, Jarrad Schofield, Phil Matera and Fraser Gehrig were other young guys I'd sit next to on the bus or the plane, all of us knowing our place.

We had plenty of time to get to know each other, because of the amount of travel involved in being an interstate team. It took a huge toll on me personally, mainly due to the regimentation of the lifestyle. I hated the plane trips, which were like torture for someone like me who couldn't sit still. All the waiting in line, the sitting and doing what you were told was suffocating. You lined up to load the team bus, you lined up to unload it, you waited in line to get taped, go to training, eat your dinner. Every step you had to fight your way through it. It was kind of competitive and as a kid you were a whipping boy, getting pushed to the back. I certainly knew I wasn't allowed to push in front of a Glen Jakovich or a Peter Sumich at dinner. It was a lot like school camp – and I hated school camp. Some guys really love that highly regulated environment, but not me.

I didn't dwell on any of that yet, because I was still fresh and we began winning. It started the week after the Carlton loss, when we beat Melbourne by 106. Then we took on Wayne Carey and North Melbourne, who were looking like premiership favourites, and beat them by sixty-seven. We were on a streak, and I was playing my part as a goal sneak. In our seventh straight win, over St Kilda at Subiaco, I kicked five goals in the last quarter and people started talking about us as dark horses for the flag. Glen Jakovich and John Worsfold suffered season-ending injuries, and Malthouse told the media that we were hundreds of games short, in experience, of the premiership teams of 1992 and 1994. But with Malthouse, the more he talked about rebuilding and just wanting to season his youngsters, the more everyone else said he was foxing.

In my first ten games I kicked eighteen goals. I was never a better kick for goal than I was that year. But at the same time, probably as a self-defence mechanism against the accolades that started coming my way through the press, I was savage on myself after any effort I didn't consider my best.

While Sam was my greatest source of comfort, she wasn't really into footy. She had no idea who John Worsfold was, which suited me just fine. The last thing I wanted after yet another three-day interstate swing was to sit down with my girlfriend and talk more football. I had football coming out of my ears, and the valuable thing Sam gave me was time away from it.

But if I'd played what I thought was a bad game, I couldn't get it out of my head. My confidant was Dad, who was a master of subtle sport psychology. The day after a game, I'd walk down to the oval at the bottom of our street and take some shots at goal. Dad would wander down with our dog, a beautiful golden retriever, and casually chat about the game.

There were a few interstate games in that first year when I got the footy but didn't use it well. I started to get bashed around a bit, and I'd be stewing on it until the next game. Most kids would forget it, but I couldn't. That's what Dad was good at, talking it over.

I remember one game in my first season, against Adelaide, when I failed to fire. While we were waiting for our flight home – more waiting, and it's always worse when you haven't played well – I rang Dad from the airport.

'What did you think?' I asked, knowing he'd watched me on television. The beauty of having such an involved, knowledgeable Dad was that he was someone with whom I could talk about my game, and the team's too – he wasn't a one-eyed parent who'd fixate on his own child.

'You had a pretty quiet one, pretty tough old day,' he said. He'd never feed me bullshit to make me feel better. Even though I'd always yearned for an easy compliment from him, his honesty was the key to our relationship.

I got defensive. I was in that mood where if Dad had said I'd played well, I'd have protested that I hadn't. Whatever he said, I was going to contradict.

'Yeah, but in the first quarter I got it a bit.'

'I think you're trying to talk yourself into it,' he said. 'It was a pretty average effort.'

'Do you reckon they'll play me next week?' I said, all brittle insecurity.

'I wouldn't be surprised if they dropped you back to let you run into a bit of form.'

When I got home, I had good news for him.

'I'm playing next week. Mick had a yarn to me on the way home and said I'm struggling but I just have to hang in there.'

Dad could see my relief, and he was happy for me. He'd just been engaging in some psychology, to help me straighten up my attitude for playing away from home.

'When you're away,' he said, 'you've just got to work on the little things – the smothers, the chases, the tackles. Don't be thinking about kicking five goals. Just the work rate, and if you can get those little things up to the same rate as when you're playing at home, then the rest will follow.'

It became another challenge. *Because* I didn't enjoy the travel, I set myself to play better on interstate trips than in Perth. Later, Dad said that I actually became a superior player away from home. It was becoming hardwired into my brain that I wanted the toughest possible challenge in order to show my best. It wouldn't be long before, unconsciously, I would be toughening up the challenge through artificial means.

AFTER MY debut, I played every game until August, when I hurt my ankle against Essendon and missed the next two rounds against Geelong and Richmond. Two weeks before the finals, we were looking at finishing in the top half of the eight, with a crucial double-chance. My comeback game was against Carlton at Subiaco, and I kicked five goals, which made it thirty in eighteen games in the regular season. I was doing my job, and we'd beaten the premiers by ten goals.

As an impressionable kid, I learnt things that would never leave me. Often they were buried deep beneath the headlines. Malthouse would have meetings in which he'd ask blokes what they loved most about playing footy, and of course some would say how they loved winning, or kicking goals. But Tony Evans, a rock-solid guy who'd later become the club's number one ticket holder, said: 'What I love most is giving the ball off to set up a goal for someone else.' It was the first time I'd heard that kind of sentiment – that teamwork can light a bloke up more than being the goal scorer – and it stuck with me. I still think about it.

In the first week of the finals we played Carlton at Subiaco again, and beat them again. Ron De Iulio was on me, as in the earlier game, and I added three more goals; we won by fifty-five points and were installed as premiership favourites.

But due to agreements on the playing of finals in Melbourne, we had to travel to the MCG to play Essendon the next week. Even though Essendon had finished two places below us, and even though they'd lost in the first week of the finals, they got a home game and we had to travel. The winner would play Sydney for a place in the grand final.

First, though, was the Norwich Rising Star award, for rookies under the age of twenty-one. I thought Shannon Grant would win. He was having a dynamic year for the Swans. The judges were a daunting bunch: Kevin Bartlett, Ross Glendinning, Malcolm Blight, Gerard Healy, Leigh Matthews, and the top officials Ian Collins and Ross Oakley. Watching by video link from Perth, I couldn't believe it when I won by one vote over Grant. I chose the moment to tell the world that I wanted to spend my entire career playing for West Coast.

WE FELT we were up for the semifinal, but were never in it against Essendon. Gavin Wanganeen, the champion Brownlow Medal-winning defender, was put on me. I guess I should have been flattered that I was now being marked by the game's best small defender, but it didn't feel good to be kept in check and beaten by seventy-seven points.

Still, it had been an amazing season, way beyond expectations. I'd played twenty games when I'd been hoping to play one. I'd played in two finals, and kicked thirty-three goals. I'd finished fourteenth in the best-and-fairest voting in a team of all-stars. It had been so sudden, and so surprising. A year ago I'd been a schoolboy player who'd spent most of the winter getting over an injury; now I was judged the best rookie in the country by a panel of legends.

What do you do after such a year? You shrug off the back-slappers and get into training, because now you're under pressure to go even better.

8

TAGGED

The better you play, the harder to follow it up. I guess I'd heard that often enough, but I didn't understand how true it was until my second year.

Having gone so well in 1996, we were one of the early premiership favourites. I'd started as a kid who could sneak under the radar and grab a couple of goals, but now I was a target for opposition coaches, who figured the way to control me was to put a tagger on and make my life difficult.

I enlarged the bullseye on my back by starting the season well, with three goals in a big win in Sydney in the first round, then five goals when we trounced Melbourne at the MCG. Aside from a rolled ankle and a virus that had me coughing up blood against the Dockers, I was going fine.

Then, on a Friday night in May, we played the Western Bulldogs at the WACA and I had Tony Liberatore on me.

Liberatore had been a prolific ball-getter who won a Brownlow Medal back in 1990, but now that he was thirty-one and nearing the end of his career, his new coach Terry Wallace had switched him to a totally negative role. Liberatore had one job, which was to scrag and harass one of the key players in the opposing team. I guess his coach and his fans loved him.

The Bulldogs had a team strategy where they'd nominate a young opposition player with a particular slogan. They'd say: 'He's in the gun.' Every Bulldog would have a crack at that player.

That night it was my turn to be 'in the gun', and Liberatore was on to me from the start. I got an early free kick and a goal, and told him it would be the first of many for the night. But I only got one more, and they beat us by fourteen points.

Unfortunately, my quiet game sent out a signal to other clubs. The next week Brisbane put Andrew Bews on me, and then Richmond put Chris Bond on me. From Melbourne it was Paul Hopgood. Week after week I had someone bashing me. Playing in a good side made it easier, but not too much. I always got the most irritating and persistent taggers. Some were fair players, given their role, and others were just doing what they could to survive in the AFL. But the strategy – as if all the fifteen other clubs were collaborating – was to shut me down, hamper my enjoyment of the game, and stop us scoring, and overall it was working.

By late May I felt I was just getting some form back. We were playing Essendon at home. I kicked three goals and felt my confidence returning, when ten seconds before the final siren I was tackled from behind, by Paul Barnard. His knee went into my calf, and at first I thought it was a hard cork.

When the siren went, I was down. Rod Moore, the club doctor who was also our family doctor, and the Eagles' legendary head trainer Billy Sutherland came out and hoisted my arms over their shoulders.

'We've won! We've won!' they were shouting.

All I could gasp was, 'Get my mouthguard out.'

I was in such pain I knew I was going to faint. I'm not sure why it is, but my body reacts in this way to extreme pain. Over the years I became renowned at West Coast for fainting. This was the first of many times I'd pass out in Rod's and Billy's arms. They got my mouthguard out, and I hit the deck. My body just shut down. I don't know how long I was unconscious, probably only a few seconds, but when I came to, Rod said, 'Don't get up, we're bringing out a stretcher.'

I was taken away in an ambulance to hospital. Malthouse thought it was a pinched nerve – wishful thinking, maybe – but X-rays showed that I'd broken my tibia.

For four weeks I was off my feet, and when I got up I needed crutches to walk. This would be tough for anyone, but given my nature, it drove me mad. Not only did I feel caged in by my inactivity, I could literally feel my leg muscles withering away. After all the work I'd done on my fitness, I was beside myself with anxiety that even when I could walk again I'd have lost too much condition to get up for the rest of the season. I'd worked so hard to get into shape, but it was going away in a flash. I'd broken the leg in round eleven, and it would be round seventeen or eighteen, at best, when I could come back. I could feel the whole season slipping away. The boys were going well, maybe not premiership well, but definitely heading for the finals. I couldn't bear the thought of missing out.

It was during my recuperation that I dabbled with ecstasy again. I'd been so committed to my footy, it always took precedence. But then, when I was injured, I just got bored. Totally unplanned, as a kind of release from my boredom and frustration, it happened twice during my seven weeks off. Looking back from here, I realise it was never as good as the first time and I was always chasing that feeling. But to be honest, at the time it felt great, and that was why I kept doing it.

But then I got fully into rehab and refocused on my footy. At that point, drugs and football didn't mix. They were in sealed-off, separate boxes. My football was too precious to me, and the idea that you could sample that thrill I'd got from ecstasy while also functioning at your peak as a footballer did not seem possible.

A SOURCE of relief around the club that year was that one of my best mates had joined the Eagles. In his first year Michael Gardiner was good enough, as a ruckman, to make his seniors debut – an amazing achievement, because ruckmen normally take years to mature.

But Gardy was one of a kind. I'd played a bit of state under-age footy with him. He was that rare animal: a huge bloke who was as nimble and skilful as a little guy. He was a fantastic basketballer, and brought that quickness and agility to football. Watching him play for Hale, Dad had long been saying he'd love to work with Gardy, who he thought could be the most dominant player in the history of the Alcock Cup, and in 1996 he'd recruited him to Wesley.

Bill Mitchell had alerted the old man that Michael was on the verge of being expelled from Hale. Dad rang up Michael's old man, Renny, who said Michael was desperate to stay at Hale, but he'd call Dad if it didn't happen.

Gardy was a bloke after my own heart. Being entrepreneurial in spirit, he'd somehow found out where the exam papers were kept at Hale. A week before the exams, he copied some of the papers and, with a mate, marketed them to the 120 or so kids who'd be sitting them. I think they made a couple of thousand dollars. Of course, it wasn't long before the whole school knew. The teachers were the last to catch on. Gardy, a boarder, was that brazen that he was sitting in his dorm the night before the exams, filling out the papers, when a boarding master came in and asked him how he was going with his homework. Gardy said he was having some trouble with some questions. The master sat down and helped him with the exam, thinking it was his homework. So the next morning, Gardy pulled the whole exam he'd finished the night before, with his teacher's help, out of his pants, put it on the desk, slipped the unmarked exam paper down his pants, and left an hour early. That's how well he had it orchestrated.

He and his mate got caught and called in by John Inverarity, the former Test cricketer who was Hale's headmaster. Renny drove to Hale to see if he could save Michael from being expelled. They struck a deal: Michael could stay at the school as long as he gave the names of all the other blokes who were involved.

Gardy said to his old man: 'That's not how you brought me up. If I rat on my mates it won't be worth staying at the school anyway.'

So he came to Wesley and became the school's star recruit. From hearing that story, I already knew I liked him. Gardy would cop a lot of criticism over the years but he's got a lot of great qualities. As with some of the sillier things I've done, Michael's attitude to his exam stunt was that he probably shouldn't have done it, but if the chance came around again, he'd probably do it all over. It was just boys being boys. He never saw any reason to apologise for a lark.

Ironically, after all that, he broke a bone in his foot in his first game for Wesley and didn't play again for the rest of the year. But he was always at training, encouraging the blokes, helping out with the coaching. He didn't have to do that, but he couldn't have handled himself any better.

*

WHEN I was ready to train again in July, it took me a while to work my lungs open. I couldn't have played midfield; I didn't have the tank. So I was back in the forward pocket to grab goals opportunistically, be more of an impact player in bursts than a hard runner for all four quarters.

The plan went well at first. My first game back was on a wet day in Sydney. I scored a goal with my second touch, and even though we lost I felt quite relieved by how I'd handled the ball and the pace of the game.

But for the rest of the season, I couldn't maintain that form. An AFL season is incredibly attritional – it's a marathon. Getting yourself up to play at your sparkling best week after week is tough for anyone. Malthouse was always drumming into us that we'd be judged on our consistency, not just our best games. This is a lesson for anyone who plays the game, but when you're a kid it's unbelievably difficult to keep doing it week after week for six months.

When I felt sluggish before a game, I went to Port Beach. If it was a nice day I'd go for a walk, have a stretch, and go in the water. I've always found a special healing power in salt water. I'd jump in, do three or four porpoises, then hop out and have a hot shower and get ready to go to the match.

But it was a tough, tough season. To make matters harder for me, playing up forward relies a lot on factors beyond your control. Sometimes you're out of the game for long periods, even though you're very active. I felt I was working really hard and doing everything right, but the ball just wasn't coming my way, and my position felt like a graveyard. When you're already down on confidence, as I was, the natural lulls in playing forward aggravate it. I started asking myself whether I was up to it.

Then the bashing restarted. Against Fremantle, I was belted from behind by Andrew Wills before the opening bounce.

I couldn't even remember the first quarter. A couple of weeks later, I faced Liberatore again for round two.

After subduing me in the game in May at the WACA, Liberatore had received a lot of praise. A lot of the media were enjoying his destructiveness. During the week after the WACA game, when Liberatore wasn't at training, Terry Wallace told reporters he thought Liberatore was 'still with Cousins'.

Now we were playing the Bulldogs in the last-ever match at the Western Oval, before they were to move to the new Docklands Stadium. The match was a bloodbath. Peter Matera was punched in the jaw and ironed out. Michael Gardiner got charged viciously from behind. And for my sins, Liberatore scratched me with his fingernails, sledged me, elbowed and scragged me, did everything he could to put me off my game. He wasn't there to play football. He just wanted to negate me. Big deal. The hardest part for me was to resist the urge to do what he wanted me to do, which was punch his lights out. He was only a little guy, not much more than 5 foot, and if you're in a pub and a bloke's doing what he was doing you'd love to smash him. But that was what he wanted: put me off, get me reported, stop me thinking about what I was meant to be doing, which was helping my team win. If I'm spending half my day fighting, then that's a victory for the opposition.

It was a horrible day, and the officials made it worse by reporting only one player – our ruckman Jason Ball, which was ridiculous. I ended up covered in bloody scratch marks, and Peter Matera and Gardy were badly knocked up. The fact that I kicked the last-ever AFL goal on the Western Oval didn't console me one bit.

When I got home I was ranting and raving.

'I fucken hate that bloke, I can't believe what he was doing!'

When I'd simmered down, Dad came to my room and said I wasn't playing very smart. He gave me a few suggestions, but I didn't want to listen, I was so angry. Dad had a way of hearing me out, waiting for the storm to pass, and then quietly having his say.

'Mate, I can tell you one thing without a shadow of a doubt,' he said. 'Next time you play the Bulldogs you're going to get him again. We can sit here and feel sorry for ourselves, but it's probably better to do something about it. You played to his strengths. Next time, get him out one on one. You're a skilful player and he's a dogged little bloke, highly irritating, but he can't match you for skills. Test him out, run, take him on.'

What Dad was saying was, I'd been sucked into engagement with Liberatore, chasing him up the ground when he had the ball, when what I should have done was take a few risks, run away from him, make the play. I could outrun him, and if the ball was in the air I could certainly out-mark him. My problem, in that match at the Western Oval, was that I was so tied up with frustration about my game generally, and so lacking in confidence in my stamina and pace after my injury, that I'd let Liberatore dictate how I'd played.

I'd remember that advice for the next time we played the Dogs. But for the moment I was as close as I ever came to being dropped. I just hadn't come back from the broken leg with any consistency or any luck – funny how they seem to go together.

We were in the finals, but in an eliminator at the MCG against the premiers, the North Melbourne Kangaroos. For West Coast, the choice of who to drop came down to me and Andy Lovell, the former Melbourne grand final player who was reaching the end of his career. We had a beer, and Andy said, 'If it was down to form they'd pick me ahead of you. But I reckon because I'm at the end and you're the future of the club, and you've worked so hard, they should leave me out.'

I was grateful, and impressed. It wasn't up to Andy to choose the team, but it would have been a hard thing for him to say.

Every match would have been like gold to him. It was a measure of the quality of the guy that he sat down with me and said that.

The match committee did choose me ahead of Andy. We travelled to Melbourne but were outclassed. I kicked two goals but we went down by thirteen points. My feeling about the season was: 'Good riddance, let's put that one away and start again.'

9

IF I HAD MY TIME AGAIN

I'd finished 1997 feeling more disappointment than I'd ever had as a footballer. I'd felt a lot of external pressure to exceed my rookie year, but that was nothing compared with the pressure I heaped on myself. Not only had I not improved on 1996, I'd gone backwards. I could blame the injury, and I could say that teams bashing and tagging me were paying me the ultimate compliment, but that kind of thinking could only take me so far. During the summer, I got hungry again. The disappointment of 1997 became the spur for 1998. I trained maniacally in the pre-season. If I'd been full-on before, it was nothing like the summer of 1997–98.

I grew closer to Malthouse. One of the things I admired about him was that he wouldn't become complacent himself, so there was no way he tolerated complacency among others. He knew how hard I worked and how desperate I was, how I wouldn't accept my performances, how I had to keep punishing myself. It's a weird way to be, but for Malthouse it was the road to success, and I lapped it up. After training I'd 'touch' with him for five minutes: I'd hand pass the ball and he'd punch it back. I'd read the bounce, pick it up and hand pass it back. He was intense, and so was I. We wouldn't need to say very much. It was our way of communicating our hunger. I sought him out in preference to some of the assistant coaches, because his aura created a game-like intensity. You could never lapse into a false sense of security with him.

By the time the new season kicked off, I was probably ready for a finals series. This time, unlike 1996, nobody was worried about me. That's a strange thing, looking back. My intensity as an untried seventeen-year-old rang alarm bells. But my doubled intensity as a nineteen-year-old who'd had a good season followed by a mediocre one was seen as healthy preparation. I guess people thought I was in control.

IT TURNED into my breakout year. We lost five of our first seven games, but often by tiny margins, so our percentage was still better than 100. From April we began to convert good play into wins – six in a row, getting us up to third on the ladder and justifying some of the pre-season hype.

I felt good all year – injury-free, or as much as you can be in the AFL, and achieving the week-on-week consistency that Malthouse asked for. I was wearing the number 9 jersey now, Peter Wilson's old number, and that also gave me a lift. Even though I was still only nineteen, I was getting closer to feeling like a fully-fledged senior player. In May, Malthouse moved me from the forward pocket into the midfield, where my training really paid off.

I was still learning the requirements of playing on the ball. I was no natural aerobic athlete, no Robert Harvey or Shane

Crawford. If I ended up as a renowned runner, I didn't start that way. The demands of the midfield were taking me to places I'd never been, where I was so exhausted my mind began playing tricks on me and I had to push on through what was almost an altered mental state.

My fiftieth game showed me how far I still had to travel in this new role. We were playing Hawthorn, who had the Brownlow Medallist in the corresponding position, also wearing number 9. We won, but Crawford outplayed me, teaching me a lesson in midfield football.

In June I signed a new two-year contract with the Eagles. After my initial emotional reservations, I was now firmly committed to the club. Most AFL footballers will tell you that in a perfect world, they would be one-club players. I was no different. I hoped and believed I'd be an Eagle for life.

We were patchy in the second half of the season, wins alternating with losses, and ended up seventh on the ladder. We had a better than expected away record, with six wins and five losses, and probably a worse than expected home record, also six and five.

Our final was against the Bulldogs in Melbourne, and the media was revved up all week about another Cousins–Liberatore clash. He'd missed our first match that season, and in the second, following Dad's advice, I'd run him around the park and we'd broken even. This time, in the semifinal, after all the anticipation, he wasn't put on me. For the rest of his career, he'd never spend more than a quarter, or even a few minutes, tagging me. I'd won. My role models in that regard were Dean Kemp and James Hird, blokes whose temperament was never rattled. That was what the Liberatore contest had taught me. For all that you can say about being harassed as the highest compliment an opposing team can pay you, it's an even higher compliment when your harasser is taken off you and given an easier job.

Although I won that personal battle, the bigger one was thoroughly lost: the Bulldogs smashed us by seventy points. We were out in the first week of the finals, and the Adelaide Crows went on to win their second straight flag.

I was selected in the All-Australian team, a huge honour I was happy to be sharing for the first time with our fullback, Ashley McIntosh. I was flattered and a little overwhelmed by that kind of recognition. I'd had a good year, I knew that, but to be picked among the best in the country was a big leap from my moderate 1997 and an unthinkable one from where I'd been at the beginning of 1996. I also came second to McIntosh in the club's best-and-fairest, and got eighteen votes in the Brownlow, not too far behind the winner, St Kilda's Robert Harvey.

At the end of the season I was approached by the well-known Melbourne player agent, Ricky Nixon. Most of the prominent Victorian managers had paid us a visit at some point to try to sign me up, but I didn't think they could give me anything I didn't already have with Dad. I liked that I was Dad's only 'client', and it didn't make sense to send management commissions outside the family when Dad was doing a great job anyway – and Dad always forgot to charge me management commissions.

Nixon was an all right bloke; I didn't form any strong opinion about him one way or the other. He said he could really help me broaden my opportunities and income, but when we told him what I was already doing and what I was getting paid, he was staggered. Perth was a two-team town and West Coast had all the money. I had an endorsement from Puma, retainers with Channel Seven in Perth and radio 96 FM, and even a gig to promote the West Australian Trotting Association, courtesy of the old man. (I was the 'face' of the association, to draw younger people into the sport; what I couldn't admit was that with my asthma, I couldn't go anywhere near Dad's horses or stables! I was so sensitive to horse dust that Dad, when he came home, had to take his work clothes off before he went anywhere near the bedrooms.)

Even Ricky had to admit that from Melbourne he couldn't do better than Dad. But we ended up doing a kind of side deal, where Ricky would look for opportunities for me in the eastern states and leave Perth to Dad. The big carrot Ricky held out was his 'Club 10', this select group of some of the biggest names in AFL, which he could market together, and it was flattering to be considered in that league. Gary Ablett, Jason Dunstall and Greg Williams had been in it, and were retiring. Coming in were guys like Wayne Carey, Michael Voss, Mark Ricciuto and Matthew Lloyd. I felt under-qualified. They were all superstars, and I signed up to join them because I felt honoured that someone saw me as being at that level. But to all intents and purposes, Dad remained my real manager.

WITH THE good side of the off-field action came another side that I wasn't so sure about. In 1998, I became conscious that I was getting more media attention than the two-time premiership players at the club. Everyone wanted to interview me and make me the focal point. I didn't really understand the news media – that they were doing this because I was a novelty. They'd done the Worsfolds, Mainwarings, Kemps and Jakoviches before, so now they were moving on to me. I didn't see it that way; instead I saw myself getting an amount of attention that was unwarranted compared with the senior players. My first loyalty was to my teammates, so when I'd see headlines saying West Goes Wild for the Kid, I'd cringe. One report said I was the most famous person in Western Australia. It embarrassed me. Two years earlier I'd been playing in front of eighty people at Beasley Park. What the hell were they talking about?

I was so worried about treading on the senior players' toes, I didn't know how to react. I belonged to a team, and didn't want to be singled out. The result was that I developed a prickly relationship with the media. They'd want an interview, and in those days the club didn't have a full-time media officer controlling these requests. I had to respond to them myself, and the only way I could see to protect myself and not offend the senior players was to say no. Talking myself up to the public wasn't the way I was raised. I was superstitious, too, afraid that whenever I gave an interview I'd be setting myself up to play a shit game the next week. The footy gods, I was convinced, would punish me.

But my strategy ended up being counterproductive. The more I thought I was doing the right thing by saying no, the more I got a reputation for being difficult. I just didn't want the attention, but the more I ran away from it, the harder it chased me.

THE ATTENTION I received during 1998 had the effect of refocusing me on working for the team. Whenever I was over-praised (and to me, all praise was over-praise), I felt I had to compensate by running harder, training harder, playing harder. Whenever I got worried that I was getting so much attention that senior players would be put out, I worked my arse off to be the guy who never let them down on the field. I tried to restrain myself around the club, making a deliberate effort not to seem like a lair. I just wanted the team to swallow me up. I had no interest in being singled out as an individual. Still, your best efforts can only go so far. Beyond that, people will form their own opinions. As a kid, everything I did was scrutinised. I understand that now, but back then, I was quite hurt when Brett Heady pulled me aside and said, 'Listen, mate, understand that not everyone around the club loves you, you're not everyone's cup of tea.'

That year was my real education in how different you look from the outside compared with how you look to yourself. From my own point of view, it just didn't make sense that I got recognised by strangers in the street. Being shy, I didn't like it. But I hid my awkwardness behind a grin – which, to me, was just a grin to keep everything at arm's length, a smile like a fence, but to others it looked like the cocky grin of someone who was lapping it all up, revelling in the attention. But it was a misunderstanding. If any of my teammates thought I was enjoying the attention, they couldn't have been further from the truth.

On weekend nights, after games, I'd want to go out to bars or clubs like any other bloke my age. I often had Sam with me, which I thought would seal off a bit of private space.

It didn't. Girls would come up and ask for an autograph or a photo, or just want to start a conversation with me, right in front of Sam. Or, if Sam wasn't there and I didn't want the attention, I was backed into a bit of a corner. I couldn't just tell someone to leave me alone. It wasn't in my nature to seek confrontation, and the last thing I wanted was for people to go off saying Ben Cousins was an up-himself dickhead. So I just grinned, appeasing. I was a people-pleaser, because that was the easiest way. And I thought it was part of my responsibility, as a West Coast player, to be polite. But there were limits. Girls would come up and say things like, 'I hate football.' It amused me that so many of the same lines got trotted out again and again. I guess they just wanted a reaction. I'd say, 'Yeah, I hate it too, I just do it because I can't do anything else,' and look bored until they went away.

I don't know if anyone really enjoys that attention without being suspicious of how genuine it is. I was getting more adulation than I'd ever received as a kid, especially from girls, but I was smart enough to realise it was fickle. I'd never had very high self-esteem when it came to girls, so I told myself that they were interested in celebrity, not me. In my mind, I was still the kid who'd been knocked back by girls behind the rec centre.

Sam knew I wasn't interested in being the young-man-about-town, and she let it wash over her in her typically mature way. I don't think I ever acknowledged how hard it must have been for her, though, to rise above it. I had trouble seeing things from her point of view. And because she never made a fuss, I never thought she was bothered by it. But that was the convenient thing for me to believe, and if I had my time again I'd recognise that it was a struggle for her.

If I had my time again . . .

IT WAS at the end of the 1998 season that I broke through a kind of barrier with my drug-taking. Up till then, it had only been occasional. But after all the attention that was heaped on me that year, I craved the life I suddenly felt I was missing out on. My mates from Wesley, or from the Leeming area, were doing what normal twenty-year-olds were doing. A bunch of Wesley guys went to London to travel around and work in pubs and enjoy their freedom. They stayed in Covent Garden, worked at a place called Belushi's, and lived the life. I couldn't do that. My Leeming mates were up to all sorts of tricks right through the year. I couldn't do that either. I resented it, and all the school-camp stuff we had to do at the Eagles, all the travel and regimentation, only deepened my resentment. I was missing out on a special stage of life, the beginning of freedom. All I had was a window of about ten weeks after the footy season finished, and before the pre-season began. Into those ten weeks I wanted to pack a full year's worth of the life I was missing.

I got to go to America with Mum and Dad, who wanted to take all of us kids to California for one last big family holiday. I paid a brief visit to the blokes in London. Travel gave me even more of a taste for what I was missing out on. I wished I could take a year off and get it all out of my system. I played with the thought of taking that year off when I was twenty-six or twenty-seven. It wasn't feasible to do that at nineteen or twenty, which was when my footy career was taking off – though that was probably when I needed it most. By the time I was twenty-seven, it would be too late. As it turned out, I'd have my year off at thirty, but not in the way I'd planned.

Ecstasy still did it for me the way no other drug did. I loved the warm feeling of euphoria it gave me; they don't call it the love drug for nothing. I liked to combine it with speed, which I began snorting in that off-season. Speed didn't change the way your mind operated, but it gave you incredible energy and charge. When you were on speed, you could do anything, go anywhere. Usually this meant going to a club and raving.

Later, people would say that I got into drugs because all the fame went to my head. This might be hard to believe, but the opposite was true. The public attention pushed me towards the drug-using culture not because I wanted to enhance the 'excitement' of being recognised in public, but because I wanted to escape from it. I took drugs not with my football mates, but with people I knew from school and around home. It was a separate group, a separate life. Being high felt like being in a group within a group, an inner circle that I escaped into. When I took drugs, I thought I was being a bit clever, hiding in full view. If I was straight and sober in a bar or a nightclub, with people, blokes and girls, always coming up to me for something, I hated it. When I had chemicals in my system, I could tell myself, 'I'm not really here, I'm enjoying my privacy even though nobody knows about it.'

It was during that summer that I became 'connected', and learnt to how to get gear, mainly speed or ecstasy. To be honest it wasn't hard. You'd go through a club and there was gear every- where. When I walked into a club, people were virtually throwing it at me. Tough guys, bikies, gangsters, small-time or big-time dealers alike, they were all willing to give me a leg-up. I became acquainted with cocaine. It was much more expensive than speed, but I loved how subtle it was. It didn't rev you up like speed, and it didn't give you that almost psychedelic euphoria of ecstasy. It was almost like the drug you did when you didn't want to have a big night; coke wore off and left your system. It wasn't long before I fell in love with it. It was the drug most conducive to a professional footballer's lifestyle, where he wants to feel really good for a few hours and then have a chance to sleep it off and be clean again. A night on coke didn't have to turn into a whole weekend.

And the cost wasn't much of a barrier for me at the time. I'd like to get back a quarter of what I spent on it.

If I had my time again . . .

10

SUBTLE SHIFTS

By 1999 the old order was on its way out. Each year we lost two or three blokes from the 1992 and 1994 premiership teams, and the remaining ones were slipping towards the end. John Worsfold's retirement was one of the most noticeable changes for 1999; he'd been a steady influence as captain as well as the toughest backman you could imagine. Single-minded, unhesitating, a man who'd sacrifice his own game for others, he epitomised what I thought of as a good captain. Peter Matera, Chris Waterman, Chris Lewis and Chris Mainwaring were also reaching that point where an injury, or a run of indifferent form, raised the question of whether it was time to go.

For me, that only sharpened the edge. I was coming under more scrutiny from opponents because I was playing better, and also because they had fewer and fewer other Eagles to be on the lookout for.

I approached the new challenge the only way I could, which was head-on. If I was ambitious for one thing, it was to improve on 1998. My bad year in 1997 had taught me a lesson: if you're not going forwards, you're going backwards. There's no such thing as sitting on your previous year's form and trying to guard it. You have to keep improving to stay ahead of teams who think they've worked you out.

In the pre-season, Malthouse kept stressing to me that the great players get judged over time, not on one or two good years. 'You have to play good-quality footy for ten years,' he said. 'Only then are you a champion.' He'd talk about guys like Carlton's Craig Bradley, playing great footy year in, year out. I had such respect for Malthouse, I wanted him to rate me with guys like that.

For a lot of that year, we looked like another premiership was a real possibility before the guard changed for good. Scott Cummings had been recruited to give us a focal point in attack, and he was kicking goals. Although I was a rover now, I was still contributing handy goals, sometimes bags of three or four. I was being heavily targeted: in the opening round, a western derby, there was a brawl, an inquiry, and $45,000 in fines handed out; but the important thing was that we won by four points.

After fourteen rounds, we'd won eleven games and were at the top of the ladder. I'd played all over Liberatore at Subiaco in our game against the Bulldogs, one of the last times he got to have a crack at me. Things were sailing along well until the weekend after my twenty-first birthday.

Being born on 30 June, for a serious footballer, is a bit of a curse. As far back as I could remember, I hadn't had a big celebration, because it was smack-bang in the middle of the season. In any case, I preferred a family roast. The year I turned twenty-one, my birthday fell on a Wednesday, three days before our game at Subiaco against Melbourne. We did nothing special that night, but Sam and I planned a dinner out after the match.

In this Melbourne game I was shadowed by the rugged Paul Hopgood, who didn't bend the rules as far as Liberatore but was a real obstacle nonetheless. I corked my thigh late in the game, which we won, and came off.

Then, during my birthday meal out with Sam at Alto's restaurant, I suffered a reaction. My thigh was swelling up badly. As I got up to go to the toilet, I got dizzy and my legs went out from under me. I passed out and ended up in an ambulance going to hospital, where I was kept overnight so they could drain fluid from my leg.

Perth is a small town, and the rumour mill cranked up immediately: that I'd gone out partying and had somehow overdone it that night. The foundation of that rumour was quite funny, actually. There was a doctor in the restaurant who ran across and knelt by my side when I fainted. When I came to, my mouth was bone-dry and I had an intense craving for sugar. I was gasping loudly, to her and anyone else who might have been listening: 'Coke! Coke!'

I just wanted a drink, but someone thought I was speaking about the other coke, and one thing led to another. Small town.

I missed the next game, against Richmond, which we lost. From there the team imploded. For the rest of the home-and-away season, we only beat Collingwood and lost our seven other matches. I got charged by Joe Misiti in a ten-goal defeat by Essendon, hurting my hip when he ran into it with a raised knee. But that was only a small part of the picture. We'd been almost unbeatable for the first two-thirds of the season, and in the last third just forgot how to win.

Having slipped from first to fifth, we had our first final against the Bulldogs, a top-four team throughout the late nineties. Against Liberatore again, I did enough to get him moved off me – he just couldn't keep up now – and we won by five points. But it was a last gasp. The next week, against

Carlton, we went down by nine goals and that was it: my fourth season out of four when we'd made the finals but been knocked out in either the first or second week.

There were some personal accolades again. I was third to Bluey McKenna in the club's best-and-fairest, and was picked in the All-Australian team again. This led to my one and only appearance in an international rules series.

I took my brother Matthew to Melbourne for the series. He'd been just as passionate as me about footy, and I found it hard to see the bad luck he'd had. I'd always hoped for the best for him, and had desperately wanted both of us to succeed. But in those big development years, ages fourteen through seventeen, his shoulders kept popping out, his body wasn't going to hold. I was blessed with all the luck he didn't have.

We had a good time in Melbourne, and then as always he never made me feel guilty. He's an outstanding bloke, which he showed in how he handled adversity. He handled disappointment a lot better than I would have. If he'd succeeded and I hadn't, I wouldn't have been anywhere near as mature about it as he was. He remained very cluey about the game and we'd talk three or four times a week. While I dropped out of uni, he did a commerce degree and got into property development. He was always happy to see me do well, even when his heart was broken by the setbacks he'd had. He'd grown up like me, wanting to be an AFL player. It's not everybody's dream, but it was for Matthew.

In Melbourne, I said to him, 'Footy's not everything. You get to do all the good things in life which I can't.'

Before long he'd be looking at me and thinking maybe he got the better end of the deal.

I PLAYED international rules so that I could sample the experience of a round ball and represent my country. But I didn't believe in the concept, which seemed artificial to me, and I couldn't get my head around the complex hybrid of Australian and Gaelic football. I hated it. There was a lot of school camp in the way it was organised, and I couldn't think of anything worse than more travelling, on top of a season as a West Coast player. A lot of Melbourne blokes jumped at it, but I couldn't get motivated. By that stage, I was champing at the bit to get together with my mates, charge out and have my idea of a holiday.

Not that I'd waited until the off-season. That year, I was having the odd binge during the football season. Although my football was going so well, and was giving me great professional satisfaction, I wouldn't say I was *enjoying* it the way I had as a kid. This wasn't accidental; in fact, not enjoying it was almost planned. I'd figured out, through my four seasons in the AFL, that I had to live in a place where I was constantly hungry. I had to make myself uncomfortable, ambitious, in order to motivate myself. Malthouse was like this: a guy who approached each season, each match, as if he'd achieved nothing in his career and it was all on the line every week. That was how I wanted to be.

So, for example, I was watching what I ate – vigilantly, every minute. The right amount of carbs, protein, sugar. Every single meal had a point to it. I could only eat junk food when I was pulling up after a bender. I could enjoy junk food then – not because it was a release, but because it had a point. I could rarely just exist and do nothing, never go on a holiday and sit down and think. Every conscious hour was targeted towards some effect on my body and my game.

But my basic nature was to be happy, so forcing myself to be dissatisfied created an imbalance that needed redressing. This was where my double life worked, I thought, to my advantage. The only time I didn't live in a state of discomfort and hunger was when I could be in the exact opposite of it. So I needed to do something to let off steam in a fast, efficient way. That's where the drugs came in. When the moment came for me to let loose, I'd really let loose, get on the gear and charge until I was the last man standing. I was as competitive about partying as I was about footy. It was insane, but I saw myself as something of a machine. So it'd be train hard for a match, play on Friday night, go hard on some combination of coke, speed, ecstasy and alcohol until Sunday night, then crash for twelve hours, wake up and go for a run so hard I'd almost make myself vomit. Then drag myself out for a week's training.

My weekends would start out with Sam. She was my girl – also my wingman. But pretty quickly she made it clear that I was driving the pursuit for full-on benders. She wasn't the type of character to party like I did. Sometimes she'd party with me, but not all the time.

We were both very co-dependent, though, and I needed her desperately. After being together for four years, we moved into a place I bought in South Perth, a nice duplex near Wesley College. Sam looked after me, nurtured me. I wouldn't have been able to keep my football together without her picking up the pieces after my partying. Some weekends, having gone out after a Friday night match, I'd stagger back home at eleven on a Sunday night, and she'd be there to feed me and put me to bed and make sure I was all right. In turn, I supported her. We were a partnership. There's no questioning how much she contributed to my career. And when I look back on those days, there is not a single memory I treasure more than shutting the world out on Sundays, turning the phone off, cocooning in our bed, watching television, just being in our nest. It was my way of surviving the Mondays, but it was also special. My problem – one of my problems – was that I'd had to go through all of the drug-taking and drinking to get to the point where I was unwound enough to just *be*.

I didn't take drugs every weekend. I had to plan methodically, looking for windows when we had a Friday night or Saturday afternoon game and I'd know I had enough time to rest and get the drugs out of my system. Six-day breaks were too hard, but if we had an eight-day break I'd be rubbing my hands together. There was a urine-testing program in place, but I'd learnt that I only got tested once or twice a season, and the testers never came on Mondays, when I was at my most vulnerable. For my first few years in the AFL, they only tested on game days. As I never took drugs within four or five days of a game, and as I concentrated on cocaine, which I believed was the quickest out of my system, I thought I was safe. Once every five or six weeks, three blokes out of our squad of forty would be taken for testing on game day. So I just rode the odds.

The whole scheme of planning when I'd get on it, which matches had a bit of clear space after them, how long I'd binge for, all appealed to my meticulous side. I was highly organised and controlled in all things, and a drug bender was another facet of that. I was stimulated by the cat-and-mouse game drugs forced me to play with testing and performing on the field. I promised myself never to take short cuts and never to let my teammates down. I rationalised my drug use in this way: if I trained harder than every other bloke, played harder, performed better, then I could excuse my little holidays. In fact, the logic soon became inverted. *Because* of my holidays, I was actually forcing myself to be a better footballer. Every time I had a binge, I had to purge myself with hard training and a great game. In a perverse way, during that year I began to tell myself that my good performance as a footballer was dependent on the binges. I was proving it with All-Australian selection. I was operating in the opposite way to how I thought a regular drug user operated. No way was I taking my foot off the gas. If anything, I was going harder. In my naivety,

SUBTLE SHIFTS

I thanked my drug use for making me a better footballer. And that was the real beginning of the end, though the end was a hell of a long way off yet.

11

BOTH OF MY TWO LIVES

For half of my career at West Coast, I built a wall between my football mates and the people I took drugs with. My drug mates were well outside the club. They were my 'real' social life, which I kept private. I couldn't afford to let it get out. Obviously it could hurt my career if it did, but part of the fun, also, was the secrecy. Eventually it became the worst-kept secret in Perth, but for a long time it wasn't.

My best mate within the club was Gardy. That friendship wasn't about drugs. We had a similar attitude to authority, and he always made me laugh. Like me, Gardy hated the off-field restraints and the meetings; we couldn't sit still. We both walked a fine line between what we could get away with and what we couldn't. We were committed footballers first and foremost, and Gardy had the wit to go with it. If we were called into a meeting and asked to sit in a circle, Gardy would give me a look. He had this saying: 'If it involves a circle, it can't be good.' He cracked me up.

The friendship I had with Chris Mainwaring was completely different. He was my role model and mentor, in more good ways than bad.

People at the club looked up to Mainy. He was like a magnet: a fun, knockabout bloke from Geraldton who loved his surf. He looked like a laid-back surfer, but he was a gifted and extremely tough footballer, a star wingman in the Eagles' premierships in 1992 and 1994. Twelve years older than me, he was All-Australian twice, and had played with the East Fremantle Sharks, like I had. Of all the senior blokes who were at West Coast when I started, Mainy was the one who took me under his wing, offering encouragement and advice.

He was different from the rest, too. He led a bit of a double life. Socially, on weekends he'd often go off with his own mates and run his own race. John Worsfold said that in the early nineties, when they went on end-of-season trips to Hawaii, they'd lose Mainy on the first night and not see him again until the end of the trip. 'But,' Woosher said, 'he was also the guy who, if you looked over and saw him in your side going onto the field, you'd be totally rapt that he was there.'

When I started at the Eagles, the stories of what Mainy got up to on Thursday nights before games were legendary. If the team was going to be flying interstate on a Friday afternoon for a Saturday match, he'd go out all Thursday night, come to the Friday training session reeking of piss, get on the plane, fall asleep on the tarmac and sleep solidly the whole way to Melbourne, get off the plane, not talk to anyone on the bus, have another sleep, eat his dinner, not have much to do with anyone, sleep all night, then get up on Saturday a new man. He'd bounce around, have breakfast with the boys, a couple of coffees, then go out and smash it. That was Mainy.

Mainy's legend was still revered even when he'd retired and the very straight and straight-shooting Woosher was coach. Woosher and the blokes who played with him loved Mainy, and spoke about him with great affection, because no matter what he did with his nights he was the bloke who never let them down. I remember thinking to myself: 'That's the bloke I want to be. I'll never let this club down.' And I never did. I never let the club down on game day. Mainy was the same. Seeing how he flogged himself made a great impression on me.

From the very beginning Mainy saw a bit of himself in me. He sensed that I kept a second life separate from the club. Another thing we had in common was extremely solid relationships with our women. For me it was Sam, and for Mainy it was Rani, who he married about the time I started at the Eagles.

He wasn't one to run with the foxes and hunt with the hounds, but of course Mainy got a lot of female attention socially and he revelled in it. He had a great way of entertaining women but keeping them at arm's length. Some footballers see fame as an opportunity to put notches on the bedhead. Mainy wasn't like that; he loved Rani, so it wasn't about girls. In seeing how he was with them, I saw a model I could follow.

In the pre-season of my first year at West Coast, we travelled to Melbourne for an Ansett Cup game. We were staying overnight, and we won. When that happened, you'd go out as a side. Mainy teed up a visit to a strip joint called Bar 20, which was owned by a good mate of his called Robbie Bottazzi.

As we were gathering at the hotel lobby ready to go out, I realised I was wearing the same clothes as Mainy – a V-neck grey top with a white T-shirt and blue jeans. I looked at the two of us and got embarrassed. Mainy let out a big laugh. He didn't give a stuff. We went to Bar 20, full of gorgeous girls being very attentive to all the boys, and I wondered, 'How long has this been going on?' It was a different world: free drinks, strippers everywhere, a real eye-opener for me. Mainy pulled Robbie aside and introduced me to him.

'This kid's going to be anything,' Mainy grinned, 'so keep an eye on him.' It was the beginning of a great friendship with Robbie, and there were others too, such as Craig Belcher, who owned the Imperial. All these guys were a few years older than me, successful blokes who owned clubs and pubs. Mainy just opened their doors to me so that I'd always be looked after and allowed to enjoy myself when I was out. I know that some people thought nightclub owners were the wrong types for me to be hanging out with, but I make no apologies. They were good loyal mates, and I had Mainy to thank for them.

The dynamic of our friendship replicated what I'd had as a kid: running with the older guys. Ever since I'd hung out with Rick Mulligan at the Leeming rec centre, I'd been attracted to the excitement of what the older crew was up to. Now that I was at the Eagles and my career was taking off, I was so conscious of everything I was missing out on, I wanted to make doubly sure that I caught up with it. I looked for action in all the right and wrong places. I wanted to live life, just like my non-footy mates were, but I had to pack it into small and intense packages. And that was exactly where Mainy was coming from, too.

By 1999, things weren't so good for Mainy on the field. He'd injured his knee badly in 1997, had had a couple of operations, and spent his last three seasons on and off the field. He worked his arse off trying to get back, and it wasn't happening. He still had the ability to switch back on, like the old Mainy, and drive a team meeting or get-together. When he was on, he was the life and energy of the party, with the influence to make things happen for the group. But in 1999 there were periods when I felt we lost him. He was so low, you couldn't even get a 'g'day' out of him. Looking back, I now see he might have been struggling with depression. But at the time, I couldn't understand how not playing could affect a bloke, and was confused by how aloof he could seem.

I was confused about a lot of things; I just didn't know it yet. One thing I already knew from football, and learnt a different dimension of from Mainy, was how you develop a system where you don't listen to your body. When you're training in the pre-season or playing a hard game, your body is screaming at you: *I'm tired, I can't get there, I can't make that contest, I can't keep going.* But as a footballer, you call your body a liar. You say, *No, you're not tired, you can keep going.* And it turns out that you're right and your body is lying to you. You block out what it's saying. That's part of being a top endurance athlete: ignoring your body's screams, getting yourself up week after week even when you don't feel good.

But it's also part of being a regular drug user. When your body's saying it's had enough, it needs a rest, you say: *You're lying again, you can keep going.* Midway through some binge, I'd be in a state of oblivion, unable to pick my head up off the couch, my body shutting down. Then six hours later I'd find myself storming around, dancing on a table. *How did that happen? A few hours ago I was in the gutter dying! Now I've had a full-body rebuild, and I'm away again.*

Pushing through. Endurance. It was the way I approached both of my two lives. I thought they were in perfect balance.

12

THE CYCLE STARTS

Late in 1999, rumours started to circulate in Perth that Malt-house wanted out. There was a lot of cat-and-mouse being played over whether he would or wouldn't go. At social functions, the club's powerbrokers were murmuring that he was on the verge of dumping us.

By the time he announced that he was moving back to Melbourne to coach Collingwood, I'd swallowed the club's line. I took his departure badly. Just when we were losing some of the greats, like Woosher and Mainy, the coach was leaving us in the lurch. I felt personally offended and never spoke to Malthouse about it.

When I look back now, all I can see is politics. The reality was that Malthouse had given ten seasons to the Eagles, winning two premierships and annual appearances in the finals. It was an incredible record of achievement. He had family in Melbourne, the offer of a new challenge at Collingwood, and every reason to take it on. You couldn't ask more of him at the Eagles, but instead of thanking him for a decade of his life, the club fuelled a perception that he'd been dishonest in his dealings. It was true that he was fox-cunning in how he negotiated his exit, but he did have to leave the state without being lynched. You can't give a whole season's notice that you're going to Collingwood. You've got to walk out with your back covered. That's what he did, but for a long time after he left I didn't see it that way, and held a grudge against him.

His replacement was Ken Judge, an East Fremantle man who'd played VFL for Hawthorn and Brisbane, and came with a pretty good recommendation from coaching the Hawks for four years. At East Fremantle, I'd come across Judge to say hello, but hadn't known him well. He wasn't an effusive person. It wasn't just me; he didn't warm to many people. You wouldn't have said Malthouse was best mates with any of the players, but he built a rapport through one-on-one work he did with you and the trust he placed in you. From the start, I felt Judge gave off a vibe of insecurity. I guess he knew he had big shoes to fill. He was taking on probably the hardest job ever in Western Australian football – by taking over from Malthouse.

He and I got along well at first. He challenged me a bit. He was more about negative reinforcement than positive, the stick rather than the carrot. Going into 2000 was a time in my career when I was upping the ante on my work rate and intensity, and Ken would motivate me by giving me a spray. Initially, it helped spur me on.

My career had begun at the end of a great era, and each year from 1996 to 1999 we'd spent some part of the season among the premiership favourites. We were talking of going better each year, but the reality was we were crumbling, bit by bit, losing big personalities and household names that we couldn't replace. We tried to hang on to them, and the club couldn't let go of its heroes. There was this hope that the younger blokes like me, Gardy, David Wirrpanda and Phil Matera could form a kind of bridge with the veterans like Guy McKenna, Glen Jakovich, Dean Kemp, Peter Matera and Mainy, but that chance probably came and went in 1998–99. By 2000 we had to bottom out.

Superficially, Judge's first season was a bizarre one. At the top of the table, Essendon were winning everything. Meanwhile, we looked world-beaters one week, wooden spooners the next. We beat Adelaide by 114, then lost to Geelong by 81. We beat Fremantle by 117, and lost to Brisbane by 88. Towards the end of the season we smashed St Kilda by 86, keeping them to four goals, then went down to Melbourne by 70.

Even that makes it sound better than it was. We ended the year with six wins and a draw, and thirteenth place: the first time the Eagles had missed out on the top eight since 1989.

I played some good footy, and reckon I worked my guts out for Judge. I didn't make All-Australian, but put a particular effort into how I played away from home, where we were really struggling.

There is no doubt that Judge was a very capable coach but, looking back, I think that it may have been bad timing for him, the club and the players. While there were positive moments with him, my strongest memories are of the 'sprays' the team or specific players received. Judge's response to the pressure was to rip into blokes, not excluding me. One of his 'motivational' techniques with me was to harp on about Shane Crawford, who'd had his Brownlow year under Judge in 1999. I'd been touched up by Crawf a few times, and he was a great benchmark against which I could set myself. Judge used the example of Crawf to motivate me.

After we were thumped by Geelong in Geelong, we got straight onto the bus and drove to the airport for our flight. We were a pretty subdued group. I went off to get some Hungry Jack's in the terminal. On the Monday at the team meeting, Judge glared at me, in front of the whole team, and said: 'Crawf wouldn't eat that if it was the last fucking thing in the world.'

I had a bit of a chuckle to myself. Hungry Jack's was our main sponsor, wasn't it? But Judge went on and on, the biggest bake he ever gave me, so long that the effect wore off. He went past the point where I was thinking, 'Hey, you're right, Crawf wouldn't do that', to where I was closing my eyes and thinking, 'You've made your point, Judgy.'

He was hardest on the younger blokes. Senior guys can take some tough talk, but not everyone is responsive to that sort of coaching. Some young people, you have to build them up, not tear them down. On that same Melbourne trip, poor Rowan Jones, still a fairly young player, was on the receiving end of a Judge spray. Rowan was a quiet, educated bloke, the ultimate team man, who never did a thing wrong. We were in the Golden Wing lounge and he was reading a novel instead of watching Melbourne playing Essendon on the TV with everyone else.

Judge collared him.

'Do you know everything about every fucking player for Melbourne and Essendon?'

I felt for Rowan. The bloke was just trying to read a novel, take twenty minutes out of football while we were waiting for a plane, and the coach had given him the biggest spray of his career. But footy's not always fair.

WHEN JUDGE started, there were other changes. Stuart 'Knackers' Cormack came in as fitness coordinator, and Glenn Stewart was made head of fitness, which was more of an office job. Knackers, a military type of bloke with short cropped hair, was from the

Australian Institute of Sport, highly controlling about what we did and the way we did it. He knew his stuff, and I respected his knowledge, but he was a my-way-or-the-highway type.

Of course, I had a big personality clash with him. I was set in my ways and had played a lot of good footy. At first he'd treat everyone as a herd, without allowances for players knowing their own bodies. Under Glenn Stewart, West Coast had pioneered the specialisation of training for different players with different needs. Knackers had good ideas, but his communication with blokes like me wasn't the best.

It got to the point where we had a couple of heated arguments. He reminded me of those school teachers who didn't get me. I irritated him, and he irritated me. I wasn't trying to get out of hard work. I wanted to go over and above the hard work, but I wanted to do it my way. I hated being put in a box, and as soon as anyone did it to me I rebelled.

Like Judge, Knackers wanted to impose his methods. There was no pulling blokes over and making them feel good about themselves. What drove me mad was how he treated recovery. It's an important session, loosening out the kinks and bruises from a game. We'd normally come into the club and do three laps of Kitchener Park, 900 metres around, walk it or jog it, then go to the pool for a swim. Knackers would be that anal, he'd be putting out cones for us to jog around. You might do that with fourteen- or fifteen-year-old kids, but we were exhausted and usually downhearted after a loss. His intense training methods might have been all right at the AIS when you're getting athletes up for a world championship, but Knackers didn't start out with any concept of how long an AFL season was, how attritional it is, especially with all the travelling interstate. Half the trick is switching yourself off, and timing your week so that you're getting up mentally on the weekend. Recovery is a session where you back off, and he didn't understand that.

I couldn't really take him on directly, but I could try a bit of guerilla warfare. Stuart Cormack and Glenn Stewart – the two Stueys – shared an office in a little bunker next to the gym. By 2000 we'd moved into the new Subiaco Oval facilities, with a state-of-the-art, gleaming 25-metre lap pool, a couple of spas, a beautiful gym overlooking the pool, a players' room with pool tables and table-tennis tables, huge indoor warm-up areas, a theatre with a big screen and projector, a fully fitted-out medical and physio room. It was a great place. I'd walk straight past Knackers to go to Glenn's office, which was like pulling rank on him. It was a bit pathetic of me, but we had so many run-ins that I'd go out of my way to yank his chain a bit.

I'd never go further. Knackers was experienced at judo, and I'd say tongue in cheek to the boys, 'The only reason I haven't whacked him is because I'm petrified of him putting me in an arm bar and throwing me on the ground.' He was the bloke I banged heads with the most, but the fear of humiliation kept me from doing anything.

By THE end of the 2000 season, I was jumping out of my skin to take my idea of a holiday. But it wasn't as though I'd been living like a monk. Through the winter, my benders had crept up in frequency. I was into a cycle. After a Friday or Saturday match, I'd track something down, then go to one of my mates' houses and get on. That meant the next day was a write-off, but I was meticulous about knowing how far I could go. Planning was paramount: short or long break, travel, who we had coming up. Only if I ticked all the boxes could I give it a nudge.

The cycle fed my love of planning and control. I could have been a general in an army or a chief executive of a big corporation given how much fastidious planning I put into my drugs-and-footy lifestyle. I wanted to control every last thing: how much coke or speed I'd take to get high, how long I wanted to stay high, how much alcohol or Xanax I'd have to help come down. When I had one of those windows coming up, I'd get excited just thinking about it. That excitement, and the business of scoring high-quality gear, were as addictive as the substances themselves. Even if I didn't feel like getting on it, I'd still do it, because I knew that if I abstained on a Friday night I'd wake up on the Saturday regretting that I'd missed my window. It was more powerful than me, this need to attack my little windows ferociously, to make up for all the times when I was unable to do it. It wasn't like I was a nine-to-fiver, or a student, who could get on with relative flexibility. I had to take advantage of the opportunities as they presented themselves. In my increasingly fucked-up way, I was developing a deal of self-knowledge.

I don't blame the legal-drugs regime of the footy club for my recreational drug use one bit. I take full responsibility. But as far as chemicals are concerned, my two lives had a lot of common ground. Since 1996, I'd been initiated into a professional life where there was a tablet to cure any problem. Every week had a drug storyboard: pills like caffeine to get up, sleeping pills to come down, antibiotics if you've got a head cold, anti-inflammatories for injuries. We used to live on cold and flu tablets, if we had so much as a hint of a cold. If you had any sign of a headache they'd bung you on Panadeine Forte, something strong to mask the pain. If your stomach felt funny, it was Amoxil, one of a number of substances that left me with stomach ulcers from which I'd suffer for years.

It's no excuse for how I let my substance use get out of control, but the two drug regimes worked hand-in-glove. If I was racing the clock to get ready for a match, I wouldn't think I'd have to go home and rest. I'd think: *What pill should I take to get up for this?*

Letting off a bit of steam through the season didn't seem to mean I'd have no steam to let off at the end, though. That's the journey towards drug addiction; I was building up tolerance, steadily losing my grip on the difference between an occasional dabble and a bad habit.

After the season, I went on a ten-week twister. To give you a picture of what these episodes were like, I have to fight my own lack of interest. I remember fleeting moments of humour, and have great memories of the mates I spent my time with, but when you try to narrate the heavy drug user's life to someone who hasn't been there, the fact that stares you in the face is that it's boring, it's pointless and it's stupid. My greatest regret, aside from the pain I caused to other people, is how many beautiful days and nights I threw down the toilet.

At the start of this planned end-of-season bender, I didn't leave anything to chance. I knew who was 'Frankie J' – as in Holden, or holding drugs – and if I hadn't scored from that person, I'd made sure I knew where I could find him.

If there was coke around, I was expert at sourcing it. I'd drop over to where some blokes were having a few beers, we'd start talking about gear, and hey presto, someone would pull something out of his pocket and we'd start racking up. From there we'd go to a bar, on to a nightclub, and so on.

While I like to remember these periods as hell-for-leather, they weren't actually like that. The psychology was not just, *Yes, yes, yes*. There are so many mind games in a drug user's life. After a couple of nights of carnage, I'd crawl home and swear to Sam that I was going to pull up for a while, not do any drugs for a few weeks. I'd get through a few quiet days, and we'd plan to go to a movie together the next night. But first, I had to run a few errands.

Funnily enough, my planning in avoiding drugs was never as thorough as my planning in acquiring them. So while I was running my errands, I'd get on the phone to one of my mates.

'Trying to stay out of harm's way?'

'Yeah, me too.'

'How long have you been fresh?'

'All week, haven't touched a thing.'

'Same here.'

'Few of the boys are having beers down at the beach.'

'Yeah? Might drop in on them. Just for a beer.'

'Me too.'

'But only one. I've got to get back to take the missus to a movie.'

'Yeah, and I've got to pick up a car for the old man.'

'See you there.'

So I'd go down to where some blokes were having a beer, with the best intentions of staying fresh. But then, when I got there, we started joking around, and when this group of people got into a room together all the best-laid plans would inevitably go out the window.

'Where have you been?' someone would ask me.

'Ah, just lying low, staying fresh.'

'Bullshit, your hands are shaking.'

'Serious, I've been quiet.'

Then we'd all start laughing, and just by chance, someone would be Frankie J.

'You wouldn't believe it, I've got something in the car.'

'Serious?'

We'd all be pretending it was unplanned, and coincidental. 'Oh, who'd have guessed you were holding?' Yeah, right. Water finds its own level, and in a town like Perth the blokes who were like that knew each other. So then I'd have something – 'But only one, okay? I have to get home to take the missus to the movies' – while knowing right then that I wasn't going to get to any movie, I wouldn't be home for a few nights, and before long I'd be thinking, 'What the fuck have I done here?'

In the initial stages, we'd be roaring with laughter, most of all at the charade we'd been trying to play about having a quiet healthy night doing the right thing. In a twisted way, the humour was about bluffing each other and ourselves before discovering how weak we all were.

As these binges went on, they lost shape and got more and more disorganised. Doing coke and speed for day after day can be called 'partying', but it's not really a party after a while. With coke, you could never have enough because it always left you on the brink of where you were trying to get to. So you'd sit and do a few lines, and then someone would think of some place to go, which sounded like a great idea. That's the thing with coke and speed: everything sounds like a great idea. We got ready to go there, but figured we'd better score first because we were in danger of running low. There would be a frenzy of phone calls and arrangements. Meanwhile we'd have some more. More arrangements and talk. It was a full-time job trying to stay high. Then we'd be on our way to score, but someone would have left his phone somewhere, so we'd be going back. Then we'd have to sort out a disagreement somewhere, and pay someone somewhere else. Then we'd have some more gear, and come up with another great idea. The party, the action, was always somewhere else. We didn't have time to party. We were having fun, but in reality it was a whole lot of organising, going places, losing things, going backwards, making calls, getting set to do the next thing, but rarely actually doing it. It was ridiculous, a comedy of errors. I spent so much time looking forward to partying, and even when I was partying I was looking forward to partying. I'd be stomping around on my feet for so many hours I'd spend the last phase of a bender in ugg boots, just to give my feet a break. I look back on those weeks with memories of humour and mateship but also this overwhelming sense of the pointlessness of it all. Anyone who says being a drug addict is easy is wrong.

As well as running like a squirrel in a wheel, I was fending off a background dread of small obligations. While I was rushing to do nothing, I was putting off important duties. At the start, I knew I had to take Sam to the movies, make phone calls, return messages, pay bills, talk to Mum and Dad. But as soon as I got on, I thought: 'Can't do that now, I'll do that later.'

A few days in, I was flogging a dead horse. I was wasting drugs, still using but not getting high. I'd be saying, 'Why didn't I go home and take Sam to the movies?' But in the next breath, I'd be making a case to stay out. I'd phone her, apologise for going missing, and say, 'Listen, there's a game on TV that I've been looking forward to for weeks. I swear I'll come home after then.' By this stage I was kicking on out of fear of going home and facing up to all the obligations I'd been putting off. So I kept pushing forward until I finally ran out of steam.

But even then, I didn't necessarily stop. I knew that after I pulled up, all my obligations would be stacked a mile high. There was so much to do, where would I start? The answer was to keep putting things off.

At home, I'd take a couple of strong 2mg Xanax, but they wouldn't put me to sleep. So I'd get up, race off and join the boys again, charge into a room and say: 'Come on, let's go!' They'd be looking at each other thinking, 'This bloke's not right in the head.'

'You think I'm joking?' I'd say. 'Back to work, boys!'

At the end of those episodes, I was thinking, *I need a holiday from my holiday*. It had nearly killed me. So I made a vow to pull up, start running again, go surfing, and get ready for the new season.

But it's one of life's little injustices: how long it takes you to get into peak shape and how quickly it goes away. The damage I had done to myself in my end-of-season bender was frightening – it undid months of fitness. When I meet God, one of the first things I'm going to ask is why he set things up so that it takes so much to get our bodies into condition and so little to lose it.

So the pre-season was testing for me on many levels. Not only was I getting back to fitness physically, which is always the hardest patch of any player's year, but I was battling with the mental demons as the drugs I'd been taking were leaving my system.

After a ten-week bender, it's not a pleasant thing to pull up and start an AFL pre-season. I went from not running at all to running every day. I'd drag myself down to the river, dreading it but also knowing I needed a break from what I'd been doing. My first run would be eight minutes, then stopping for five, and running for another eight. The first five days I'd do five runs and they were frightening, painful. Some of the places I went in my head in those runs I can't even describe; they were like waking nightmares. I couldn't control my thoughts, which were full of a painful anxiety tumbling around all over the place, with no order or logic. I had deadlines coming up, and my body was screaming: 'Abort! Abort! Abort!' I was in places of shadows and fear, a personal hell. I had no control over my body. Someone who went running once a fortnight could have galloped past me, I was so uncoordinated and weak.

But eventually I broke through. Every day I'd been dying to quit running. All I wanted was to give up. If I could have done that, I'd be happy. But no: if I had given up just once, it would have been symbolic. I'd have lost my battle. I'd never given up on anything. It meant everything to me to survive these sessions and defeat the voices in my head. It had become a test of my mental toughness. And so the feat of surviving, keeping my body moving through that mental and physical torture, became a positive. It's amazing how you can rationalise things to yourself! After all the hell my drug use had put me through in those first weeks, by the time I broke through I was able to tell myself that it was all good, all positive. The end-of-season bender had been part of my challenge, and I'd won. I got to the point where not only had I conquered my demons but I loved them, and loved where they came from. I got so clean and so fit that I started feeling dangerous again.

That was my biggest problem with getting fit: it made me feel so good I wanted to get high. There's something about Perth in summer. We were training in beautiful weather, then swimming at City Beach. A few days earlier I'd been thinking, 'I don't think I'll touch a drug ever again.' But after Friday's weights session, the end of the week, I couldn't wait to hop in my car and grab a beer from the drive-through on the way home. *Fuck*, I'd think, *this is going to be a good weekend. How good is this?*

I loved that feeling of being dangerously fit. Looking back it was frightening, the adrenaline from life I was getting. I was diving headfirst into everything. After pulling up from a bender and getting into pre-season work, I got so fit, and fresh, that I could only think of one way to burn it off. And so the cycle went on, football and drugs, two insatiable beasts feeding each other. Little did I know that there was a clock on my drug use, and it was starting to pick up pace towards midnight.

13

SENIORITY

Guy McKenna left the club at the end of 2000, along with Mitchell White, two more premiership-winning veterans. Bluey had had enough, but Mitchell left because he'd fallen out with Judge. Mitchell was a good club man, a bit of a lateral thinker, to whom Malthouse used to look for alternative ideas. He was relaxed, cool, loved to go for a surf. For some reason, Judge just didn't like his manner. If you got in Judge's gun he wouldn't leave you alone, and so by the end of the year Mitchell White was off to Geelong.

Bluey's retirement meant the captaincy was open. Glen Jakovich, also nearing the end of his playing days, was I believe pretty keen for the job. He was very popular with the public and had a great image due to his on-field heroics over the years. The *West Australian* ran polls, and he was always the popular favourite. But among the football department, Dean Kemp was the universally accepted leader. Kempy, who hadn't been striving for the captaincy, put his hand up for it out of a sense of duty.

In a surprise move, they made Kempy and me co-captains. It was probably a good idea, to bridge the generations, and Judge deserves as much credit for it as the match committee who ratified it. But it made me, at twenty-one, the youngest player to be an AFL captain. I was having a shower afterwards, when Jako came up and said: 'I wanted that captaincy desperately, but I've lost my father, I've been through tougher things than this, and I want to tell you I'll be the first bloke to back you up. I'll never undermine you.' It took a big man to say that, and then act on it. It also strengthened my resolve to get over my trepidation and live up to the loyalty he was giving me.

I was hugely proud, of course, and so was Dad. But he was a little concerned. He went and saw Trevor Nisbett at the club, to tell him he wondered if things weren't moving too fast for me. I'd never had a burning ambition to be captain, and we wondered if I could handle the extra expectation. The old man remained my main confidant and mate, even if he didn't know what I was up to in my extracurricular life. He'd taken a few phone calls from people passing on rumours that I was getting into drugs, and Dad knew that my idea of a big night out wasn't to drink a dozen beers and leave it at that. He knew a little, but until 2007 Dad's knowledge probably lagged two or three years behind what I was really doing.

Like most people, Dad assessed my health by how well my footy was going. In those years, my footy masked the extent of my drug-taking – from others, from my mates, even from myself. It didn't make sense to me, how well my footy was going. Looking back we were all naive, because it was always going to go pear-shaped, but I thought I was rewriting the rules.

It wouldn't compute with Dad that I could play as well as I was and be regularly using drugs. He did speak to me about thinking I was bulletproof. He cautioned me against being sucked in. I remember him using that term: *bulletproof.*

And now I was captain to go with it. I'd started at the Eagles in a side that more or less led itself, it had so many natural leaders. So I'd been able to go about the business of looking after myself, being a good player. Now I was being challenged to take responsibility for others.

Up till then, I'd never given much thought to whatever influence I might have at the footy club. It was like school. Some guys would follow me down whichever path I chose. But now I had to broaden my thinking: I was co-leader of the whole squad, not just my crew.

I'd never given pre-game talks to the team, public speeches or media appearances, but now I had to. Malthouse had put a great premium on leadership, placing particular demands on the senior players. I'd thought that was tough on them, but now that I was a senior player myself, I understood what it meant to feel like you owned a stake in the team. Out of my comfort zone, my response was to take it head-on. When the easier option felt like crawling into my shell and focusing on my own game, I did the opposite. I got up in front of the guys and promised I would work on some especially challenging aspect of my game, and expected the same from others. I'd look at someone and say, 'I want you to run your opponent's legs off, because I'm going to do the same.' Like Mainy, at those times when he took over team meetings, I was using these exhibitions to get myself up as well as the others.

One responsibility of the captaincy was to lead Monday meetings where new guys to the club would have to stand up and give a two- or three-minute spiel on where they'd come from, how they'd come up through the junior leagues, whether their family was big or small, religious or not, educated or whatever. At the end, we could ask questions. Invariably and quickly, the questions came down to 'What's your best sexual experience?' and 'When was the first time you had sex?' It didn't bother me, but it was awkward for some kids.

Two of our new players in 2001 were Troy Wilson and Mark Seaby. Although they both came from country Western Australia, that's where the similarities stopped. Wilson was twenty-nine, about as old as a draftee gets, and he'd earned his call-up after several seasons as an uncompromising full-forward in the WAFL. He was a tough bloke who liked to barrel his opponents out of the way, and Judge had got him in as a target forward.

Seaby was much younger, a third-string ruckman behind Gardy and Dean Cox. He was a quiet bloke, and serious about his religion. I respected guys like that and loved playing with them, even if they weren't part of my social crew.

After Seaby gave his talk, of course someone asked him about his first sexual experience. He'd mentioned that he'd had the same girlfriend for a number of years.

'I haven't had one,' he said. There was a bit of murmuring, but for most of us the penny dropped: of course, that's part of his religious beliefs.

But Troy Wilson made a smart-arse comment, something really ordinary. And then Mickey Gardiner did one of those things that I loved him for. In his time in Perth, Gardy would manage to upset everyone in the city about three times each. But he would not tolerate teasing. He grabbed Wilson by the scruff of his neck and said, 'Pull your head in or I'll give you a slap.'

I remember leaving the meeting full of new respect for both Gardy and Seaby. And I was ashamed that I wasn't the one who stood up and grabbed Wilson like that. I went up to Seaby and said, 'For what it's worth, I have a lot of admiration for what you did, because I know myself that if I was in that situation I wouldn't have the balls, or the courage, or the dash, to stand up and say I haven't had sex. Mate, I admire that. You have a rare quality that virtually none of us do, and I hope you're proud of it.'

A football club is a tough place to be different. They've improved a bit since then, but the mentality is still there. It never sat well with me that a bloke couldn't feel safe standing up and saying who he was. I also felt like I was back at my first day at Wesley, when I'd had to act sick to cover up my fear. In the club, you were terrified of looking as inadequate as you sometimes felt. And when it came to girls, what Seaby said made me think back to how I'd been in such a hurry to do things only because I felt so inadequate. When I saw his sturdiness of character, I regretted my own rush as an adolescent: by rushing to get some things out of the way, I'd missed out on something else.

EVEN THOUGH I was so young, I enjoyed the challenge of captaincy, not for any personal glory but because it made me a better player. That season was one of my best. I remembered the dominant West Indies cricket team in the 1980s, how they would target the opposition captain. Chop off the head and the rest of the team will fall over. That reinforced how important my role was, and it took my footy to the next level.

We set ourselves to use the travel factor to our advantage. As hard as it was for us to go to the eastern states, we had to make it even harder for visitors to come to us. We all lifted when we were at home, but on top of that I prided myself on getting my hands dirty in Melbourne. I remember one game fondly from that season, when I played a huge quarter against Carlton in Melbourne and helped drag us across the line.

The season plan was this: if we won our ten or eleven games at home, we only needed to win four or five away and we'd be in the top four.

SENIORITY

That was the theory, anyway. Although I made All-Australian for the third time and was the club's best-and-fairest for the first, the season was a shocker. We won five games and came four-teenth, the worst in Eagles history. Our average losing margin was seventy points.

During the season, Dean Kemp retired. He was a ripper bloke, a Norm Smith Medallist, and he helped me shoulder the load. But through the season it was clear that he'd suffered too many head injuries in all his years at the top. It was part of most of our warm-ups that we'd do some bumps and tackles in pairs, and that was enough to rattle him, even though by then he had to play wearing a padded helmet. By the end, he had been concussed so many times that the doctors told him another heavy knock might do him irreparable damage, a risk he was wise not to take.

Kempy's retirement was sad, but far from our biggest problem.

I was getting along as well with Ken Judge as anybody was. However, the team was playing poorly and the players generally were not responding to the coach. It probably comes down to who do you blame: the players or the coach?

The club had brought in Tim Gepp on the match committee to help Judge. Tim had been at West Coast before, and had worked with Dad on my contracts. Tim had been good mates with Judge in the past, but when he came back, Judge was under so much pressure that he thought Tim had been brought in as a board spy.

Judge's apparent paranoia about the West Coast board was not completely unfounded. When it became clear that we weren't going to make the 2001 finals, I took a call from Dalton Gooding, a senior board member. Dalton wanted to take me to lunch at Coco's, a fancy restaurant on the Swan River. He said he wanted to sound me out about the coach's predicament and what I thought. I said it was inappropriate for the captain to talk about the coach with a board member over lunch. I said my opinions shouldn't be used by the board against Judge.

There was nothing to gain from this kind of meeting, and when he probed me for more information, I backed off.

'I feel uncomfortable about it,' I said, 'and I don't want to be part of it.' As captain, I felt it was important for me to show solidarity with the coach.

At the end of the season, the board sacked Judge, which was the right thing for the club. But I saw echoes of the politicking that had taken place around Malthouse's departure. Football club boards sometimes look for others to carry the can. I don't know what they said to Judge, but he thought he'd been done in by Tim Gepp and, by inference, me too, because I was close to Tim. The board, which had taken the decision, intrigued for it and pushed it along, was happy for Tim to be the scapegoat. It ended his friendship with Judge. The board just wanted to make it look like they were carrying out due diligence, and their idea of due diligence was to make Tim look like the axeman.

Judge blamed me as well. On top of knocking back any approaches from the board, I was one of the few blokes playing my best despite getting battered and punched and scragged every match. After playing good footy for him, I was disappointed that he held me and others responsible. Players don't appoint or sack coaches.

It's INTERESTING to look at the legacy of Judge's two years. A football department makes lots of decisions, and for better or worse the buck stops with the coach. During Judge's tenure, West Coast had a policy of bringing in second-chance players from other clubs. They recruited Michael Prior from Essendon, Mark Merenda from Richmond, David Sierakowski from St Kilda, Michael Collica and Richard Taylor from Hawthorn, and Greg Harding and Trent Carroll from Fremantle. As a policy, this didn't work particularly well, and left a bit of resentment that the Eagles weren't developing their own juniors as fully as they had in the past.

But we also made some great acquisitions during the Judge years, like Dean Cox. Coxy was a beanpole from Dampier who couldn't get out of his own way. He was like a big, gangly colt. In 2000 he was brought in as Gardy's ruck understudy.

Gardy was a phenomenon. For a ruckman, he'd developed very quickly. Because of his background in basketball, his greatest strength was his ability to tap the ball. It was caressed, put down your throat. He and I enjoyed a great understanding of where it was going. Even when we were struggling in those years, a footy game still starts in the centre, and more often than not we'd get first crack at it, thanks to Gardy's strength and touch.

By comparison, you could have wondered what Dean Cox was doing there. In pre-season training at City Beach Oval in 2000, we had to go under 3 minutes 30 seconds for the last kilometre of our long runs. Coxy virtually couldn't get one leg in front of the other, he was in such agony. If one player didn't make 3 minutes 30 seconds, the whole group had to go around again. I was in his group, waiting for him, hoping against hope that he'd beat the clock.

'Fucking come on, Coxy!' Judge was barking orders, being really harsh on him. No way was Coxy making it, so we had to do it again. But we found out soon after that he had an iron deficiency which had limited his stamina. Once that was rectified, he turned into one of our best runners, for a big man. From that moment I learnt never to be quick to judge a ruckman.

There were other new players coming in with sound credentials. Andrew Embley joined the club under Judge, and progressed steadily. Darren Glass, a defender from the Perth WAFL club, was our first draft pick in 2000. Like a lot of defenders in struggling sides, he did it tough at first. Our veteran Ash McIntosh was one of the great blokes in footy, relaxed, loved a drink, naturally gifted, and as a fullback he was unbelievably reliable. When Glass took over Ash's fullback position he was under huge pressure each week, and got some touch-ups from the likes of Sydney's Tony Lockett and Brisbane's Jonathan Brown. But he was destined to develop into one of the best fullbacks in the competition.

In 2001, Daniel Kerr came in from the Alcock Cup, having played under Peter Spencer at Aquinas. Quinten Lynch was their ruckman and Kerr was rover: a famous school combination. Lynchy was as big at fifteen as he is now, a well-developed monster, and he'd join the Eagles a year or two later. At eighteen, Kerr was a natural runner – he won the interschool 800 metres – and a hard footballer. You never know if a kid's going to be able to bring that to AFL footy, but he was one who did it straight away.

His father, Roger, was an Indian-Australian who'd played for East Fremantle. We were family friends, and Daniel knew my sister Melanie, who went to Aquinas' sister school, Penrhos. Before long they were going out together. Daniel and I would have our ups and downs, but in 2001 he made an immediate impact, being among the best first-year players in the AFL.

As I'VE said, I'd kept my party life pretty much separate from the football club. Around 1999 I'd bumped into Fabian Quaid, a bloke I'd gone to primary school with, in a restaurant. Fabian was an Australian tae kwon do champion, an athlete who loved all sport as much as I did. When we met up again, Fabian was working in security, having a fair impact in the nightclubs. He introduced me to his companion at the restaurant, John Kizon, who the media liked to describe as a 'colourful Northbridge identity'. Nightclubs were a big part of my social round, and I'd met owners, bouncers, and tough guys. JK dressed sharply, and had a bit of a shady reputation, but I only knew him as a good bloke and loyal mate. I wasn't naive about the darker side of his life, and knew that I was sailing close to the wind by having him as a friend. But that wasn't reason enough to shun him. Our friendship was always light-hearted. Perth's a small town, and I was brought up not to discriminate. I just took people as they came and didn't ask for their CV.

In 2001, Gardy and I met up with Fab after the Brownlow Medal presentation and were photographed going into Crown Casino. JK and his crew were also there. Trevor Nisbett called us in and carpeted us. He said that as captain, I'd hurt the club's image and brand by associating with a 'criminal'. He gave us both one last chance and warned us about the company we kept.

We weren't going to dump a mate just like that. It was a bit controlling. We thought hard about what kind of people we were, and what kind of friends, and came to the conclusion that friendship was stronger than 'brand' and 'image'. I told Nisbett I would try my best to avoid being seen in restaurants or casinos with JK, but I'd still cross the street to say g'day if I saw him.

We weren't doing anything wrong, but we began to attract attention whatever we did. One day Gardy and I went to Fab's unit in Northbridge to watch UFC on cable. We had a good laugh, made a bit of noise, and went to training. By the time we got there the club had been tipped off by police that we were still knocking around with blokes we shouldn't.

14

BULLETPROOF

In the middle of that 2001 season, we'd gone to Melbourne and been smashed by Carlton. John Worsfold was their assistant coach, but he was also a caring guy and an Eagle at heart. He called me after the game and asked how I was handling it.

'We're not going too well,' I said.

John said it was obvious we were under huge pressure. 'Some of the Carlton guys said you weren't very West Coast-like,' he said.

'How do you mean?'

'New faces, a lot of young guys, not much left of the old era.'

He was right, but facing up to it was a bit of a turna-round for me. Year by year we'd been losing two or three of the premiership players, and I felt the loss of those big personalities, none more so than John himself. You didn't feel, as a young bloke who hadn't been part of those premierships, that you ever could fill their shoes. I'd been feeling inadequate about it, and it caused me to doubt my ability as a captain. Woosher knew Ken Judge was under the pump, but he definitely wasn't angling for the job. He was sincerely wishing me well and checking on our welfare as a club.

And it wasn't good. Everyone was unhappy, not only the players. Everyone wanted answers – this was an organisation that was not used to losing. A lot of the staff and directors who'd been there when the Eagles were flying were still there, and they couldn't cope with it. It was a really hard time to get through. I don't know how to describe it other than to say the club felt like it was collapsing under the tension.

A decision needed to be made on the coach. It is always a difficult time when a coach is sacked. All AFL coaches have huge responsibility and give an enormous amount of time and effort to the job. When Judge was sacked, the initial tip to replace him was Neil Craig. I wasn't party to any of the negotiations, but some-thing went amiss there and Craig went to the Adelaide Crows; we got Woosher, who had been the popular favourite all along.

As far as I was concerned, the club couldn't have made a better choice. Woosher had already had a big impact on my career. When I was starting out in 1996, he already had a coach-type aura about him. That aura and respect would ease the transition from playing with him to playing under him.

The moment he walked through the door, something changed in the place. You could feel the clouds lift. He was the returning premiership captain, and he had a rapport with people around the club, and the members. He automatically brought back hope.

He sat us down as a playing group. He said he wanted us to enjoy training and playing. He wasn't going to hammer us with meetings. He brought our minds back to the thing we actually loved doing: playing footy. It sounds obvious, but at the time the club had become such a nightmarish place, our minds were filled with everything but footy.

As captain, I sat down with him in one-on-ones, and he really gave me a new lease on life. He had this Clark Kent thing going on: very quietly spoken, didn't say a lot and didn't need to.

He was different from Malthouse, who had more charisma and a bit of a fear factor. With Worsfold I was older, too, and he was my third AFL coach. He wasn't an intimidating God-like figure like Malthouse; the coach and I were more like partners now.

That said, when you sat across the desk from Woosher in his office, he was the master of the staring competition. He'd just sit there staring at you with this half-smile on his face and big unblinking eyes. I don't think he even knew he was doing it, but the effect of his stare was to make you so scared of the long silences that you'd throw anything out, just to fill the space. I'd known him for a long time, but I experienced it as much as anyone. You just wanted to jump out the door and get on the field and play for him.

He realised there was a lot of work to be done, so he wasn't going to try to do it all in the first year. He had a long-term plan to build up the side bit by bit.

One of those 'bits', arriving in the pre-season of 2002, was Chris Judd. The Eagles had drafted him from the Sandringham Dragons in Melbourne, where he'd grown up playing at Caulfield Grammar. He was a deep thinker, with interests that went far beyond football. More than with any other kid who came to the club, I felt I could automatically speak to him as an equal. He was incredibly mature, switched on, and in that pre-season he gained everyone's respect as a phenomenal athlete, a natural runner with a turn of pace like I'd never seen.

*

WITH WOOSHER, and our sense of a new team, I became infatuated with pre-season training. I was fixated on what I was doing, what I needed, when I'd do it, how it fitted in with the footy season. Glenn Stewart put me in a power group with Drew Banfield and Quinten Lynch, and we'd do sprints and weights to add power and pace. It was all scientific, and the methodical, obsessive side of me loved it. The more the better.

Diet was part of that too: everything was about low-fat, lean foods and staying at my optimal weight. For me it was 80.5 kilograms – precisely. I was typically anal about my need, on game day, to weigh not 80, not 81, but 80.5 kilos.

As we knuckled down in the pre-season, our lactate sessions became a focal point. I felt that if I could augment my football by turning up the screws on my fitness, diet and training, no opponent could get the better of me. We had sessions that were like training for an Olympic 400-metre race. We did sharp sets running between the two behind posts – you'd sprint for seventeen seconds flat out, then have only seventeen seconds' rest. Then you'd do the same out to the 50-metre line, flat out there and back with a short rest. That was two repetitions. Then you'd do four reps with two minutes off. Then the same again, then two reps. If you could sprint 100 metres in fourteen seconds, you'd only get fourteen seconds' rest. It wasn't enough rest to get your air in. My heart was going through my chest – and then I had to go again. By the end of the fourth set I was trying to run, but everything was falling apart, like I was in the last 50 metres of a 400-metre race. The veins on my neck were bursting out.

By the end, I doubled over, vomiting. These lactate sessions, which I'd do after a light skills session, I loved and hated. They were shocking, but they were also the single most important thing I did for my running. When the season started, with the long 100-metre runs up and down the ground, I could blow out nearly any opponent. With that sort of running, I'd never lose the feeling of the lactic acid, but my body learnt to cope with it. We talked about superlative runners like the world and Olympic champion Michael Johnson: how he'd be feeling the lactic acid in the end of his 400-metre races, just like anyone else, but his body and mind could tolerate it. That was what I was aiming at: not being free of the pain, but being able to ignore it.

ON THE eve of the season, I was knocked over by pain of a different kind. I'd known Ben Hollioake since he'd arrived at Wesley in year ten. He hadn't known anyone, and we clicked immediately. An incredibly talented sportsman, he was one of those blokes who never saw any need to talk about himself or let people know what he'd done. He was just a good, funny, down-to-earth person, and during the years after school when he'd gone to England and represented them at cricket, we'd stayed mates.

In March 2002, we went out for dinner. The next day, he lost control of his car in Perth and died. I was absolutely gutted. His funeral the following week was one of the most emotional days of my life. I'm not ashamed to say I lost it and cried my eyes out. He was such a good bloke, and the shock of seeing him one day and losing him the next was something I took a long time to get over. I'm not sure if you get over it at all.

FOOTBALL, AS always, was my sanctuary. By the time the season started, we were ready to go. Our foundation was one-on-one footy. We would take on our opponents as individuals, and each of us would try our best to beat our man. It was easy to coach, easy to implement, and we aimed to become a side that was very successful at it.

The season started with the western derby. I had twenty-nine possessions and kicked a goal as we edged out Fremantle.

We still had four premiership veterans – Drew Banfield, Peter Matera, Glen Jakovich and Ash McIntosh – and they seemed to be combining well with the new order.

But from the second round, when we lost to Collingwood by one point, we went into a strange pattern. For eleven rounds, we went win-loss-win-loss-win-loss-win-loss-win-loss-win. We just couldn't establish any consistency. A lot of the losses weren't even close. In round five, we hosted the Brisbane Lions, who'd won the 2001 premiership and were on a run of twenty wins in a row. They knew about consistency. But we kicked eighteen goals against them, and won by forty-six points. It was a really great day for us. Then, the next week, we got beaten again.

We finally strung three wins together from rounds eleven to thirteen, but were up and down for the rest of the season and ended in eighth place. Our win-loss record, no surprise, was 11–11. We were almost even in our records at home (6–5) and away (5–6). In our elimination final, we just weren't good enough against Essendon and went down by thirty-three points.

THROUGHOUT THAT winter, I was flying – in both sides of my double life. I'd play a month of footy where I'd have thirty touches and kick goals every week, and would be smashing myself on coke afterwards. The better I played, the more I figured that the drugs weren't doing me any harm. Both sides of my life were reinforcing each other.

It's hard to put my finger on exactly when or how my drug-taking became that regular. It's a thing that creeps up on you. I wouldn't actually say to myself after a Friday night game, 'Okay, I'm going to get on the gear and stay out until Monday.' But once I did it – then recovered through the week and put in a blinder for West Coast the next weekend – it changed my parameters of what was doable. Things were going well for me. No matter how long

I stayed high, my footy kept going well. I continued moving with it, just because I could. There was no reason to change direction.

One important thing changed in Woosher's first year. Because I'd played under him when he was captain, and thought he was the ideal, I was very critical of my own captaincy. I just didn't think I was measuring up to the example he'd set. I didn't think the younger kids in the club were looking up to me the way I had looked up to John. Partly this was because I felt guilty about my double life. I knew I was living a lie, and it was eating away at me.

As I've said, legal drugs were part and parcel of a footballer's routine. Taking caffeine was a way of manufacturing an alert, sharp state for a match. It wouldn't guarantee you'd play well, but it stacked the odds in your favour. Then there was Sudafed, which was widely used in the AFL. The pseudoephedrine pepped you up for those games when you weren't quite sharp. Drugs were already an accepted part of our playing life, so what, really, was the difference?

If I got wind that young players were experimenting here and there with drugs, I'd pull them up and tell them it was a shithouse thing to do. I knew it was hypocritical, but my duties as captain were pulling me in both directions, and I still thought it would have been ordinary of me to go out on a twister with young guys. My approach to life wasn't something I endorsed for others. Playing good footy was the measure of success, and if kids were putting that at risk, they were mugs.

With older blokes in the team, my long-term mates, I decided that I didn't want to get to the end of my career with them not knowing who I really was. For me, it was part of the honesty of friendship. This is who I am. I figured my drug use was the worst-kept secret in footy anyway, so why keep up the charade? So, around 2002, when the football and the drug use in my life seemed to be in perfect sync, I let my guard down. I never flaunted it, but there were guys at the footy club with whom I shared confidences.

BULLETPROOF

*

Ironically, I had my only drug-testing scare in a decade that year. The testing was still in-competition and for statistical purposes. Two or three guys got tested on game day, every five or six weeks. That year, I tested positive once, but the club wasn't told which of six players it was. They called the six of us in, and I imagined they knew it was me, but all we got was a general talk.

I'd always ridden the odds on the drug testing, knowing the angles and loopholes. They said they'd only test the All-Australians and leading Brownlow vote-getters, which I thought was a bit rough, but I got through with a bit of luck, a bit of plotting. I'd flush myself with water, get my system going, training hard to get any trace of the drugs out of me. There were plenty of times I thought I was gone, but I squeaked through.

Meanwhile, a few of the ground rules were changing. Cocaine was my drug of choice because I believed it was only in your system for one or two days. If I snorted it from Friday night to Sunday night, I thought that by Tuesday morning I stood a good chance of being clean. If I was going to take ecstasy or speed, that could only be a Friday night thing, and only if I had some extra days up my sleeve before the next game.

Then a counsellor came and told us that cocaine was the worst, because they tested for the drug's metabolites in your system, not just the drug itself. I was devastated. I had to change my whole outlook. But soon I settled down again, because it became a three-strikes system. Even if I got caught, I'd have a couple of strikes up my sleeve. There was so much momentum in the way I was doing this, I thought I'd address it when I got two strikes. And I never needed to. I was lucky – or unlucky. My footy and private life were going well, I was earning money, I had good mates, and I had no positive tests to stop me. There were no red or amber lights, only green.

TRADITIONALLY, WE'D start our end-of-year celebrations at a pub called Steves Hotel, then moved to Club Bayview, a nightclub in Claremont. As a player, Daniel Kerr was one of my teammates I admired the most. He was gifted and tough, and with Juddy and Gardy, we were beginning to form a midfield that could rattle anyone, including Brisbane.

But Kerry and I had our differences. I can't lie about that. When we were at Club Bayview at the end of the 2002 season, the tension between Kerry and me, which had been bubbling along for the whole season, busted open. One of the things about stimulants is that they increase your impulsiveness at the same time as they reduce your capacity to control yourself. So it's like hitting the accelerator and cutting the brake lines at the same time. I let loose at Kerry, punched him in the face, and left him lying on the floor. I went outside, then back into the club, and there was a bit of a melee that ended up with someone throwing me down the stairs and me breaking my arm.

The club put out a statement saying I'd slipped, but the truth couldn't stay buried for long. It got out that I'd hit Kerry and been pushed down the stairs. We were counselled, and it was put down to the occasional sibling fights that go on in a football club. And they do. I'd fought with my brother Matthew all our lives, which never stopped him being my closest buddy. I couldn't say the same about Daniel Kerr, but that was where we let it rest. From that point on, he and I had a strictly professional relationship: we'd play football in perfect harmony, but steered clear of each other socially.

So I WAS at the Brownlow Medal night with my arm in a sling. I came sixth behind the winner, Brisbane's Simon Black.

Simon had grown up not far from us, and I'd played with his elder brother Ben. Simon had been behind us at Bullcreek Leeming, but even though I tended to run with blokes older than myself he and I had been mates. He had exceptional endurance and was silky with his hands, a real ball-magnet, and in 1997, when he was being drafted, we'd hoped that he would come to the Eagles. Dad had even spoken to the club about what a big talent and great bloke Blacky was.

In the end, he got drafted to Brisbane. I remember the day the news came through, and Simon was in tears: he just didn't want to leave Perth. We didn't want it either. Dad and I visited him and, as much as we'd have liked to say, 'Bad luck, you'll come back here one day,' we emphasised the positives, building him up about the adventure he was about to embark on. It had taken a while, but he'd settled down and seen it as a challenge. Now he had a premiership – a week later he'd have two, and a year later three – and a Brownlow Medal. I was rapt for him. It was one for the Bullcreek Leeming boys.

15

FROM THE GROUND UP

By my eighth year as an AFL footballer, I'd had plenty of provocation to punch blokes, and got away with what I could. But I'd never been reported until, in the first round of the 2003 season, I was given a one-match ban for striking.

The match in question was at Subiaco, against Port Adelaide. In the summer and autumn I'd gone through the usual off-season hell, accentuated by the fact that I was suffering from tendonitis in my foot, a pain with which I'd played through the previous season. Near the end of the first quarter of the game, I was also struggling with a knock to the ankle and the constant attentions of Kane Cornes, one of the fittest taggers in the AFL.

At a boundary throw-in, I was going for the ball when Damien 'Dimma' Hardwick came into view. Dimma, as tough a nut as any I'd come across, had been a premiership player with

Essendon in 2000 and was now anchoring the Port backline. We were grappling for possession when I pushed him in the chest, with two open palms. One caught his chest and the other slipped higher, brushing past his face. It was a legal shove, so you can imagine my reaction when Dimma fell back clutching his face, an Oscar-winning performance that surprised me from such a hard defender.

That was nothing compared with my shock when three umpires ran up simultaneously and put me on report. To one of them, Mark Fussell, I shouted: 'You can't be serious, there was nothing in it.'

I was convinced they'd been conned by Dimma's dive, and hadn't actually seen the contact. We won the match by forty-eight points, a solid start to the season against one of the stronger teams, and I was fairly confident that when my case went to the AFL Tribunal I'd be cleared.

It was my first appearance before the tribunal – a virtual appearance as it turned out, as I went to Subiaco to sit in a room while a video camera linked me with Melbourne. The hearing went for seventy minutes. The important thing was that Dimma gave evidence in support of me, admitting he'd dived.

'It was probably one of the best ever,' he said of his act, 'and I got a free kick for it.' Later, he said: 'When I saw he was being reported, to be honest, I was quite embarrassed. It would be embarrassing for me and bad for the game if Ben got reported.'

Bert Gaudion, the barrister who was defending me, asked the tribunal to let me off with a warning. He said a player like Damien Hardwick was so tough that 'he wouldn't give you a smile if he owned a fun factory'. His point was that Dimma had been upfront by admitting his mistake, and I shouldn't be punished for it.

Despite Dimma's admission, and my evidence that I'd pushed him with open palms, the tribunal's inspection of what

I thought was unclear videotape resulted in them giving me a one-match ban.

The ban blemished my behavioural record which had been spotless after 146 games. I wasn't overly precious about the record, but it was unfair to get reported for something I hadn't done.

So two days later I was on a plane to Melbourne for an appeal. This time the Eagles had got in touch with a company that had produced technology for slowing down and enlarging digital video. They'd used it in cricket telecasts. At the appeal hearing, the enlarged video showed my open hand casting a shadow on Dimma's face as it passed it. There was no contact, and it certainly wasn't a punch. The appeals tribunal reversed the decision, and my slate was wiped clean. I was grateful to be exonerated, but it shouldn't have got that far. When I said I'd never struck him, and Dimma said he'd taken a dive, the original tribunal should have taken us at our words.

I could never have guessed that several years later, Dimma and I would become great mates working side by side at a different football club.

THE SEASON was almost a repeat of 2002. We were up and down at the start, put together a run of five wins in the middle, and then lost consistency in the run-in to the finals. I took the first couple of months to sort out injuries to my ankle and thigh, but once we played Brisbane at the Gabba in round twelve I was feeling good.

Brisbane were the super side of the early 2000s, winning flags in 2001, 2002 and 2003 and being runner-up to Port in 2004. But for some reason we had a better record against them than any other team.

We just seemed to match up well. Their biggest strength was their midfield of Michael Voss, Simon Black, Nigel Lappin and

Jason Akermanis. But that was also our strength, with Chris Judd, Daniel Kerr, Chad Fletcher and me an upcoming crew trying to rival them. We really looked forward to playing them. Brisbane was invariably a fast and hard track, which we liked. If you asked me what temperature I'd like to play in, I'd say the high twenties, which is hot, but I loved getting warm and my body feeling so hot that it seemed like I was all fluid. When I was cold, I felt brittle. Playing Brisbane, whether at the Gabba or at Subiaco, we were almost sure of having warm weather and fast conditions.

At the Gabba that June, we beat the Lions by eleven goals and I got thirty-five possessions. Not that I was a big possession-counter – there were players who used to go for a lot of low-hanging fruit to rack up their possession stats, and I didn't have a lot of time for that attitude – but having a good game, and winning well, against a side like Brisbane gave me a lot of satisfaction and gave us all, as a club, the belief that we were capable of beating any team in the league. Two years earlier we'd barely won a game, and now we were beating Brisbane, in Brisbane, by sixty-nine points. Something was changing.

A crucial new string to our bow was the recruitment of my old mate Daniel Chick.

When I'd got drafted from East Fremantle to West Coast, Chicky had gone to Hawthorn. It wasn't long before Ken Judge, who was coaching Hawthorn at the time, would play Chicky on me. He didn't quite have the tank that I had, but he was very quick, a bit more mature than I was, and as time went on he'd invariably go out of his way to belt me.

In one season in the late nineties, the football photograph of the year was one of me kicking the ball while Chicky was tackling me. It's a magical shot, one of my favourites from football. After that game, Gardy came up and said, 'I thought Chicky was supposed to be your mate?'

'So did I,' I said with a laugh, 'until he started belting me.'

Off the field, Chicky and I caught up whenever we could. In lots of ways we were running in similar directions, but on different sides of the country. Whenever we'd speak, we'd say how at some point in our career we'd like to play with each other.

Chicky was famous during his Hawthorn years for having his finger amputated. In one game he broke his finger, but their club doctor said it was only dislocated. The club let it go for a month, giving him painkilling jabs to keep him playing. Broken, it fused out of shape. When they realised what had happened his finger was a bit of a mess, but to rectify it surgically would have cost him his season. He was playing well and they were in the finals, so he chose to have it taken off rather than miss games. It added to the Chicky legend.

By the end of 2002, he'd just got married and wanted to come back to Perth. From 2003, when we started playing together, he was as valuable a teammate as anyone in the club. Running out of defence, he used his body as a battering ram. He sacrificed a lot of potential personal glory for his team, and became a protector for us in the midfield. And he was one of my real good mates off field, as rock-solid all the way through as he had been that long-ago night on Rottnest Island.

A COUPLE of weeks after the win over Brisbane, I inked a new deal to stay with West Coast for the next three years, from 2004 through 2006. The money was good, but it surprised a lot of people that I had no money increase on my previous deal. I'd been club champion twice in those three years, All-Australian twice, and gone from a player to co-captain to sole captain. It was widely commented that if I'd gone on the open market, I could have earned an extra $200,000-plus per year.

But the thing was, I could see what Woosher was building at the club and wanted to be part of wherever it led. I was hell-bent on being a one-club player. And I wanted the other guys coming through to be with me. Most notably, Juddy and David Wirrpanda were going to be off-contract in 2004. To me, having those guys was essential to realising our potential as a club, and when I was told that the club might not be able to afford to keep them, I told Dad that I would take an effective salary sacrifice if it meant those blokes would stay.

I don't want to make too big a deal of it. The money West Coast offered me was very good, and I wasn't being a martyr. But it gave me a huge boost when, in the days after I signed my new contract, Judd and Wirrpanda followed suit. We were sticking together. I understood list management, and my aims were all about team success.

We celebrated by beating Carlton by 116 points at Subiaco, their biggest loss in more than 2000 matches and our biggest win at home. It was also satisfying for Woosher, having been at Carlton as assistant coach himself. We could all remember that low day two years earlier when Carlton had smashed us. It was another marker that things were turning around, though not enough for us to make a credible charge at the premiership. We finished the regular season in seventh place. We won twelve, lost eight and, unusually, had two draws, with the Bulldogs and Geelong. Those draws weren't necessarily indicative of the season. Our wins and losses were more often than not blow-outs, either for or against. We would have been a tipster's nightmare.

Our elimination final, at Football Park, was against the sixth-placed Adelaide. In many ways they were on a similar cycle to us, holding onto the last of their dual-premiership players from the nineties while regenerating with a new group. It wasn't a good night for us, with Judd, Kerr, Fletcher and Gardiner all picking up injuries in the course of play. I held my own, kicking three goals, but we were well beaten. Another season, another almost-satisfying result. In my eight years, we'd finished in the finals six times, but only progressed once past the first week of September – and in that year we'd been knocked out in the second week. It was starting to annoy me. But that was that for season 2003. I went off into the summer, set to celebrate in my usual style. I couldn't wait.

16

TESTING NEW LIMITS

We'd been building for a couple of years now, and felt that 2004 was the season for our breakthrough. In early summer, we trained at the grass athletics track marked out at Perry Lakes. I'd just crammed twelve months of hedonism into eight or ten weeks, then crammed eight weeks of running into a fortnight of sheer hell. I was always cramming. Then, when we were straight into the 'beep tests' to assess our fitness, I was well behind the elite runners: another reminder, in case I needed it, that I wasn't as natural an athlete as some of my teammates.

The first part of pre-season was running, about which Knackers Cormack was fastidious. This was where he was at his best. We'd go in groups of five or six and burn up the track. They were tough sessions but we'd do it on the clock, to the second, to match each group's running time that Knackers had written on a board. We were definitely ahead of our time in that sort of running, and became super-fit, resembling an athletics squad more than a football team.

When we were doing 1-kilometre and 800-metre runs, I was hanging on for dear life to the top group: the supreme runners like Daniel Kerr, Chris Judd, Rowan Jones and Josh Wooden. They could put themselves to sleep over 800 metres, while I'd be fighting a grim battle with my body to keep it from quitting.

But as the pre-season progressed, and became more football-specific, I loved it. We brought the distances down gradually from 800s to 100s and 50s, and started doing runs in which we had to stop and turn and burst. By the time we got to the last two or three weeks of running training, I was just about the best in the club. My body was more suited to shorter 'football running' than distance running.

I loved training on my own, and was a good self-motivator, so the more the pre-season became individualised the better I went. We talked a lot and learnt the science of why we did what we did – research was another of Knackers' strengths. He wouldn't give you a punishment run, because he'd designed our programs to the metre. Everything was tailored. Each bloke had to be super-fit for the position we played. It wasn't just the midfielders building up huge tanks. The key position players had to be fit for what they did. In this way, we built a foundation for our team on our work rate. We had talented players, but that wasn't our foundation. In our pre-season, we identified moments where we were making a statement about how tough we were going to be that year. We got competitive, each of us trying to become the hardest, most durable runner. By the time the pre-season ended, I had the utmost confidence in our group. We had to be the fittest team in the league.

*

I STILL had my limits. As scientific as I knew Knackers was, his commitment to his methods rubbed against my rebellious side. I'd clash with him not because I disagreed with his aims, or because we weren't on the same page, but because I had to clash with anybody who was so rigid about telling me what to do. It was a temperament thing, not a brain thing, beyond my control, and even though I couldn't admit it at the time, it probably stemmed from how much Knackers' personality and mine had in common.

Each January, we'd go on footy camps, which I hated as much as school camps. If it wasn't hiking through the bush for five days, it was something else hyper-organised, and that wasn't me. I didn't mind being flogged day after day, but at least at the end of the day let me go home and have a shower and sleep in a nice bed and eat some nice food. As for staying out in the bush, sleeping on the ground in a tent, with crap food, forget it. Like a lot of the regimentation of a football club, there are guys who love it, and those who may not love it but cope with it. I was neither. But as captain, I knew I had to set an example, so usually I struggled through them. The one time I tried to be a bit too clever with it, I received a serve of justice.

The 2004 camp was going to be held at Kalgoorlie, from a Monday to Thursday. Hot, middle of nowhere, a community camp, really rough: not my cup of tea. I needed to have my wisdom teeth out, which might hurt, but my plan was to arrange the timing of it to get me out of the camp. West Coast had a minor sponsor, LifeCare Dental, where Sam, Mum and my sister Melanie all worked at some stage, and the dentist there was good to go.

I arranged to have all four wisdom teeth out on the Friday before the camp. I figured I'd be recovering until Sunday night, when I'd be coming good. But I'd tell the club I was in shocking pain and couldn't get on the bus to Kalgoorlie. It wasn't the right thing, as captain, and I knew that, but I also knew that I wasn't going to be any use to the team unless I had a rest. I really struggled with the idea of letting the boys down, but I was at breaking point. This was how I justified it to myself, anyway.

I went in on the Friday and had the teeth out. Instead of the recovery I'd planned, my head blew up and I was in agony. On Sunday night I rang Rod Moore, the club doctor, and said, 'I don't know how painful this is meant to be, but something's not right.' I was on the verge of going to after-hours emergency.

So I missed the camp, as planned, but for my sins I ended up having the toughest week of my life, sheer agony from Monday through Thursday, hideous pain, the nerves in my jaw like I was having needles stabbed into them. I'd been planning to go to the movies, catch up on my sleep, freshen up, have a great week.

When the boys came back from Kalgoorlie, I couldn't even train. I thought I was going to die. I'd thought I was being clever, but I guess the lesson was, be careful what you wish for. I deserved what I got.

AFTER NOT having a vice-captain in 2002 and 2003, I now had three: the club announced a 'leadership group' comprising me as captain, and Andrew Embley, Gardy and Rowan Jones as my deputies. That suited me fine, and we went into the season feeling solid. We had an unusual first four rounds, with each match being decided by seven points or fewer. We beat the Bulldogs by seven, lost to Port Adelaide by three, lost to Essendon by six, then beat the Lions, now three-time premiers, by three points at Subiaco. It was an incredible run of finals-type matches, and built a certain spirit into the team. We began to relish a close game, and look forward to those times when you've got nothing left, you're playing exhausted, everything's on the line, you can't think clearly, and you discover what you and your teammates are made of.

But we were two and two, and then hit a rough patch. Gardy did his cruciate and had to have season-ending surgery. He was the reigning All-Australian ruckman by then, the best in the league, and I'd been feeding off him. Dean Cox and Mark Seaby, his replacements, were developing but not yet in his class. We lost a bit of confidence as a team and were defeated in four of our next five matches, including a 101-point thumping by St Kilda. Our only win in that stretch was at home over the Swans, Glen Jakovich's 276th and last AFL match.

It was a huge symbolic moment, the retirement of the last of the premiership players. He'd been one of the greats, but part of the legacy of their achievement was the shadow they cast. It was inspiring to play alongside Glen Jakovich, but also a reminder of all the things you hadn't done in the game. Not his fault, of course: it's just generational change, and the inadequacy the younger brigade inevitably feels. But when he retired, it was the first time that I could look around the changing room and say, 'Hey, this is *our* team now.'

I WAS always trying to lift the boys, which became all the more important after losing two giants. One of our debutants that season was Ashley Hansen, a tall, gangly forward with curly blond hair.

In one of his first games in 2004, before the opening bounce Hansen was already getting roughed up by the opposing centre halfback. I kept running over to the guy and putting a word in his ear.

'Mate, we have a special video on you. We knew you'd do this, and we've been watching it. When you play on Jonathan Brown and Warren Tredrea, you don't touch them, you hand the ball to them meekly, good as gold. But when you're on a rookie, you're the big hero. We're all watching you and laughing at you.'

I let him know he wasn't like John Worsfold, who would intentionally square up to the hardest opponent, not seek out a novice. This defender became more worried about me heaping shit on him than about his own game, and lost his focus on Hansen because he was fixated on me. Which was just how I wanted it. I'd been able to do for Hansen what a teammate like Chicky would do for me.

It was something that ran pretty deep in me. In my first years as an AFL player, I'd copped plenty of shit from older opponents, and the usual approach was just to let you sink or swim. I didn't see things that way. I felt that younger players needed protection from the senior men. You're mates, right?

AFTER NINE rounds, we weren't having the season we were hoping for: thirteenth place with three wins. We picked up a few games in the middle part of the season, but I was struggling more and more with back, ankle and hamstring injuries. I was missing Gardy and not running as well as usual. By July, my body had had enough.

We were playing Hawthorn at York Park in Launceston, and I thought I put my ribs out when I was tackled late in the game. On the plane home, I drank a fair bit of alcohol and took some Valium. At training on the Wednesday, I felt like I was ninety.

X-rays found that I'd damaged a disc high in my upper back. An operation was a bit perilous, as I'd hurt the disc on the front side so they'd have had to go in past my heart and lungs. The alternative was to rest for a month or more.

I'd had a great run of luck with injuries since 1997. Nothing tests a player's mettle more than sitting out matches with injury, and I knew how blessed I'd been compared with some of my teammates. Our round sixteen match with Essendon was my first missed league game since 2000. Each week the club was putting out a statement that I might be able to come back, saying it was a 'back-related hamstring injury', but I wasn't up to full-tilt running. I eventually missed six games, coming back to play Melbourne the week before the finals.

In my absence, the boys had done extremely well, winning five out of six. A key reason was Juddy. He tore opponents up in the midfield, by reading the ball off the packs to perfection and speeding out of reach with that amazing acceleration. Even if someone caught him, he had such core strength that he could break free of a tackle. Then, to cap it off, he would invariably use the ball well. He was the complete midfielder, and would prove it a few weeks later by becoming the first West Coast player to win the Brownlow Medal. As a talent and as a leader, he was a once-in-a-generation guy, the X-factor we needed to go forward. You never know when a Chris Judd's going to walk through the door, but the occasions are rare.

In my comeback match we beat Melbourne and snuck into the finals in seventh place. It wasn't a bad result considering where we were mid-year, but was far short of where we'd hoped to be. We flew to Sydney for the elimination final at the Olympic Stadium. Going out onto the field before the match, we were taken aback by the size of it. Sydney trips had always meant playing at the SCG, which was shorter and wider than most AFL grounds, an idiosyncratic shape and very loud when the stands were packed. At the Olympic Stadium, the playing surface was longer and larger, and the seating, more than twice the capacity of the SCG, was enormous.

My back felt all right, but a freak thunderstorm hit during the game. There was lightning everywhere and the rain drenched the ground. Playing Sydney in Sydney was a tough assignment at the best of times, let alone in a final. We had a nightmare match, never in it against a team who were as much on the upswing as we were. We only kicked 4.10 for the game, and went out by forty-one points: my ninth AFL season, seventh time in the finals, and sixth time out in the first week. Now it was really giving me the shits. All I could do was go out and blow off some steam.

IT WAS during that off-season that I got into crystal methamphetamine, or ice. It had taken off in Perth a couple of years earlier, and I'd tried it once or twice but didn't find it any different from speed.

In that off-season at the end of 2004, I finally had proper crystal. I'd been snorting coke for two days, and then had a pipe of this stuff, and it took me where I'd been trying to get all along. My reaction was: fuck me, where have *you* been? It was like speed, but super-charged. It had a bad rap, even among heavy drug users. It sent you proper-fucked. It seemed so good – no blocked nose, no anxiety, and you didn't have to keep on smoking pipe after pipe to get an effect – but before you knew it you'd been up for days. When you got on the rock, you were locked in. On an ice bender, I'd be up drinking and smoking for a day and a half, and then I'd say, 'I have to go home. I have to shower up, then get a massage, then clean the house, then meet Mum to drop something off.' The incredible thing about the rock was, you could do all that, and do it with a manic energy and efficiency. I had *clarity*. I'd make all my necessary phone calls and pay all my bills – knowing I'd be in no shape to do so before long – then reload and get back into things. I'd go back to whatever apartment or nightclub or boat my friends were on, and start out on a new ten-hour session.

I'd be out in public at these times, feeling fantastic, and talking to anyone. I thought the whole of the city knew what I was doing, and that I didn't have to apologise. It was my time, my precious little slice of freedom, and as long as I was performing for my teammates during the season I could do whatever I liked with my private time.

As good as it was, there was something about crystal that I had yet to discover: it was the one drug you couldn't beat.

My mates and I called racking up 'ironing', just an in-word that assumed more sinister overtones when it got out, when a newspaper reported me and a friend mentioning it. It was one of those words that seemed very funny at 4 am on the second day of a bender, and it stuck with us. Sometimes the benders became competitive. On day four I'd look healthy and still be functioning well. If any of our group wanted to go home, I'd call them weak and urge them to join me in another pipe or line. I attacked it as I attacked a football game. For those first four days, I always seemed to be going better than I was the day before. But then the wiring would start to break down, and I'd start having black spots. I'd forget where I'd been for the previous few hours. Basic things were impossible to keep track of. When I'd hit a wall, I wouldn't think of going home: I'd think I could fix my motor with another pipe, until finally, when the sleep deprivation and, frankly, the sheer toxicity of what I'd done would force a halt to proceedings. Days after I'd started, I'd crawl home feeling like I'd been dragged through the bush. As ever, my beautiful Sam was there to put me to bed and shut the door for a few days.

When I first discovered good crystal, I didn't become hooked. I'd only seek it out if there was no coke around. I wasn't so stupid that I didn't realise it was something to steer clear of. With your first ice pipe, you mightn't intend to go on for five or six days, but inevitably things would get out of hand. It meant trouble and fear. But it was the kind of fear that, at the end of 2004, I felt sure I could master. Self-confidence is a great thing for a footballer. But for a drug user who's tasted the rock, self-confidence is going to be your undoing.

17

ON THE BOIL

When I'd started at West Coast, I'd had a privileged AFL apprenticeship in a premier team. Even though it had been a long time since then, I'd kept the memory fresh in my mind of what a flag-winning team looked like. They were driven by the players, with many leaders on the field, and had the best training methods in the game. As a junior guy, you just had to fit in and play your role.

I remembered what a premiership team felt like. If my senses weren't deceiving me, our 2005 squad had that same feeling.

With Jakovich having left in 2004, and Drew Banfield the only 1994 player left, it truly felt like our side now. The midfield of Gardiner, Cox, Judd, Kerr, Chad Fletcher and myself had proved against the Lions that we could compete with the best. Up the back, Darren Glass and Adam Hunter were a great tall fullback combination, with David Wirrpanda and Chicky – who'd moved into my home after his marriage busted up – running it out. Quinten Lynch, Ashley Sampi, Ashley Hansen, sometimes Gardy, and Phil Matera gave us options in the forward line. With wingmen like Andrew Embley and Michael Braun, we had good players all over the ground.

The final piece in the puzzle was the club's recruitment of Tyson Stenglein from Adelaide at the end of 2004. He'd been my direct opponent a lot over the years, and I found him one of the hardest negators. A lot of blokes could run with you, but you could outplay them on the ball. With the bigger, rangier blokes like Stenglein and Geelong's Cameron Ling, it was much harder, because not only could they run with you, at the stoppages they could also push you out of the way. Guys like Ling and Port's Kane Cornes would also get a lot of the ball themselves. Their teammates would go out of their way to give them a lot of touches, to keep you honest, and it would give me the shits. If they got the footy, I'd have to hedge my bets and think as much about stopping my opponent as getting the ball for myself. I'm sure Mark Williams, Port's coach, drilled this into his team, to get the ball to the tagger and force the tagged player to change his game and chase the ball to places he wouldn't normally be running.

For Adelaide, there had been a few games when Stenglein had got the better of me. He was a big strong bastard, he'd just plant his legs and you couldn't get around him for a run at the footy. Out in space, even if I got a yard on him and reached the ball first, he still made it hard for me.

A Perth boy, Stenglein was good mates with Chad Fletcher. When the opportunity came up to draft him, I gave him a big endorsement.

*

FOR THE first time, a West Coast team made the final of the pre-season competition. It wasn't normally our focus, but we were riding our momentum from a great summer of training. We lost to Carlton in the final, but went into the season brimming.

The early signs were all good. In round one, we beat Adelaide at Football Park for the first time in seven years. I dislocated my finger and missed the next round against Geelong, but we put them away and set off on an eight-match undefeated streak. We lost to Collingwood at the MCG in round nine, but then bounced back against the premiers, Port Adelaide, kicking 27 goals and smashing them by 117 points.

It was all looking rosy until an unnecessary off-field distraction threatened to derail us in May. Gardy and I were asked to go to the main police building in Perth city. When we got there, we were sat down and told that certain phone records connected us with an incident during the summer at the Metropolis nightclub on the edge of Northbridge.

There had been a serious fight at the nightclub during which, Troy Mercanti had been slashed and critically wounded with a knife. Troy was in the Coffin Cheaters bikie gang. The guy who knifed him was allegedly shot by Mercanti, and two mates of ours, David Morris and John Kizon, had been charged as accessories after the fact over the disposal of the gun.

Gardy and I didn't know what it had to do with us. I'd been in Melbourne when the incident happened, and he was in Fremantle at Ashley Sampi's twenty-first. I didn't even know about the nightclub incident until I was back in Perth. A lawyer sent by the football club gave us the standard legal advice: say nothing. All we knew about it was what we'd read in the papers. Our only connection was that we'd had phone calls with Dave and Troy around the time it happened, but we'd just been bullshitting away, and neither of them had told us about the incident. As it's not a crime to talk on the phone with a bloke you know around the traps – I'm one of those people who make about a thousand phone calls a week to various friends – Gardy and I asked if we could leave, and the police let us.

The coppers were gunning for the gangs, and no doubt saw us as young smart-arses. Which we were. We weren't clueless about the risks we were taking, and knew we'd cop a whack sooner or later.

It came sooner. Even though we'd only been in the building for ten minutes, when a grinning policeman put an arm around us and led us outside, a photographer from the *West Australian* was waiting for us. No wonder the copper was so cheerful. That really pissed us off, because the newspaper was obviously tipped off by the police, and we knew we'd receive a lot of negative publicity over something that had nothing to do with us. It was the police's way of telling us to pull our heads in.

Trevor Nisbett called us in and lectured us once more about harming the 'image' and the 'brand' of the club. He criticised Gardy for a gesture he'd made while celebrating a goal in an early-season match, holding up his wrists as if they were handcuffed. He was sending a message of solidarity to Mercanti, who was sitting through a pretty grim time in jail. Say what you like about him, Gardy was loyal; he wouldn't hide his friendships just because his buddies were in trouble. We saw ourselves as cheeky kids playing with fire, full of bravado, but were out of our depth. We didn't realise how many people we were rubbing up the wrong way, or how hard they'd eventually come down on us.

As with the photographs of us leaving Crown Casino with JK a few years earlier, there was no mention of us actually having done anything wrong. We were in trouble for being photographed – but we'd only been photographed because of the police tipping off the paper. The logic sort of went round in circles.

But each of these incidents was adding up to something. Gardy and I saw a lawyer, Peter Momber, who helped us write public statements to put an end to the issue. I came across as more contrite than Gardy, apologising to my family and club for 'the public perception of my continued association with people who are regarded by others as underworld figures'. That was as apologetic as I was going to get. But we did know that these guys were so hot they were tropical. We were testing our limits, and knew it.

We told Nisbett what he wanted to hear, which was that we'd do the right thing with the police and not associate with 'criminals'. We said what we had to say. Dalton Gooding, who'd become club chairman, was in Italy at the time. He put out a statement saying Gardy and I were on our last chance. It added to the pressure and complication we were bringing down on ourselves. The public was divided on whether I should be allowed to keep the captaincy. I thought I was a lot smarter than I was: it was taking time to dawn on me how the responsibilities of my job were changing. Gardy and I were clinging onto a world where our only obligation was to turn up each game day and play good footy; a world that belonged to the past, not the present and definitely not the future. A part of me was aware that the football world was moving in the corporate direction, but another part, the part in denial, still clung to the romantic idea that I was an old-fashioned knockabout footballer, rough around the edges and loving it. I wanted it both ways.

The next weekend, down in Tasmania, we beat Hawthorn. I had their captain and best tagger, Richie Vandenberg, on me, and picked up twenty-five possessions. When Gardy made his comeback from injury a week later against St Kilda, he kicked four goals in the first half. That seemed to do the trick – in our minds, anyway. A little more smoke and mirrors.

MY 200TH LEAGUE game came up in July, against the Lions. We'd still only lost once that season, against Collingwood in round nine. I gave the obligatory press conference for the game, and surprised a few people by saying my career didn't have a highlight yet. I didn't mean to be ungracious. It was just that I'd never had any finals success. It was eating away at me that we'd been in the finals year after year and been bundled out.

But this year was feeling real good. I was getting more satisfaction than ever out of my footy. With Juddy and Kerry so dominant in the midfield, I had a chance to drift up forward more. Early in my captaincy, when I'd played in struggling teams, I'd got a lot of the footy in less damaging positions, on or behind the ball. Now that Judd, Kerr and Fletcher were taking up so much of our opponents' attention, and Stenglein had become a permanent fixture in the centre square, I had a chance to move forward of centre and set things up. I resisted it at first, and there had to be a bit of give-and-take between the midfielders, all of whom wanted to play on the ball. But it was the best thing for the team. Opponents, knowing we had great delivery out of the midfield but no superstar forwards, would try to clog our forward line and frustrate us. My role, as a link between the midfield and the forwards, was to get the ball through the traffic and ensure we didn't turn it over and give up a goal on the rebound. The better we became as a side, the better quality ball I got, in more and more damaging positions, and consequently the more we looked after each other when under scrutiny and the more we shared the ball among ourselves.

We had a great ethic of selflessness. There was one game against Fremantle, where Matthew Carr, my direct opponent, decided to run off me whenever the Dockers had the ball. The object was obviously to keep me accountable. But Rowan Jones foiled it. He was our other half-forward, and he tore off after Carr. It left me free, and disrupted Fremantle's plan. I ended up getting the accolades, but Woosher made a point of recognising Rowan's contribution. Others may not have seen it, but we prized self-sacrifice above all other virtues.

This was also the time when on-ball players were increasingly coming off for a rest. I'd do fifteen minutes on, with three or four minutes off in the middle of every quarter, then back on. It gave me the chance to do the ballistic running I was best at. When I was on, I wasn't running at a constant three-quarter pace, in a groove that a natural 10-kilometre runner would do; I was going full-tilt. If opponents played a halfback on me, he wouldn't have the running base to keep up with a midfielder. But if they took their best tagger or midfielder out of the square to cope with me, they lost one from the centre and it suited us beautifully, because it left Judd free to cruise through the middle of the ground. They were reluctant to do that, so their best tagger had to go back to him, freeing another of us up. We all had a turn at getting off the chain. No wonder we were having a good time.

I got the flu early in the week of my 200th game. Dad's filly Innocent Eyes won the Australasian Oaks in Melbourne that week, so we were having a double celebration. I got myself right for the game against the Lions, who were still the competition benchmark, and kicked three goals in the first quarter. It was one of those games where everything fell into place, and having played 200 I knew how rare they were. We won by twenty-three points, confirming ourselves as flag favourites.

We won fourteen of the first fifteen rounds, but, ominously, it was the Swans who snapped our run in Sydney. The AFL's chief executive, Andrew Demetriou, had joined some commentators earlier in the season in making some derogatory remarks about the Swans' style of play.

I didn't agree. Paul Roos was an outstanding coach, and I saw the Swans very much in our image: really honest workers playing one-on-one footy. We'd been on a collision course for a couple of years now, moving through the rebuilding cycle at the same rate. We both had an even spread of talent across the ground, and founded our games on hard work. It may not have been pretty in some eyes, but I had great admiration for the way they played their footy.

After such an amazing season, we got the wobbles in August, losing three of our last four rounds. In our final regular season match we hosted Adelaide and lost by eight points. Having been runaway comp leaders all season, we didn't even win the minor premiership, finishing level on points with Adelaide but behind them on percentages. Sydney were third, St Kilda fourth. On the eve of September, it was a good kick in the arse for us and a reminder of so many finals campaigns gone amiss.

OUR FIRST final, a qualifier to get the second week off and go through to the preliminary final, was against Sydney at home. Superficially, we looked prettier than we were and they looked uglier than they were. The truth was there was nothing between us, as the next eighteen months would show. That night, they got ahead of us, as they had in the previous year's final, but this time we clawed back. A few decisions went our way in the last quarter and we won by four points in a very low-scoring match.

It gave us a week off. Adelaide had dropped their bundle against St Kilda, but they won their next match to come up against us again. Sydney, meanwhile, looked gone for all money against Geelong but a freak Nick Davis goal in the last minute, plucking the ball out of a crowded ruck, got them through to a preliminary final with St Kilda, which Sydney won comfortably.

We'd learnt our lessons from the round twenty-two match against Adelaide and this time came through by sixteen points. Tyson Stenglein, stopping Mark Ricciuto, was instrumental against his old club.

So: THE grand final week I'd always dreamt of. Most previous years, I'd been dealing with my disappointment at grand final time. I'd only been to Melbourne to see the grand final twice: when Brisbane beat Collingwood in 2002, and Collingwood's win over Essendon in the grand final of 1990.

I'd been close to winning the Brownlow Medal before, but knew too much about the vagaries of voting to think about it. As a kid, it had always seemed far beyond my abilities. I didn't believe winning one would complete or validate me as a foot-baller, but later in life, when things went pear-shaped for me, I'd value having won it more and more. Thanks to the Brownlow, at least my football couldn't be completely wiped from the record by my other actions.

Even in such a good team, I was the favourite in 2005. Juddy had been ruled out of contention back in May, when he copped a one-match suspension for elbowing St Kilda's Steven Baker. I said the medal didn't matter to me, and I believed that. Personal acco-lades are hollow if your team's not doing well. I'd found that was the case in 2000 and 2001. I wasn't one to buzz around happily if I'd picked up thirty possessions in a ten-goal loss. This week was about Saturday, not Monday.

But you never know, do you, until it happens? Maybe I was just full of shit, and the Brownlow did actually mean the world to me. There was only one way to find out. It was another thing sent to test me, to show me what I was really made of.

On the Sunday morning we all went to the club for a brief review of the Adelaide game. Monday morning was light training, followed by a swim in the crisp salt water down at City Beach. Having knocked back the AFL's generous but easily resistible offer to fly me to Melbourne on a private jet, I was always going to watch the Brownlow by videolink at an Eagles function at Burswood Casino. I was nursing a black eye from the Adelaide match. I don't know what the atmosphere was like at Crown, but at Burswood it was quite tense. In plenty of the early games, when I'd played well, I didn't get a vote. In the second half of the season, I emerged as leader, but my nearest challenger was Daniel Kerr.

After our bust-up in 2002, Kerry and I were at peace with each other. No matter what our differences were over the years, I loved playing footy with him. The smallest bloke in the team, he had the biggest tank. Plus, he was going out with my sister Melanie. During the vote, I'd look across the table and shoot Kerry a wink. Mel, who didn't know who to barrack for, couldn't bring herself to look at me.

The final votes came in for the final round, when I knew Kerry had played well. To show how chancy these things are, he didn't poll one vote. I finished one ahead. I went to the bar and bought a bottle of Moet for my folks, who were there, had a lemonade, and was asleep by midnight. It was a huge thrill to win the Brownlow, don't get me wrong, it was an honour to join the great players who'd won it and the many other better players than me who hadn't. But in that way of standing outside and looking in on myself, I was pleased to see how quickly I was able to put it away and maintain my focus. Saturday, not Monday.

The week, as I've said, went like a dream. Our only hitch was that Michael Braun and Rowan Jones, two of our real stalwarts, couldn't beat injuries. But on the flipside, Travis Gaspar, who'd inspired us all with his determination to overcome foot and ankle problems, would be on the field.

Tuesday was a day off, but a lot of us went to the club for a massage or some light weights. On Wednesday we had a last training session at Subiaco, and on Thursday flew to Melbourne. Gardy sat next to me on the flight and tried to bait me into losing my calm, but he was unsuccessful. Nothing could shake me, not even my best mate driving me mad. On the Friday we had a grand final parade, where I posed with Sydney's co-captain Barry Hall and the trophy. I was pleased to see so many Perth people lining the parade route, but at the same time didn't want to feel *too* pleased. We had an afternoon training session at the MCG, then our team meeting and dinner, and for me eight hours of perfect nothingness.

18

PAIN

You can't manufacture confidence. You can't manufacture belief. It comes in stages, and it's earnt. By grand final day 2005, we felt like we belonged there. This was the culmination of a four-year campaign since Woosher had come back as coach, and for me the culmination of a lifetime's lessons in football.

I ran onto the field with great optimism, thinking, *We're a real chance here.*

It's true that grand finals go faster than any other game. I remember we started well in the sunshine. In the second minute, Juddy made a burst and got it forward to Mark Nicoski for the opening goal. I was vaguely aware of Kerr picking up a leg injury and going off, but everything was moving quickly and we seemed to have the momentum, never more so than when Dean Cox, on his way to the interchange bench, found himself in clear space, picked up a mark, ran 30 metres, and kicked a 50-metre goal. It was a bonus, the kind of uncanny luck you like to be getting in a grand final. You're looking for signs everywhere, and this seemed to be a bright flashing one.

But the Swans were looking for signs too. They played with a more open forward line, leaving Hall and O'Loughlin with plenty of space. Despite us having dominated the first quarter, Hall and Amon Buchanan jagged goals in the last few minutes and they finished the quarter leading by a point.

As at each break, Woosher was calm, going through everything as he would in any other game. It steadied us, but Sydney came out with all the energy in the second quarter. Kerry came on but went off again, clearly hobbling. Roos had started Sean Dempster on me, a young guy with a big tank, but I'd been breaking free so they gave me Paul Williams, the former Collingwood premiership player who'd become an All-Australian at Sydney. Williams, a good ball player, matched me step for step and I didn't get the space I wanted. Cox and Judd were having huge games in the midfield, but by half-time we were trailing by twenty points.

The third quarter, the premiership quarter, was ours. I got the ball six times in the quarter, mostly good possession going forward. Embley kicked our first goal since Coxy's in the first quarter, then Ashley Hansen got one. In another of those great turning points, we felt things were going our way when Woosher moved Adam Hunter from fullback to full-forward and he got the last goal of the quarter. Gardy and I sometimes joked that West Coast's signature move – Hunter forward! – was West Coast's only move. But it worked more often than not. We went to the final break two points behind. Sydney hadn't scored a goal since half-time.

So it was all down to this. Kerry was back on, breaking through the pain barrier to get his head over the ball in the centre, as only he could. I floated forward. In the third minute, the Swans' Luke Ablett, who'd worked his arse off tagging Juddy, had the ball in the Swans' back pocket. I was having a breather in front of the goal square. Nobody was more surprised than I when he chipped it dangerously across the face of goals towards Leo Barry, and I intercepted it. I didn't have time to feel sorry for Ablett. My first goal in a grand final put us four points ahead. *Fuck*, I thought, *they can't beat us now.*

When you're as tired as we all were, you're highly sensitive to momentum shifts, and we thought we had it when Hunter followed my goal with his second. At the ten-minute mark of the final quarter, it was just our seventh goal, but we had the momentum and were getting away from them.

I should have been smart enough to realise how much time was left. The Swans were amazingly resilient. Although Mick O'Loughlin was missing shots, Hall kicked a long one and they were four points behind. We then had the run of play for a few minutes, but Brent Staker missed and then Banfield hit the post at the sixteen-minute mark. We were one point ahead, until Buchanan snapped Sydney's eighth goal. At least ten minutes still remained, and both sides were flogging themselves. It was the footy we lived for: when nobody can think straight and you can barely move your legs. With about a minute to go, Nicoski almost scored the winning goal but Tadhg Kennelly rushed it through for a behind. Four points in it.

The last act – it's unbelievable that your whole season, your whole life almost, can come down to that. It's a famous moment, I guess. I was near Dean Cox when he grabbed a mark about 75 metres from goal. He was going to kick towards a big pack forming in our forward pocket. I was running towards the pack, still close to Coxy, when he let it go. Everyone held their breath.

The only way I can describe how I felt when Leo Barry ran in from the side, flew above everyone and came down with that ball was: *This is the end*. And it was. The siren went before he had to dispose of it.

*

I'D PREPARED for every last thing that week, every moment fitting into my scheme of mood control. The one thing I hadn't prepared for, I realised now, was losing.

I'd never even thought of it, which was probably a good thing, because it was so much worse than I could ever have imagined. The moments after the siren were a blur. We stood around to receive our runners-up medals, and I said a few words about this being not the end but the beginning. I meant it, but it was just a cardboard cut-out of me standing on the podium. The real me was somewhere else, numb and wanting to escape.

In the rooms, Woosher said a few words which I can't remember. I do recall the vacant stares on everyone's faces. Often you feel like that after a bad loss, but you feel it alone. You don't know what you look like. That day, looking around the rooms, I could see my emptiness mirrored in my mates' faces. Mick Gardiner, Daniel Chick. Drew Banfield. Everyone: just this terrible collective pain and complete exhaustion.

ALL I wanted was to hide from it. We knew that Leo Barry's mark would be replayed all summer on television. It would be in the highlights promoting the next season. We'd see it a million times, as if someone was trying to twist the knife. The disappointment wasn't in that great piece of football – and it *was* great. The disappointment lay in the knowledge that so much had gone our way in 2005 and we'd missed our golden opportunity. The hardship, the work, the luck with injuries, the luck with results, the skill and synchronisation of how we'd come together as a team. It had taken us half a decade to get here from 2001. How did we know it wasn't going to take as long to get here again?

PAIN

But there was no hiding from it. I suppose that was the first thing that helped me to dust myself off. I had to give interviews straight away, where I repeated my hope that we hadn't come to the end, but were still at our beginning. We got into our suits and went to a dinner at the Melbourne Convention Centre. Everyone has his own way of dealing with this kind of grief. I'd made my arrangements. I got through a one-minute speech at the function, had a night out, nearly missing our flight home, always trying to keep the pain at arm's length.

In Perth I addressed our fans. Being captain, I still had to get the words out. I wasn't celebrating, I was trying to destroy what had happened. It's amazing that I could function. I was wrecked from the experience of the grand final. I was so focused on this thing, this match, and it hadn't turned out the way I wanted. My way of dealing with it wasn't the best way, but it was the way I dealt with everything. Hyper-focus on the match, get it done, then wipe it out.

And that was the summer for me, a sunny season with a big black cloud of anxiety hovering over us. This team and I were about to learn something new about ourselves.

19

LITTLE THINGS, BIG THINGS

The big end-of-season hit-outs had become a test I put myself through, a hurdle to jump over when I started training again. Would I make it this time, or had I wrecked myself beyond repair? I know it doesn't make sense, but that's the way I was. I used the experience of the bender to make myself a better footballer, by giving myself a new opponent to beat. Of course, this was also a rationalisation for my drug use. It's how an addict thinks, when you start to see your substance use as a thing that's helping your professional life.

By late November 2005, I'd squeezed as much into my break as I could. October and early November was my time away from footy, my time to be a normal bloke. The lunacy was that I was doing what no normal bloke would do.

Then, more cramming. Two or three weeks before we'd start training, I'd see if I could do eight weeks of running in two and a half weeks. Go through hell, then train like an animal. I'd also run around to see my family and reassure them that I was okay, touching all the bases to maintain illusions, running around like a maniac in the effort to put on a show that everything with me was all right.

WHEN THE team got together for the first time after losing the grand final, we were trying not to be downhearted. We'd missed our opportunity, but our performance on the day was something we could be proud of. Losing in the way we had was nothing to be embarrassed about. We'd given it everything. But we didn't watch it. A grand final loss is the one match that a team doesn't go back and review in detail. I've never watched it.

We didn't know if it would ever heal fully. We could come out in 2006 and be the best side, and still not win it. There was so much doubt and physical pain, and so many unknowns, before our next chance. We had to be patient, and lucky, and determined beyond belief.

But those were just words. Beneath the surface we were all feeling pain. Steadily, through November and December, we got fit again. When Woosher spoke to us, he stressed how the experience of losing so narrowly clarified how much every little thing counted. We became fanatical about the little things – because we'd learnt, when you're a good side, they're not little things. They're big things.

I GUESS at Christmas 2005 I lost sight of the line between little things and big things.

I've always loved the magic of Christmas: the anticipation of what we'd get, how we'd spend the day, the joy of time with Mum, Dad, Matt, Mel and Sophie. Perth is stunning at that time of year, and that summertime feeling got me excited about everything. That's why I can't forget how I fucked up Christmas 2005.

Any drug user's family will tell you Christmas is a minefield. This one wasn't just a fuck-up, but fuck-ups setting off more fuck-ups, each one getting bigger.

Christmas Eve had always been a night that Sam's family and mine spent together. I loved her parents and brothers, and enjoyed the tradition.

The key to a great Christmas, like a footy match, was timing. My feelings of anticipation at Christmas were a lot like they were for game days. I'd be at my best for the event itself, in the knowledge that I'd made my preparations for Boxing Day. I'd have a week off before training restarted, so Boxing Day was always the start of a bit of a twister. But this time I jumped too early, having some drinks out with the boys a couple of nights before Christmas. It got away from me, and come Christmas Eve, I was in a bit of a state.

After dinner, when Sam went to bed, I told her I had to go out.

'I'm going out to get your Christmas present,' I said. She was fuming, and it did sound a pretty lame excuse.

But it was true: I'd put a lot of thought into it, and had bought her a moped. Now I had to go and get it from my parents' place so she'd have it in the morning.

First, though, I had to hook up with some mates. Then I got waylaid (I was easily waylaid), and it was about 5 am before I got the moped and rode it home, with a mate driving my car behind me. I thanked him, parked the moped out front, and went inside.

I woke Sam gently. 'Happy birthday,' I said. 'I've got your birthday present out the front.'

She saw the condition I was in, and what should have been a nice moment turned bad very quickly. She whacked me across the face.

'It's not my birthday, you idiot, it's Christmas!'

LITTLE THINGS, BIG THINGS

There wasn't much I could do. She knew what I'd been up to and I'd already fucked up her Christmas, so I took off with my mate in the car to Gardy's place. Gardy wasn't there – he was spending Christmas with his family in Albany – but we knew someone else who was staying there, and by six-thirty I was breaking in, jimmying a window while holding an ice pipe in my free hand. I found the bloke asleep in bed. I fired up, and woke him by blowing smoke into his face. He opened his eyes to the sight of two of us, wide-eyed and out of our trees.

'What the fuck are you doing?'

'Merry Christmas, champ!' we chirped, lunatics on the loose.

We were smoking; that was obvious enough. We sat for a bit, had a bullshit, and left.

We shot back to my parents' place, where we arrived at about seven-thirty. My sisters were asleep, Dad was out training his horses, and we said Merry Christmas to Mum before ducking out the side of the house for a smoke.

'Oi, what are you two doing?'

Having pulled the wool over Mum's eyes for so many years, I'd lost track of when she'd woken up to me. My mate just panicked. He looked at me, horror-stricken, jumped over the fence and bolted.

I went into the house and calmly lied: 'Come on, it's just pot. If I can't have a smoke on Christmas Day there's something wrong.'

There was something wrong, all right. One of the many effects of smoking ice is that you lose perspective. It's a hard drug, so you think smoking marijuana is nothing at all, and you think other people are going to see it that way too.

It was pretty important for me to get out of there before Dad arrived home, so I went to Sam's family's house, where I did a reasonable job of holding it together for a few hours. Sam wasn't too pleased with me, but we kept up a front for her folks.

At midday I had to go back to my parents' place for lunch. It was a different situation there. It was a hot day, and Mum, Mel and Sophie had made a beautiful Christmas lunch, with a ham, salads and nice bottles of wine, crackers with paper hats, a Christmas tree, the feel of old times. I was trying to psych myself into the spirit but I couldn't help noticing how edgy everyone was with me.

It overwhelmed me during lunch. I was at the table, talking to Sophie, when my eyes rolled back into my head for a few moments. I came to, and what I saw was her frightened face. I looked down the table at Matthew and Dad, who were furious. I felt like I was about to faint.

'What the hell do you think you're doing?' Dad erupted. 'Why do you want to come here and wreck Christmas Day? Just get out of here, mate, just get out of here.'

He couldn't take me. Nobody could, and I don't blame them. But at the time, in my wired state, I thought, *OK, fine, I'm off. That's a win.* I got on the phone to a buddy.

'Mate, where are you?' I said. 'What are you up to? I'll be back at my place in ten minutes.'

'I'll be there in five,' he said.

I thought that was it for me for Christmas Day, so we sat at my coffee table, going line for line. The only way I could put what I'd done to the back of my mind was to shovel it back behind a wall of coke.

But three hours later, the old man rang to say he'd changed his mind and expected me at dinner, a much bigger affair with the extended family, taking place at a house Dad's parents had rented on the beachfront 50 kilometres south of Perth.

Fuck, I thought. *I'm in a worse state now than I was before.* I tried to convince my friend to come with me.

'You're dreaming, mate,' he said. 'No way am I going to cop the flak for the way you look.'

LITTLE THINGS, BIG THINGS

Not wanting me to drive, Dad sent Melanie to pick me up. In the car, we had an argument because I wanted to use before we arrived. I said it was the only way I'd get through it, and Mel flipped out at me. As we were arguing, she clipped a car in front of us and ended up in a big blue with the driver. I was like a string of explosives, setting off one reaction after another.

When we arrived, Dad's extended family were already sitting at the dinner table, eating and drinking. No doubt I'd been discussed. If they were fearing that I was going to put on a show, I delivered. I walked into the house with a carton of chocolate milk in my hand, drinking it, but unintentionally holding it sideways and leaving a trail of milk from the door to the table.

I bumbled my way through, managing to talk but probably offending everyone who was there. As soon as I could, I grabbed a cousin and got him to take me down to the beach for an after-dinner swim to clear my head.

Back at home, Sam was ready for me. We had a huge argument. Over time, she'd been incredibly tolerant of what I'd been getting up to. When you're living with someone, you're probably too close to see how things are spiralling out of control. And every time I'd been unreliable or irresponsible or failed her, I'd put everything into making it up. She'd probably been in a bit of denial too, hoping, against the growing evidence, that I was the same Ben I'd been at the beginning.

But I think that Christmas was when she realised how proper-fucked I really was. I can't remember what I said to defend myself. It must have been pure rubbish. Finally she said:

'That's it, I'm packing my bags. I'm off.'

She started packing, and I said:

'Fuck you, *I'm* packing *my* bags too, we can both fucken leave.'

So there we were, both packing our bags, neither of us knowing where we were going.

A user's brain is like a vacuum, completely emptying itself out every few minutes, ready for some new idea to pour in.

I looked at her. 'What are we doing? Are we going somewhere?'

I'd already forgotten what had just happened. I thought we were packing for a holiday. *Great! I love to keep moving. Sure, a holiday!*

Then Sam stormed out and left me alone.

The beauty of Christmas was that someone was always having a drink. Manic, with no attention span whatsoever, I cast aside the fact that my girlfriend had left me and was cleverly thinking I was two steps ahead, getting ready for my next drive-by.

On my way out, though, I was intercepted by Dad, Matt and Mel.

'Enough's enough,' Dad said. 'We're past angry. We're simply worried about you now. We need you to pull up. You're staying with us.'

I was having none of it. I was just getting started. Sure, I'd pull up – in about three days. My benders were always so planned, usually to fit in around my training schedule, that to pull up at this point was like a drag racer doing a U-turn. I tried to get past them, but they forced me back into the apartment.

We sat down and argued. It was now about eleven o'clock on Christmas night, and I'd been up for days. As I fought with Dad, Matt and Mel, some pang of conscience got through to me. I agreed not to go out.

'But I can't come home with you and go to sleep,' I told Dad. 'You don't know what it's like on this gear. I'll be staring at the wall going mad, I can't do it.'

We hit on a compromise: I'd go to Sam's brother's place. I trusted him. They took me there, and I dropped five or six Xanax, managing to crash.

On Boxing Day, I was due to go to a big party on a 40-metre yacht on the Swan, 120 people going out to Rottnest. That was the day of the year for me, the day I always set myself for. After a few hours' sleep, I didn't know if I was battle-worn or had just run myself into a bit of form. Either way, I brushed off the lethargy the only way I knew and by 10 am I was on the boat, ready to attack.

I figured I was fine. I would enjoy myself. Sam would simmer down. Everything would be rosy. It was a thirty-five degree day, and there were lots of people drinking and partying to the pumping music. Someone decided that conditions weren't right to go to Rottnest, so, as luck had it, they moored the boat a couple of hundred metres offshore directly in front of the house my grandparents were renting.

My parents and family were still there, spending their Boxing Day looking out at this yacht and the people going mental, blokes jumping off the cabin roof into the sea. They knew I was onboard with my mates, at it again.

A runabout was taking people from the party in to the jetty, and I told some guy, 'Whatever happens, don't let me go to shore.' But such was the form I was in, I ended up in the runabout anyway, popping in to pick someone up. When we got to the jetty, my cousin and uncle were standing there fishing.

'Ben, what are you doing here?'

What was I doing there? I was there because . . . Why was I there again? It was Boxing Day and I was with my crew. Of course I was there. Why wouldn't I be there? This was where I was meant to be. I went back to the boat, telling myself it wasn't all that serious.

20

'BLOKE'S NO GOOD'

On 12 February 2006, the world started to catch up with me. Blair Taylor, my childhood rival, teammate at Wesley and good surfing buddy, got married that afternoon. The reception, on a beautiful warm summer's night, was at East Fremantle Yacht Club. Sam had forgiven me, at least temporarily, for fucking up Christmas, and we were back together. By half-past midnight, she and I decided to head back from the reception with three friends to our place in South Perth.

Mum and Dad were at the yacht club, and Mum offered to give me a lift. Just like the old days! But I said we'd be fine to drive, which we definitely weren't.

We got into a Mercedes I had on loan from a sponsor. I joked with Sam that she could put her feet on the pedals and I'd steer. Between the two of us we might make one capable driver. Always a partnership!

'This time I can't drive,' she said. 'I can't do it.'

Everyone else was smart enough not to drive, but it was my car so I took the wheel. We were heading up the Canning Highway, past the river in the suburb of Applecross. I hardly ever drove after a party – I was aware of the consequences. I did know that I was the last person who should be driving. But that night, I drove anyway. Going along the highway, I had a premonition. I said to the others, 'If there are any problems, I'm pulling over and I'm taking off. Just want to let you know.'

Seconds later, we came over a ridge and the flashing lights of a booze bus came into view. My first thought was to pull into a side street. But it was a fully organised operation: I could see police cars blocking every possible getaway route.

I put the anchors on.

'See you, guys, catch you at home.'

One of my friends also ran from the car. The police caught him and thought he'd been the driver. He was breathalysed and charged with being over the limit, and he wasn't telling them that he had not been the driver.

I didn't know that yet, of course. I was sprinting away from three coppers, jumping over fences into back gardens, climbing onto roofs, tearing through about twenty-five quiet suburban back gardens. In my mind I knew how stupid this was, but instinct had taken over. It was like a movie, or a football game. Once you run, you can't be half-hearted about it! The adrenaline supercharged me, but also gave me clarity. I knew what would happen if I was caught. I stopped at one point to take a drink from a tap, but heard them coming after me and started up again.

The river: that was where I'd go. Sanctuary. I could slip into the black river and disappear. I got into the water in my shirt, suit pants and black shoes. It was about a kilometre across. As I swam, my clothes got heavy and I began to tire. I tried to float on my back, but my clothes were weighing me down. I was looking at the sky, thinking, *It's important to get away, but more important at this moment that I don't go under.* So I swam back to the near side of the river and waded in waist-deep water for about 800 metres.

I aimed for the lights of a marina. There didn't seem to be anyone following, so I climbed up between the boats onto the jetty and scrambled up the hill to a restaurant, the Bluewater Grill.

The restaurant was closed, but the staff were still there having drinks. I knocked at the door until a couple of women came. I didn't have my phone or wallet, but thought they might let me make a call. I needed to tell Sam where I was.

They wouldn't open the door. It was only then that I realised how I must've looked. My shirt was tied around my waist, my pants were ripped from groin to knee, and I was drenched through. I wouldn't have opened the door to me either.

They got the chef, who came out to see me.

Luckily, I found a twenty-dollar note in my pocket.

'Mate, I'll give you twenty bucks if I can make a phone call.'

The guy looked at me inquisitively. 'You're not Ben Cousins, are you?'

'No, no,' I said. 'Bloke's no good. I've been at a buck's party on a boat and the boys chucked me off as we were going past. I just need to make a phone call.'

I called Sam, who arrived twenty minutes later. She was unimpressed with me, but also realised the seriousness of the consequences. The Mercedes had been impounded, she told me, because I'd taken the keys. I found them in my pocket. More spur-of-the-moment idiocy.

We went to our place, where I packed an overnight bag and left again. I thought the cops might come and arrest me. I thought of going to Mainy's place, but when I got hold of him he'd had a big night himself and wasn't making too much sense, so went over to another friend's place, sat back and regrouped. *Fuck, what an idiot*. My heart was thumping. We'd lost a grand final, I was captain, and now I'd fucked up trying to be too clever. Flirting with my career and the captaincy. It hit me – now, of all times – how much I valued that job. Without ever having strived for the West Coast captaincy, I'd turned it into my mission, and I loved that team more than life. Nobody had ever been stripped of the captaincy at West Coast. I was chopping our side at the knees. Fuck. But I still didn't fit it into any idea of *addiction*. The world would see me as a smart-arse, not a drug addict. And so did I.

The next morning, I asked a mate of mine who was a panel-beater to see if he could track the Mercedes down. I went along to the compound where the police had sent it. Nothing in their records linked the infringement to me, so I was allowed to take the car away. They knew it was my car, but were still piecing together who the driver had been.

I was thinking, *You're a chronic offender, you idiot, you never learn*. Then I set about weaving my way out of the mess. I even entertained the idea of going to one of my mates who'd been in the car and asking if he'd take the rap. I offered to pay for a driver to ferry him around if he lost his licence as a result, but he didn't want any part of it. I was desperate, and while I knew I couldn't get dirty at him for not taking the rap, I liked to think that if our positions had been reversed I'd have done it for him.

My heart sank on the Wednesday, five days after the event, when someone told me that Howard Sattler, a radio announcer on Perth's 6PR, was going to break the story on the Thursday morning.

The first person I needed to talk to was Dad. I called him at 9.30 on the Wednesday night.

'I'm in a bit of a pickle. Want to come over for a cup of tea?' I said, using my typical wording when we were in the trenches again.

Dad and I sat down, and thrashed it out. After what had happened at Christmas, he was waking up to how seriously I was spinning out of control. Ultimately though, the voice of reason as always, he set me straight. I'd been stupid once too often. I had to cop my fair whack.

We got Peter Momber, the lawyer who'd represented me before, to come with me to the police. Dad told Trevor Nisbett at the West Coast: 'I've got a horrible feeling that the bloke you and I don't want to have been driving the car was.'

The club called me in, and the management team told me the consequences were going to be heavy. What dumbfounded me was how angry they were that I hadn't told them what I'd done straight away. But I had: I'd told one senior manager, who'd recommended I deny the whole thing. I didn't dump on him. While they were tearing into me, I was sitting there feeling tight as a drum, fighting the urge to push some of the responsibility back to them. But it was my mess, my very own. I couldn't run away from this one. As Dad had said, I had to cop my whack.

I was charged with one count of obstructing the path of another driver and one of obstructing a police officer. I'd later plead guilty and receive a $750 fine without any criminal conviction. The club's reaction was unavoidable. I decided to jump before I was pushed. A week after I'd been running through people's back-yards and half-drowning in the river, I resigned the captaincy. I wrote out a statement saying, 'I understand that through a few errors of judgment I put enormous pressure and scrutiny on the football club. I did not intend for this to happen.'

I don't make light of my stupidity in taking the wheel of the car. In the heat of the moment it had seemed a larrikinish thing to do, a bit of a lark. But on top of the previous warnings, the responsibility of the captaincy, and another thing – the secret, burning guilt about my double life, which was a more serious indiscretion but not widely known – my resignation was inevitable. I'd spent so long battling that feeling of inadequacy, of not measuring up to role models like John Worsfold, worrying that I wasn't true captaincy material. Maybe, I wondered, they were right about me. Even more scary: maybe *I* was right about me.

21

MISSING THE ALARM BELLS

There was a common thread running through the strife I'd been in. I wouldn't stay down for long. After a few days of feeling miserable and angry, I thought, *Right, this is just a new challenge for me to beat. I'm gunna get out there and tear it up on the field.*

The booze bus incident happened just before the season started. And not just any season: this was when we were desperate to go one better than 2005. Within a few days I was using the episode to motivate me, in the way I'd been able to convert all of my self-created problems into fuel for my football.

We won our first five matches, the highlight a two-point victory over Adelaide, the other front-runners, at Football Park. It was strange not being captain, and at first Juddy was uncomfortable in the role. He didn't want to be seen as benefiting from my misfortune. But he was popular with the group, and of course everyone respected him for his play. I gave him my total support. I could still enjoy being with the team, helping us all feed off each other, without having the pressures of captaincy. It wasn't all bad. Again, consciously or not, I was modelling myself on the way Mainy had been in the teams of the 1990s.

In round six I missed the western derby with a rib injury, and it provided the customary upset: we lost our first league match of the season, by one kick. I was back for our defeat of Collingwood the next week, and we were off on another run of five straight wins. In round ten we went to Geelong, always hard to beat at home and developing a super side under Bomber Thompson. They led us early by 54 points, at half-time by six goals, and we'd only pegged that back by one goal by three-quarter time. Then we just found an extra gear. Kerry kicked an amazing goal from the boundary line to grab the lead with a few minutes left, Nathan Ablett got it back for the Cats, then Adam Hunter ran forward from fullback and kicked the clincher under extreme pressure. It was one of the most remarkable comebacks I was ever involved in; we'd kicked eleven of the last thirteen goals and tipped them out by three points. Kerry and I got thirty-one touches each, Coxy had one of the games of his life, and Tyson Stenglein kicked three goals. We had eleven individual goal-scorers. To do this against Geelong in Geelong was one of those team-making experiences. In the rooms afterwards we sensed we could do anything anywhere.

By round eleven we were on top with ten wins, until two losses, to Port and the Bulldogs, dropped us into second place behind Adelaide – a terrific team who were proving how hard it is to convert regular-season consistency into a premiership.

As strongly as the Crows were playing, the big AFL rivalry was between us and the Swans. They were chugging along in sixth place when they came to Subiaco on 15 July, our first encounter since those two four-point epics the previous September. This time they started dominantly, Goodes and Hall very sharp up front, and led us by five goals at half-time. Daniel Kerr was out of our team, but Adam Selwood stepped in and played a blinder, as did Juddy and David Wirrpanda, and we kept Sydney to one goal in the entire second half. They still shut us down in attack, and it was one of our typical arm-wrestles until we just edged ahead of them in the final quarter. We won by two points, 9.13 to 9.11. It wasn't really revenge for the grand final, just a renewal of a rivalry that got us up more than any other.

IN MANY ways, it was a good thing that I wasn't captain anymore. There were a lot of things I was finding it harder and harder to cope with.

Three days after we beat the Swans, Gardy, who'd been drinking alone on a Monday night, smashed into three parked cars in the beachside suburb of Scarborough. I was sitting with him the next day when Woosher called, telling him he was sacked. Officially, the club was fining him $5000 and suspending him from playing, but he was coming off contract at the end of 2006 and Nisbett said it was unlikely he would be renewed. Gardy and I knew he was gone. It was devastating. I'd been lucky – I could redeem myself through football. But due to a run of injuries, Gardy hadn't had that outlet. It was so much tougher for him to fight back. He'd only played eighteen games in 2004, 2005 and 2006. Dean Cox had gone past him as our number-one ruckman. This was through no fault of Gardy's, and he'd continued to put in a big effort to get himself right to play. It was tearing him apart in a way I was only beginning to understand.

A lot of our friendship had been like playing chicken – running close to danger and skipping just clear of it. A lot of that was harmless mischief, but now it hit me that things had gone to a different level.

After Gardy's conversation with Woosher, I rang Trevor Nisbett, who was with the club's media manager, Gary Stocks. I was furious. This wasn't about the bloke being a larrikin, it was about alarm bells ringing over his wellbeing.

'Has anyone fucken laid eyes on Gardy?' I asked. 'It's a disgrace. The bloke was drinking on his own on a Monday night. He wasn't at a strip club or out partying. He was on his own. He didn't go out and smash his car with the intention of sticking it up the club's arse so he could get sacked.'

While Nisbett and Stocks stayed silent, I told them their only interest was trying to control the way they looked in the media, when what they should have been doing was stop for a second and consider the welfare of a young bloke whose actions showed he was in a pretty dark place. Gardy's car crash was a symptom of problems he was having, but all they wanted to do was wash their hands of him. Rod Moore, as club doctor, knew this better than any of them and had gone out of his way to help, but the hierarchy saw things differently.

'You want to hang the bloke out to dry?' I said. 'Does anyone want to make sure he's all right? Or do you want to find him hanging from a beam tomorrow?'

They didn't have anything to say. I accused them of being too gutless to come over and have a cup of tea with Gardy and behave like humans, just say, 'Sorry it's come to this, mate, we have to suspend you but we want to offer you some help to sort out your problems.' Gardy was a loose cannon, for sure, but he had been at that club for ten seasons and had made a great contribution as a player and a bloke.

*

I WAS half-aware that by trying to fight Gardy's battle for him, I was finding a proxy for myself. My life was slipping out of control just as badly as his, the only difference being that I was still able to produce the goods on the field. Being injured had removed Gardy's mask. I was still wearing mine.

But only just. I'd been playing with broken ribs for six weeks, getting painkilling needles in order to take the field. For this reason, and after the bust-up over Gardy's sacking, it was agreed that I would miss our trip to Melbourne the next weekend to play Collingwood.

The team went down by thirty-seven, and I had a hit-out at home. My self-imposed boundaries were getting blurred. By Sunday night, I knew I had to pull up hard. The team was back from Melbourne and the week's commitments were starting to roll. It was an almighty juggle. I had to be organised. Having been hard at it all weekend, putting myself down was like stopping a train. When I got desperate for some sleep, I took too many Xanax.

I got into a state where I was walking around the apartment asleep for half an hour, my brain gone but my body still up. It was like sleepwalking. Then I hit the deck and slept through my alarm – my life was full of wake-up calls I was missing – then got up and rushed off to training, hell-bent on making amends, telling myself I was not going to get on the gear again until I'd played a blinder for the boys. I told myself I just had to survive the day, and I'd be fine. I was delusional, not fully aware of what had happened or how I must have looked. I thought I'd had a heavy night, not that I was putting my career at risk.

In my now fully warped universe, my self-esteem relied on these bargains I made with myself: play good footy, and you can get on the gear conscience-free. As long as you play good football, you are not just a drug user. My world wouldn't exist if I was *just* a drug user. So my football became a kind of currency with which I'd purchase my drug time.

Usually I fulfilled both sides of this bargain. I was so highly organised, I could time my run to perfection so that my physical peak each week was game day. It would be five days since I'd taken any drugs, I'd have trained my arse off, and the upcoming game provided the rest of the adrenaline. And then there was the knowledge that after the game, I could get on it again. Normally, by game day, I was fresh and ready, spurring myself on with a personal rewards system: if we win, if I run the four quarters right out, if I leave it all out on the ground, then I can escape, go on the hunt for those fleeting moments of feeling good about myself. Game day, vroom, here we go. It had been working that way for years. The longer I'd been doing it, the better I seemed to play. That was the craziest thing. In 2005 and 2006, when drugs were really putting their claws into me, I played the best football of my life in the best team I'd represented. And the vicious circle was such that the better things went on the field, the bigger rewards I gave myself.

But it's true what they say about drug use: you're like the frog boiling in the pot. The temperature goes up one degree at a time and you're feeling absolutely fine. Then, when you're suddenly being cooked, it feels like it's come in a rush.

The week after Gardy's sacking in July 2006 was the beginning of that boiling point. At that Monday training, a photographer from the *West Australian* snapped me, and the picture in the next day's paper told a story that couldn't be denied.

On the Wednesday morning, the whole squad had to turn up at dawn for a six-thirty swim – as punishment for the way I'd turned up on Monday. Nobody liked that wake-up swim, and you could never be dirtier at a bloke than when he was responsible for you doing it. I was sure Woosher was looking for more from me. It was still dark when we arrived. I felt like shit. On my own initiative, I stood up before the swim, apologised to the boys, and promised to totally abstain from my lifestyle for the rest of the year. As the sun came up I dived into the freezing water with those forty blokes, feeling I was baptising myself. I'd been compromising my footballing life, blurring the boundaries. I made my vow to the boys, and I would stick to it. But it was taking more and more extreme situations to get me focused again.

22

GRABBING IT WHILE IT'S THERE

Three days later, I had one of the best games of my life. We were playing Adelaide, now the league leaders, at Subiaco, and for once were underdogs at home. I remember standing in the race about to run onto the ground behind Juddy. I was wound up, jumping out of my skin, *ready*. The old pattern was never truer than it was that week: the depths of despair on Monday and Tuesday, leading up to the supreme challenge of Saturday.

Even by my standards it was a wild week. On Tuesday I'd been in the newspapers looking like death. On Wednesday I'd been in the shit over the dawn swim. On Saturday I got thirty-eight possessions and two goals. Nobody could touch me. We kicked twenty-six goals, with thirteen individual goal-scorers, and won by eighty-two points. A shocker, a game where I didn't get a kick, might have done me some good. Having a good one was, in retrospect, the last thing I needed.

From there we beat St Kilda, North Melbourne and Brisbane, before the obligatory loss to Fremantle. A last-round eighty-eight-point demolition of Richmond left us minor premiers with seventeen wins. At a function at the Perth Convention Exhibition Centre, the Eagles announced 'Team 20', a selection of an all-time team from the club's first twenty seasons. I was in it. Then, for the first time since the 1994 premiership season, four Eagles were chosen as All-Australians: Juddy, Darren Glass, Coxy and me. My life looked pretty good if you didn't know me.

SYDNEY FINISHED fourth, behind Adelaide and Fremantle, which meant we had them at home in the first week of the finals. Always Sydney. The Crows were seen as a team of stars, but we knew Sydney was the team we had to beat. The triangular rivalry was funny. We seemed to have Adelaide's measure, but Adelaide kept beating Sydney. Then, between Sydney and us, you could take your pick.

That night at Subiaco, they reversed the result from the corresponding final in 2005. This time the difference was one point. Hall kicked five goals and O'Loughlin four, running right up to our fans to show them his feelings near the end. Juddy got a lot of ball for us, but I was well held, and we were missing Kerry with injury. The thing between us and Sydney, though, wasn't about individuals: it was all down to a mysterious battle of one team's will against another.

We thrashed the Bulldogs the next week, which brought us up against the Crows again. On the Friday Sydney, who'd had the week off, knocked out the Dockers to go into the grand final. Seventy-two years without a flag, and now they were looking at two in a row. We had to travel to Football Park, which had been a finals graveyard for us for years, though we'd begun to turn it around recently. And we felt, after the previous year, that needing to stay up for all four weeks of the finals series without a week off might do us some good.

The game stands out in my memory as the most significant I ever played. We didn't kick a goal until the second quarter, and were four goals behind at half-time. Could we get a chance at redemption in the grand final? I was still bearing a load of guilt towards my teammates. I had a chance to repay a debt to them, but it was all down to this one half. 'This is it,' we said as we came out after half-time. This was when we had every reason to choke.

My second halves were often better than my first, and usually I came out for the third quarter feeling confident. Because I had such trust in my fitness, my approach to games was to intentionally run myself to exhaustion, see red in the first quarter. I wanted to tire myself and my opponent early, so we could find out who had the power to recover and endure and keep a clear head. I'd want to go ballistic early. I'd look at my opponent and my eyes would say, 'We're both fucked now. Can you go again? Can your body recover the way mine can? I'm doing this every week – are you?'

This day, my opponent was Nathan van Berlo, eight years younger than me and a super runner. I had the highest respect for his running ability, but from here it was gut running in the most important half of our lives.

As soon as the second half started, I found myself in that zone where my work rate was enormous, but strangely easy. We were both totally fucked, couldn't get our wind in, couldn't think straight, but all I needed was a yard and I just seemed to be reading the play. Time stood still for me. There weren't enough matches like this! And I was far from the only one. All twenty-two of our boys were lifting. By three-quarter time we'd halved the gap, and in the last quarter we outran them. We really found out that we had the belief, and the nerve, that day. Adam Hunter kicked four goals, and, after being behind all day, we kicked 5.7 to 3.1 in that quarter to win by ten points.

The grand final, again. Sydney, again.

I DON'T believe you need to lose one to win one, but it didn't hurt us as players to have gone through the full gamut of emotions since 2005. I guess it's easier saying that looking back. During the week, I had this nagging superstitious feeling about Geelong, the team I'd idolised back in the late 1980s and early 1990s. Four grand finals, and lost them all. So I knew that having lost in 2005 did not entitle us to win in 2006. There was no rule of fairness, or justice. The ghosts of Geelong were with me. But I was rapt to be there again, and had a firm sense that we were too good a side to be thought of as one that couldn't go that extra step.

Having been there before made the week predictable. Our routines were the same, and we stuck to what we knew. Adam Goodes won the Brownlow, so he had to find his way of dealing with that early in grand final week. I'd totally abstained from illicit drugs for a few months, and felt fantastic.

Not being captain didn't make much of a difference to me. I think the team got just as much out of me as a leader, and they got even more than before out of Juddy. He held his confidence inside him, quietly, and I walked taller knowing he was there. The bigger the game, the better he played. A freak player, he bordered on untaggable.

My feelings in the lead-up to the match were no less difficult to control than the year before. It was easier having been there, but harder in that I wanted it so much more. It could be our last shot at a premiership, and after the difficult year I'd had I was treating this as my last chance at redemption.

In an interview the week before the grand final, Glen Jakovich showed how much he'd learnt about playing with me for nine seasons. He told the *Age* he'd 'never seen a bloke who, if anything, the more trouble he gets into off-field, the better he plays'. For switched-on resolve and steeliness to play football, Jako said I had superseded John Worsfold. If that comparison doesn't humble you, nothing will.

The last Saturday in September 2006 was an even more beautiful spring day than the year before. My best memory of the day, and of all the time I played in that Eagles team, is going into the warm-up and running onto the field feeling absolute confidence in the fitness and talent of the blokes around me. I knew they were all going to rock up for the game. They'd shown it in the number of games when we'd come from behind to win, or had to dig deep in the second half, epitomised by the previous week's win in Adelaide. I think of Coxy, Juddy, Chicky, Embley, Seaby, Drew Banfield, David Wirrpanda, Daniel Kerr, Chad Fletcher – the whole twenty-two, too many to name – and I well up with love for everything every bloke brought to that team. The great thing was the trust we had in one another. No-one else was trying to play my role, no-one was trying to play Daniel Chick's role, no-one was trying to play Chris Judd's role. The beauty of that side was that we weren't reliant on our best players, but on every player playing his own role. I hadn't had this kind of confidence in my mates since I was at Wesley in year eleven. The essence of what got me up had never changed.

As with the 2005 grand final, the game went by in a flash. We started well again, and converted our dominance into points. Our first half was as clean and pure football as you could possibly play against Sydney. I had Jarrad McVeigh on me, a twenty-one-year-old who hadn't been in the 2005 grand final. He would become too good a player to use as a negator, but that day he was a young running tagger. I got clear to kick two goals in the half, and we were four goals ahead by the main break. At the other end Barry Hall was missing set shots, having a bit of a nightmare.

But it was no surprise when they came back at us. They were the Bloods. Adam Goodes started to get out towards three-quarter time, and they closed the gap from twenty-five to eleven points by the last break. Goodes kicked a goal seconds into the last quarter, and we went goal for goal from there.

It was mayhem in the last five minutes. Steve Armstrong got a mercurial goal for us from the pocket, showing how every last piece of our squad was working together. The piece of play that sticks in my mind was when Chicky smothered a kick, handballed it to Adam Hunter, who, protected by Chicky's shepherd, goaled to put us seven ahead.

But then Nick Malceski scored the Swans' twelfth goal – they'd kicked eight to our four in the second half – and we were only a point ahead again. Goodes shot for the winning goal, but Embley got back desperately. By the last seconds we were just trying to get it out and wide. I got the ball and hand-passed it to Chad Fletcher, and when it went down the ground we thought we might be safe. But then Sydney got it and Nic Fosdike hacked it forward again. Desperation. Glass got it out over the boundary line, and as the umpire threw it back in, the siren went.

The initial experience, when it happened, was strange. I went down on my knees and hands, just collapsed. Had we won it? I thought so, but wasn't sure. It was such a tense game, so emotionally depleting, that my first feelings were confusion. Not feeling *We've won*, but feeling *It's over*. I took out my mouthguard, breathed in and out, and looked over my shoulder at the scoreboard. West Coast 12.13 (85), Sydney 12.12 (84). I had to keep checking.

Then the blokes began converging on each other. One of the best embraces I had was with Woosher. I'd lost the captaincy, but we'd kept our strong partnership. He said, 'I wanted you to experience this as much as anyone.' Nobody had been at West

Coast as long as I had without winning one. He knew how long I'd been there, and respected all the work I'd put in as a player.

What a person Worsfold had been in the history of the club. He went and found Drew Banfield, the other guy who'd bridged the eras.

I felt a storm of emotions, mostly pride in my teammates. The Chick piece of play to Hunter. Chicky was great on O'Loughlin all day. Embley was sensational and deserved the Norm Smith Medal, though Juddy could easily have won it again. It's unfair to name names. Every bloke played a huge role.

One of us, either ourselves or Sydney, could have walked off with both of those grand finals, but it would have been unjust. It was fair that we won one each. It was uncanny how, regardless of the half-time score, our matches repeatedly came down to the last kick. Both sides wouldn't give an inch, we'd both keep going. It was magic footy – not always attractive but gripping. When it was West Coast and Sydney, you knew you were in for a game. I don't remember ever having an argument, a sledging match, a trash-talking day with Sydney. There wasn't time for that bullshit. You couldn't bluff anyone. It wasn't part of our game or theirs.

If I compare my feelings at three-quarter time in both years, I thought we were going to win it in 2005 but the second year I thought we'd be stretched. Instead, Sydney won the first and we won the second. Incredible. But having lost one really enriched the elation of winning the other. It was a well-rounded football experience, those twelve months. Getting through the loss and coping with some tough times, then experiencing good times. It's something to cherish.

When Juddy was called on to receive the premiership cup, Woosher beckoned me to go up and join him. One of the special things about the day is that I had no second thoughts about what might have been if I was still captain. Juddy was the skipper, and I was proud of him up there. Having said that, I didn't need a second invitation to go up. This time I was going to enjoy a win. It's amazing to think that in all the footy I'd played – this was my 231st AFL game – I had not won a premiership since Wesley College in 1994. They come around so rarely, you have to grab them when they're there. And it's not that I was thinking consciously of it, but something had been buried in me since that Wesley experience, when I'd felt detached from the celebrations, like I'd missed the moment and needed to catch up. In my football career I was never one for over-celebrating a personal achievement. In fact it was one of my pet hates. But for team achievements, there are no limits. When I got up on that podium with Juddy, some memory of that Wesley experience was exploding inside me. I wasn't going to miss the moment now.

23

'I WAS BIGGER A WEEK AGO'

When we came off the ground and down the race, the first person I remember running into was Mainy. There's a photo of the two of us embracing, of which I have a framed copy. It's one of my all-time favourites. I loved seeing how much he enjoyed our success. He was working for Channel Seven now, and had been at a lot of our games. He'd gone down in West Coast history for his great leap after the 1992 grand final, when he went up in pure joy and didn't care that he had a broken ankle. Now, with us having won one, he was ecstatic to see that we could experience that feeling. He enjoyed our win as much as we did, which showed the sort of bloke he was.

Mum and Dad and my sister Mel were in the rooms, as well as the jockey Damien Oliver, a big West Coast fan who I'd met through Gardy, and a couple of other mates, Clayton Kirkpatrick and Mark Bergio, who'd been in Adelaide the previous week and had followed us to the MCG.

After a while in the rooms, singing the song and getting showered and changed, it all became a bit too much for me. I almost felt myself overheating with euphoria. I hadn't had anything to eat, and was probably going into some kind of energy deficit. Just before we got on the team bus to go to our post-match function, I took a couple of Valium, just to calm myself down. Coming out of the bowels of the MCG, I was disorientated. The next thing I knew, we were pulling up at the Convention Centre and I thought we hadn't left the ground yet. Why were we getting off? The moment had overwhelmed me.

Given what happened later, I think it would always torture me if I hadn't been part of a premiership-winning team. If we'd lost, I don't think I could ever have forgiven myself for my indiscretions. I'd have spent my lifetime questioning what impact they'd had. Critics and others would have said I cost the Eagles a premiership. It makes me a bit shaky, to speculate on how I'd have punished myself if we'd lost two grand finals by a kick. I'm lucky to have been surrounded by such a great team.

When we flew back to Perth the morning after the grand final, none of us had been to sleep. A bottle of vodka got me through the flight. Sunnies fixed firmly, I stumbled through the crowds at Perth airport. The euphoria was city-wide, people coming from everywhere. You felt incredibly humble to have put so many smiles on faces. We stayed up for days to take it all in and not miss out on anything. On Mad Monday we were at Steves Hotel, where we went every year, but this time we were partying as flag winners.

One of the most enjoyable parts of this celebration was seeing how much it meant to everyone else, within the team and outside. So much of my hedonism had been a secretive thing, a way of escaping from people. This time it was about sharing: with teammates, with everyone at the club, with friends, and most of all with Mum, Dad, my siblings and of course Sam, who was as excited about our win as any of the team. Nobody had made bigger sacrifices to keep me on the field than Sam had. She'd shared my dreams. I was just stoked to see her so happy after everything I'd put her through; it spoke volumes about her generosity as a person.

One thing that made us laugh was a news report saying: 'West Coast are now partying like Sydney partied last year.' Our response was: 'No, West Coast are now partying like *West Coast* partied last year.'

After a few days, it became a week of attrition. Some blokes wisely snuck off for three or four hours' sleep, but then they'd wake up, hungover and limping, remember what was going on, and rush back before it all ended. The euphoria gave us a high above and beyond anything I ever found through chemicals.

WHEN I'D made my vow not to use drugs for the rest of the season, I'd also agreed with Woosher that I wouldn't go with the boys to Las Vegas later in October for the end-of-season tour. It was well-documented that in Vegas Chad Fletcher had to be resuscitated when he stopped breathing, and spent four days in hospital. By not going, it sounded like I'd dodged a bullet.

There's no question that we liked to let our hair down off the field, but our excesses didn't taint our achievements on it. We might have had a few more extreme characters than other teams, but the difference was in degree, not kind. Every team's got some ratbags, and I say that as a self-confessed one.

In my time as a footballer I never heard about or witnessed a teammate using performance-enhancing drugs. If you wanted to bring my sort of lifestyle onto a footy field, the only thing you're going to give yourself is a heart attack. Cheating with drugs goes against everything I believe as a sportsman. I'm thankful that our game is a clean game, and while that may sound like an odd comment coming from me, it's just to show what a firm line I draw between the drugs I was doing and the drugs that would help a cheat on a football field. There are so many reasons why my use of recreational drugs never encroached on game day, the very concept is absurd. Drugs were not for footy games. Anyone who thinks otherwise about our West Coast team is naive and ill-informed.

FOR A decade, my drug use and my football career had been in a kind of race. Would I fulfil my football potential before the drugs wrecked my chances? Well, on 30 September 2006 the good side had won: by being part of a grand-final-winning team, I'd achieved the thing I played the game for. Football had won.

But from that point, starting two hours after the full-time siren, the dark side was going to take its cut.

Vegas wasn't the only bullet I had to dodge. October in Perth meant temptations on every block. Sam and I tried to bust it. My best way to avoid trouble was to get out of Perth. We spent a week in Sydney, a week on the Gold Coast and some time in Port Douglas, chilling out and diving on the Great Barrier Reef. It was the perfect rest.

But having had a rest, when we got back I was bubbling with energy and ready for a bender. I got on the rock, which was like running a triathlon a day for six days. Each morning I'd wake from a nap and say to myself, 'I can't put myself through that again.' But sure enough, I was right back on it. Some wires in my brain had skipped a connection, so that I was applying all my powers of endurance to this, instead of to getting fit. I was digging deep, finding new reserves, defeating the signals of pain my body was sending me. While I was on it, I felt perversely proud of myself. But as soon as I came down, I was vulnerable, fragile and paranoid, malnourished and dehydrated, waking up alone on a couch with no idea where I was or who I'd been with the previous eighteen hours.

Dad was finding out how serious it had got. As my benders got worse, there were nights when he sat up with me until 5 am in my apartment, just talking, to keep me from getting on; and then he'd get in his car and go train his horses. He was single-handedly trying to absorb all the pain, protecting not only me but also Mum and my siblings. There were nights when Dad was the only person standing between me and mates who wanted to drag me out again. 'Guys,' he'd say, 'it's pretty obvious Ben's not doing too well. He's not going anywhere.' At my place on those nights, he'd drag a mattress to the door and sleep on it to stop me heading out.

Nobody, except for Sam, knew better than Dad how serious my problem had become. Through the years, like any parent, he'd wanted to believe my mates were the issue. During a bender, mates would turn up at 1 am to take me out, and Sam would call Dad in hysterics. 'Bryan, those idiots are here trying to take him out again.' And Dad would be straight over, in the middle of the night. Sometimes I'd already have gone. He'd console Sam, get some clues to where I'd gone, then set out to find me. Once he tracked me down in some horrible pit in Northbridge. I grinned. 'G'day, mate!' But it wasn't the time for humour. Dad was sober, seeing the place for the shithole it was.

Sometimes I'd leave with him, sometimes not. Once, he dropped me off at my place at four-thirty am, then drove home. He rang Sam to ask if I was asleep. 'What do you mean?' Sam said. 'He's not here.' I'd gone up in the lift, waited till Dad had driven off, then gone straight back to Northbridge and my crew. It was more than any father should have to take.

*

AGAIN I was testing Sam's patience. She'd been the driving force behind our holiday in Queensland, and now I was undoing all her good work. We flew to Melbourne for a friend's wedding. Another bad idea, and I acted like a tool. Frustrated with my behaviour, Sam went back to our room to sleep. After the reception a crew kicked on to Eve, a nightclub near Crown Casino. I didn't even know my name, I was so gone. The club owners put me in a limo and sent me to Crown, where they thought I was staying. But I wasn't, so when I got out of the car on the Crown concourse I was disoriented, literally lost and alone.

I'd lost my wallet and phone. There weren't many people around, so I thought I'd try to find my way back to Eve. Problem was, I had no idea where it was, so I stumbled along the riverside. Soon, hit by a wave of exhaustion, I sat down and fell asleep on a bench.

Apparently a passer-by took a photo of me. Someone else called the police, and the next thing I knew, two coppers were shaking me awake, asking who I was and what I'd taken.

'I'm Ben Cousins,' I croaked.

'No, you're not. Ben Cousins is bigger than you.'

I took my shirt off and showed them my muscles.

'I was bigger a week ago,' I said.

It was true. When you're doing ice, you lose so much fluid and you're so malnourished that you can drop from eighty to seventy-five kilos in a week. You go from being Ben Cousins, super-fit footballer, to a wasted shell.

The cops still said they didn't believe me. I didn't know if they were taking the piss.

'You don't believe me,' I said, 'let me prove it. I'll take off and you try and catch me.'

That's when they cuffed me.

When they searched my pockets at the police station, they came up with a phone. It was Gardy's. I said if they let me make a call, I'd find someone who could verify my identity. I went through Gardy's numbers and found Trevor Nisbett's. He didn't answer. I left a message. Then I found Chris Judd's.

'Juddy'll come and get me. It's the least he can do,' I joked, 'he took the captaincy off me.'

Again, no answer. It was 4 am. I left a message for Juddy, asking him to pick me up at the police station, heaping a bit of shit on him.

The cops were clearly enjoying the show by now. It had all been fairly tongue in cheek, and I was playing up to them, but now they said I was on my last call.

I found the number of Ben Sharp, a Melbourne guy who was on our rookie list at the Eagles. He answered! But so bad was my luck that night, Ben was in Perth on a dance floor.

'I can't hear you,' he shouted. 'Hang up and I'll walk outside and call you straight back.'

'Don't hang up, it's my last call!'

But he hung up. The cops said, 'That's it, you're in a cell.'

Then Ben called, and the cops answered. He told them who I was, but an argument ensued and he told them to fuck off.

'Mate,' the copper said, 'every time you fucken abuse me and carry on, I'm going to keep your mate in here for an extra hour.'

So I spent the last few hours of the evening, right through into the next morning, in a cell. Ben Sharp had arranged for his sister to pick me up. She dropped me at the house of a mate who Gardy was staying with. I didn't have the courage to go back to our hotel and face Sam.

After crashing on the couch, I woke up and was about to step outside the front door to check the day when the bloke who owned the house ran down the stairs and said: 'I wouldn't go out there.'

'Why not?'

'There's press everywhere.'

'Who for?'

'You.'

Who else, I guess.

Another mate from the Melbourne scene, Angelo Venditti or 'Fat Ange', as we called him, walked in through the front door.

'Don't worry, mate,' Fat Ange said, 'I've given them all a fucken spray and told them to fuck off and leave you alone.'

Great, I thought, I've got a public character reference from Fat Ange, a good bloke but one who'd had his share of strife. I knew what fun the press would have with that.

They camped out front, but Robbie Bottazzi eventually came over and smuggled me out the back. Sam had flown home. I stayed in a hotel for a few days to let the dust settle, but in Perth the storm broke. The bloke's photo of me unconscious in front of Crown, with a bunch of associated stories, took up the first five pages of the *West Australian*.

I couldn't avoid it now. For years there'd been rumours of my activities, but nobody had seen me face down in public, off my face. I knew the club and my family would be embarrassed, and I was dirty at myself. I'd done the right thing by not going to Vegas, I'd taken a quiet holiday with Sam to straighten myself out, and now I'd nullified all that with one ferocious bender. I guess it always had to happen. Now it seemed the whole country was talking about it, and I had no excuses, nowhere to hide. If the warnings from Sam, my friends, my family and my club weren't enough, now there was this visible evidence screaming at me: *Stop!*

I chose not to listen.

24

'AN ALIEN DRESSED UP AS BEN'

After the public embarrassment of the Crown Casino incident and spending the night in the police cell, I tried to get back into training as the boys came together for the first time after the win and the celebrations. But it was clear that I was unstable. When I turned up late for training one day, Woosher had a meeting with Dad and me, and told us I was on my last chance.

For Dad, seeing my problem acknowledged by the coach gave it a new concrete reality. Woosher and I had had a lot of meetings through the years, but none was harder than this one. Where I was at was not John's world, and it was hard for him to get his head around. He was aware that there would be blokes who'd take the occasional this or that, maybe go a bit mad in the off-season, but we knew now that my problem was far more serious. I had an illness all year round.

John was extremely supportive and empathetic. We talked about how people had noticed changes in me. Even while I'd been using drugs a lot in Woosher's early coaching years, I'd still been among the first to arrive at training and the last to leave. My behaviour with club staff and teammates was friendly and bubbly. Now I was arriving just on time to avoid being late, and would skip away quickly afterwards. I wasn't as engaged with the staff. Aware of how different my life was from the other boys', I was retreating from them. I was seen as aloof at the club. I was usually great on game day, but, John said, for me and for the team, that wasn't enough.

He said I was the most mentally tough player he'd known. I was on my knees, and he knew I'd need every ounce of that toughness to get myself back up.

By the end of our conversation, I was flooded with gratitude to Woosher. Unlike the way the club had treated Gardy, he was caring about me as a person first, a player second. He was worried for my health and my future. I told him I believed I could get on top of it, and it wouldn't affect my football.

'Never mind the football,' he said. 'Take care of yourself.'

Dad, who was becoming really concerned now, met with Rod Moore, who used the term for the first time in relation to me: drug addiction. He said that when someone got addicted to drugs, it was the family who suffered most.

'Brace yourself for a rough ride,' Rod told Dad. 'You will be dealing with an alien dressed up as Ben.'

IN A two-week period after that meeting I ran every day, hard runs, trying to transform myself from a wreck into a football player. And it was working. I'd always pulled my way out of this, hadn't I?

But I truly believe in the saying that your greatest weakness is an excess of your greatest strengths. My strength was my ability to bounce back, get fit again, face down my demons. I was so good at it that when I'd pulled myself back together, I gave myself a big reward.

I was doing a lot of different drugs, but if I could have chosen by then it would have been crack cocaine, which I smoked whether I was with mates or on my own. At my apartment, I sat on the fourth-floor balcony with its glass barrier, looking across the Swan at the city, smoking crack pipes. I sat all night listening to Neil Young, Pearl Jam or Ben Harper, chilling to the music I loved.

I knew I wouldn't sleep, so I'd call some buddies up. The gap between my public life and what I was doing was a source of endless humour. Blokes would say, 'Look at you, penthouse to shithouse in record time, hero to zero.' Nobody would find this funnier than I did.

By this point, my drug-using routines were more and more insular and, from the outside, boring. I'd sit around a coffee table having a good bullshit. I'd sit up watching English premier league soccer because it was on late, and a few of my mates would punt on it. It gave us an interest. We had a lot of laughter, but the humour was beginning to get a bit edgy. Away from that coffee table, reality was closing in on me.

AFTER OUR meeting with Woosher, Dad sat me down to lay out a few home truths. Everything was on the line now. He reminded me how much footy meant to me, and how lost I'd be without it, when my phone rang.

It was Fab Quaid's brother Mark. He wanted to meet me urgently at the Windsor, a pub in South Perth.

'What was that about?' Dad said.

'I don't know. Maybe I've upset someone.'

I was a little worried. Fab was overseas at the time, so I couldn't call him. I liked Mark, but when he called I knew something was up.

After parking the car, I was walking towards the Windsor when I heard a quick shout: 'Oi!'

In the corner of the car park were Mark, John Kizon and Troy Mercanti, who was out of jail by now. I walked over to them, thinking, *Fuck, what have I done here?*

'Come on, mate, jump in the car, we're going for a talk,' Troy said.

I jumped in the back with a bunch of fishing rods.

'What's going on?' I said.

'I'm going fishing,' Troy said.

I went pale. *Fuck. Fishing? Are they going to throw me off the back of Rottnest?*

I was a bit banged-up, not the first time I'd been caught jumpy. They drove to the other side of South Perth and pulled up at an oval. We got out and walked onto the grass.

They told me it had come to their attention that I was getting on the gear too much, especially ice. They'd heard that I'd been off my head for weeks and was putting everything at risk. They said they'd heard things were getting delicate for me at the football club – my whole future as an Eagle might be up in the air.

Ice, they said, was a big problem. There was a reason it was a taboo drug. It was associated with the loopers. These blokes didn't tolerate ice. Its stigma was like heroin's: nobody told you proudly that they used a lot of ice. I'd been a heavy cocaine user for a while, but once I'd got into ice, in the past year or so, they'd noticed that I was unravelling like so many others they'd seen. 'You can probably manage a coke problem for a while,' John said, 'but ice will catch up with you.' He was right.

'AN ALIEN DRESSED UP AS BEN'

They were worried about me. They said it was a matter of time before the press or the police caught me and I'd be sacked by the club.

We talked for about half an hour. I was lucid enough to see that they were looking out for me as friends should. That might surprise people, that they would be acting as my drug counsellors, but it was true. People might like to put two and two together, and presume that my drug history was linked to these guys. It wasn't; they were mates who were trying to get me off it.

Not even their advice got through to me, though. I listened to them. But by now drugs had me by the throat.

25

LOSING MY ANCHOR

I tried everything I could to break the cycle. That summer I went on a surf trip to the Mentawai Islands, off Sumatra. Since I'd become a professional footballer, it had become harder to find the time for great surf days like I'd had as a kid. Some Eagles players, like Phil Read, organised their lives around their surf, but I had other hobbies to attend to. Phil would surf all day the day before a game, sometimes the morning of a game, and sometimes drive down to Margaret River the night of a game and surf all the next day. When he quit football, he organised his working life to fit around his surfing.

But my number one priority was football, and my number two priority had become something else that didn't involve surfing. I understood that football paid the bills. Having said that, I'd surfed enough to treasure it, and the Mentawai trip was awesome, and put me in a better state of mind to attack the pre-season.

As I got back into pre-season training, I told myself I was back into my old structure: I have taken a lot of drugs, but I will get myself up to be the best trainer in the club and won't let anyone down.

On a hot summer's day at Perry Lakes, I planned to do twenty 100-metre sprints. The first few hundreds went all right, but then my heart began thumping so hard I thought it was going to pop through my chest. You could see it heaving around from the outside. I'd been up for five days. Meth users can be highly functional, but that's when they're working in offices or workshops or whatever. I was a functional meth user going to a job where I was training to the point where I was risking my life.

I sat down in the rooms and applied some ice – frozen water – to my body, to cool down pronto. My heart still banged away. I thought I was going to die.

Finally my heartbeat returned to normal, but I'd given myself a big scare. It was the first time my body had packed in on me during training or a match; the first time I hadn't been able to will it into submission. It felt momentous, like I really had to take this seriously.

Rod Moore saw what was happening and said, that night, that he didn't think I should come to training the next day.

I took that as an opportunity to do some more damage.

WITH A few days free, I went to stay at a mate's place in eastern Sydney and flew a friend, Anna, down from Brisbane. A former Penthouse Pet, Anna was great at parties. She loved to get things started by tearing her clothes off and becoming the centre of attention.

We hit it hard early and kept on going. The blokes I was with were loose guys, and sometimes I'd sit on a couch and feel a lump under the cushion. I'd lift it up, and find a gun. I wasn't used to this, but I could see the humour in it. Everyone had one, and I almost figured I needed one myself. I'd play with the guns, and how I didn't shoot myself in the foot I'll never know.

Whenever we felt like eating, we'd order food up from a restaurant some mates owned across the road. We were in a great part of Sydney, but we didn't want to go out and party; we wanted the party to come to us, where we were enclosed and comfortable. Every now and then I'd go to the beach and swim. I loved the clarity it gave me. It made me feel good enough to go back and start using again.

The only downside of having food and wine brought to us was that the staff didn't clean up afterwards. Three days in, the apartment was like a tip. Dishes, ashtrays, rubbish everywhere. None of us was in a fit state to pick up a dish. We were lying around like we'd been through a war, and a guy called Tom, a conservative bloke who was always trying to keep us out of trouble, came in.

'Tom, mate,' someone said. 'You mind cleaning up?'

Tom stood in the kitchen taking it all in. 'Have a good look at yourselves,' he said. 'No way am I cleaning this up.' He had a mothering side to him, and started lecturing us about how we had to get our shit together – while he started cleaning up.

As a joke, one of the blokes pulled out a gun.

'Listen,' he said, waving it about, 'just shut your mouth or I'll shoot you.'

Tom said, 'Mate, if you're going to pull that out I'm not fucking cleaning anything.'

With that, my mate picked up a pillow, put the gun into it and fired a shot. The bullet went through the pillow, through the kitchen bench and lodged in the dishwasher. Feathers everywhere. Tom was out the door, and we heard the lift bell ding. Anna was half-undressed, there was cocaine everywhere, and we were all laughing our heads off. It was a scene from a Tarantino movie.

FOR TEN years Sam had been my most loyal friend, my rock. She was the most staunch partner I could ever have hoped for, and much more than I deserved. Countless times she'd picked me up and put me back together and saved my football career; there were times when, by talking me into pulling up at the end of a bender, she literally saved my life.

But things had been difficult for the year since my big Christmas fuck-up. It was hard enough for her to live with me at home, but once my lifestyle got out into the public eye in late 2006, our problems became exponentially harder for her. As a professional footballer I knew I'd bought into that, and felt I could always redeem myself on the field. Sam hadn't bought into it, and didn't have that outlet. Perth's a small town. If I was on the front page of the newspaper for bad behaviour one day, I knew the incident would be forgotten by the time of our next big win. For Sam, the stigma was harder to shake off.

After weeks of tension and fights, we sat down one night for a long talk. Sam was simply worn out by the cycle: the bender, the pull-back, the recovery, the game, and then on again. She knew that football was driving the cycle, and had often spoken critically of how the game was affecting us. She said she wanted a break. I knew what she was saying. It felt inevitable, and I didn't fight as hard as I could have to change her mind. I needed a break from me as well. Part of me knew that I needed to be punished, I needed to bottom out before I could beat this thing. That part was telling me that I was getting what I deserved.

Sam got what she deserved in the settlement we negotiated as part of our break-up. For a decade, we'd been like husband and wife, or a business partnership. She'd done a huge amount for my career, and I'd enabled her to only work as much as she wanted. I only wished to make a difficult time a little easier for her. Looking back, I hope I made due reparations to her, financially at least. Emotionally, I have to live with the fact that I can never make it up to her.

THE BREAK-UP threw me into a tailspin. Without Sam, my emotions had no anchor, and I went into a manic state. I moved out of our apartment and in with Chicky, who'd stayed with me when he was getting over his marriage break-up a year before. He'd always been a loyal buddy, and he was taking me in when I needed him most.

The 2007 pre-season cup was about to start, and Chicky was offering me a chance to sort myself out. He lived at Quinns Rocks, the last beachside suburb north of Perth before the bush. Not only was it forty-five minutes from the centre of town, it was on the other side of the city from my usual crew. After Friday training, when I'd usually be thinking about whose place I could drop by, I'd drive up to Chicky's without going past any temptations, and the forty-five minutes in the car settled me down. By the time I got there, I was feeling relaxed.

He went to extraordinary lengths to help me turn myself around. He gave me a refuge, exactly what I needed as I dealt with the guilt and loneliness of Sam leaving me. When we had some free time he took me for a motorbike ride to the ocean. We fished and hared around on his jet skis. Although I had some big nights, for three or four weeks I was having good clean fun, away from what I thought of as the claustrophobic atmosphere of the city. I was hoping this was the turning point – being outdoors, getting fit, looking forward to the season – but it was just a momentary reprieve.

26

SUSPENDED

For all the encouragement Chicky was giving me, we were birds of a feather and it was bound to end in tears. As the preseason wore on, I couldn't maintain any discipline. After a week's training and some healthy fun with Chicky, I'd feel dangerous again.

I could no longer say I was the best trainer in the club. Once that went, a lot of other constraints fell away too. I turned up at training dishevelled and unfocused. I'd doze off in team meetings. Teammates and staff were noticing. Poor Adam Hunter, who was the first name on my contacts list in my phone, had to suffer through numerous calls at 4 am on a Tuesday or 6 am on a Wednesday when I sat on my phone during a hit-out. He picked up his phone or got a voicemail to hear me stomping around in some house. When I finally dragged myself into training, Adam would raise an eyebrow to say, 'What have you been up to?' I wondered how he knew. He was a bloke I loved playing footy with – hard, but with a sense of humour.

Where previously I could pick myself up for four days of good hard training, then peak on game day, now the routine was pared back so that I was *only* good on game day. I played in our first and fourth games of the pre-season comp, and got the old charge from running onto the field in the Eagles jersey, washing everything else away for a few hours.

But only for a few hours. I was probably our best on ground in those two games, which enabled me to lie to myself a bit longer.

The club wanted to believe it wasn't happening too. I was an integral part of a flag-winning team. I went out on game day and performed as well as ever. They'd put me on notice, but beyond that, nobody knew what to do with me.

Other incidents brought some heat early in 2007. Daniel Kerr was charged with assault over two separate incidents and was implicated in alleged drug dealing in conversations the police taped. The media targeted the Eagles, the *Sunday Age* calling us 'footy's finest – young, rich and out of it'. Their article mentioned someone known as 'the Cocaine Kid', who would snort coke off coffee tables. Was that me? I'd been known to snort coke off coffee tables, but I'd never heard anyone call me the Cocaine Kid. Maybe it was someone else. No, it was probably me.

OUR LAST pre-season game was against the Bulldogs. I was running strongly, pulling it together, I thought, just in time to defend the flag.

We had a small gathering at Chicky's place that night, but I didn't take any illicit drugs – I just drank a lot, then put myself to sleep with some Xanax and Valium.

Me: sumo wrestler, Incredible Hulk,
Geelong fanatic.

Our second home: Mel, Matthew
and me with Dad in the changing
room after a WAFL match for Perth.

For Wesley College, I was a better kick than I would be for most of my
professional career.

As a teen at the family home
with the dogs – Jack and Basil.

We played and fought together
like the best brothers: at the
beach with Matt.

Wesley College was an integral part of my adolescence: a great time in my life where my love of numerous sports was nurtured.

I was included in the grand final parade as a Norwich Rising Star Winner in 1996.

Nobody can have been luckier than I was to have a great family: with Mel, Dad and Sophie.

Like a lot of Perth people, when I needed to find sanctuary I headed south. This was taken on one of many trips to the Yallingup-Margaret River area.

Me relaxing on one of my many trips with Sam: she often tried to get me away from the stresses and temptations of life in Perth; in the end, though, there was only so much she could do.

There were moments in the surf when I found the kind of calm I was always chasing – not to mention the occasional adrenaline rush. This was taken on a surf trip to Indonesia with my brother Matthew.

'I thought Chicky was supposed to be your mate?' Gardy asked whenever my old buddy, playing for Hawthorn, beat me up. Fortunately by 2003, we were on the same side.

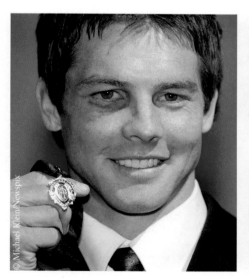

I was pleased to win the Brownlow in 2005, but my mind was on Saturday, not Monday.

The only thing I hadn't planned for was the pain of losing: grand final 2005.

Having missed my moment the last time I'd won something, I didn't need a second invitation when Juddy called me up in 2006.

As a captain, John Worsfold's boots were too big for me to fill. But after the 2006 grand final, he said to me: 'I want you to experience this as much as anyone.'

One of the first faces I saw after the 2006 grand final was Mainy's. I have a framed copy of this picture of me with my great mate.

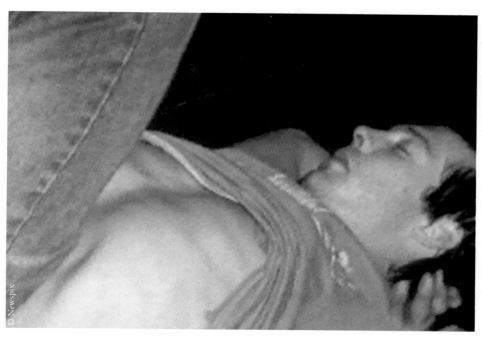

After winning the flag in 2006, my summer spun out of control. This is the infamous photo taken of me outside Crown Casino.

Trip away with Sam post 2006 grand final. Sam and I went to Port Douglas instead of the end of season footy trip to Las Vegas.

For ten years she held me together: Sam was my partner, best friend and emotional anchor.

Part of me will always be an Eagle. This was one of my last games, after rehab, in late 2007.

It was a great honour when the Mainwaring family asked me to be a pallbearer for Mainy. I was barely holding it together.

Off the rails after Mainy's death in October 2007. The police paraded me in front of the cameras in Northbridge before taking me in.

Suspended from the Eagles in 2007, knowing exactly what my next move would be.

In and out of rehab in 2007, I ran the media gauntlet at every airport I went through.

Their marriage has survived despite the problems I created for them: my wonderful parents in Perth.

Maylea Tinecheff came into my life in 2008.

Redemption came from the most unlikely quarter, but for the rest of my life I will owe the Tigers.

270 games and out. I got through my last game despite a torn hamstring, wanting to pay tribute to my teammates and the Tiger faithful.

Johnny G, pictured with Robby Bottazzi and me. Vale, Johnny G. My great friend left me with unforgettable advice: 'Take the pace off it.' Whatever flak I was going to cop, attending his funeral in 2008 was non-negotiable.

SUSPENDED

The next day, West Coast staged a family day to launch the season. I turned up pretty groggy and dusty, and did my best to avoid the kids who wanted their photographs taken with me. The person I was that day wasn't the Ben Cousins I'd like to think kids would have on their bedroom walls.

Word of the previous night's activities got around, to explain my condition, and Andrew Embley, his girlfriend and Sam drove up to Chicky's place after the family day to find out what was going on. They were concerned about me. Knowing what they'd find when they got there, I headed elsewhere.

When they got to Chicky's, it was clear what had happened. There were wine glasses and mess all over the place, a girl was in bed watching a video, and on the coffee table was a heap of white powder. It was crushed-up Xanax, but nobody was around to explain that, as if it would matter anyway. Sam and Embley's girlfriend went berserk, telling the two girls who'd stayed the night to get out.

Just then Chicky arrived, and tried to defuse the situation. He thought Embley had done the wrong thing by bringing Sam and his girlfriend there, and invading his house was out of line. They had an altercation, which I didn't see, but when I got back Chicky was still steaming.

The next morning, Chicky and I were too shabby to get to the ten o'clock training session. I didn't know there were drug testers at the club waiting for us.

Embley rang Chicky after training and said he wanted to square things up. Chicky was fired up and ready to go. But meanwhile the club was sending Steve Woodhouse, the general manager of football operations, and one of the assistant coaches up to Chicky's place to find out why we hadn't been at training. They might have been expecting a party, but by the time they got there Chicky and I had cleaned the place up and were sitting having a quiet chat. We told them what had happened between

Chicky and Embley. They said we still had to go to an afternoon weights session that day.

'If I go to training,' Chicky said, 'I'm going to belt Embley and you two will be responsible.'

Woodhouse seemed to think he was speaking tongue in cheek. He said, 'If you have to belt him, belt him, but we still want you to come to the weights session.'

So we drove down to Subiaco, and Chicky walked into the gym with one intention: to give Embley a going-over. Chicky made a beeline for him, and they were into it, possibly the first punch-up between Eagles players on club premises.

That was only the start of it. Chicky and I were drug-tested, and I must have blown it up. I knew I was in trouble, but had got to the point where I was detached from reality. I must have looked as if I didn't care about my football anymore; the truth was that my mind was so addled, I was in a kind of fog of unawareness.

Woosher called me into a meeting in his office. I'd missed training without good reason, and had been seen by others as under the weather. I couldn't defend the indefensible.

The meeting only lasted five minutes. He told me in no uncertain terms that I was suspended indefinitely and shouldn't come back until I could fulfil my commitments as a footballer.

I shook his hand at the end of the meeting and saw the sadness in his face. But the drug-fucked part of me was asserting its control. That part was rapt with how quickly the meeting went. As I walked out, I was rubbing my hands and thinking, *You beauty, I'm free!*

I felt no remorse. I didn't consider what I'd done to my club, my family, my reputation, my prospects, my earning capacity. That would all come later. As I left the meeting, all I could feel was relief. *In less than an hour, I'm going to be out of my tree.*

*

SUSPENDED

MEANWHILE, MAINY had got wind of my suspension and had called Dad. Mainy knew what I'd do next, so Dad called the club to try to get them to hold me up. While I was meeting Woosher, Dad and Mainy fought their way through the traffic on the Stirling Highway. Five minutes later, Dad called the club again, to be told I'd left.

He was furious at them, thinking I'd got away.

As I was heading for my car, I heard a shout across the car park.

Fuck, almost made it.

Dad was calling from the kerb. I went over.

'Mate, I think you should come home with me,' Dad said.

'There's no way I can do that,' I said. 'I'm going to be fine. I need to see a couple of people, do a few things. Mate, don't worry.'

Mainy, who knew exactly what I was going to do, tried to talk me out of it, but after fifteen minutes I jumped in my car, and was off and running.

FOR FIVE days the local and national media were on my tail. The night of my suspension, I went to a couple of strip joints and hung out in the back rooms. They weren't well-known places, just grimy, dark little clubs, but they were where I wanted to be. I wasn't seeing shows, just hanging out with girls and blokes at their staff drinks. I went on to a club called the Voodoo Lounge in Northbridge, made a few calls and heard that a crew was gathering after hours at a sound studio nearby.

It was a recording place, so sealed off from the outside world that once inside you couldn't tell whether it was night or day. The days and nights rolled into each other, people cruised in and out, you could hide there and be in an alternate universe. At 5 am I was leaning against the wall chatting with a mate. The owner of another Northbridge nightclub, ironically called The Rock, came, and chuckled when he saw me.

'Bro, do you realise everyone in Australia is looking for you?'

I gave him a dumb look and said: 'What for?'

We broke up laughing. His club was a second home to every reptile in town, and I use that as a term of endearment because I was one of them. I was there a lot in this period. The times I ended up at The Rock were when I was on the rock.

I hid out in the East Perth apartment of a girl I knew called Tracey. She had my best interests at heart, hoping to slow me down and get me to pull up, but I had that unstoppable momentum going. I spoke to Dad and Mainy, ignoring calls from everyone else, and moved from place to place.

The other person I took a call from was Chicky, who said he'd just had three Red Bulls pre-breakfast and was heading for the football club: Embley had said he wanted another stoush.

'You can't be serious,' I said.

'Fucken oath I'm serious. Come down.'

While Chicky had every reason to be dark, Embley was also trying to do the right thing. He was the meat in the sandwich. I wanted to keep their clash at arm's length, because it was all collateral damage from what I'd created. Two of my premiership teammates were at each other's throats, all because of me and my shit.

'Mate, I'm not going anywhere near the joint,' I said. 'I'm not even a player now.'

Chicky went to the club, and he and Embley had another punch-up. The whole thing was turning into a debacle.

I told Mainy where I was – in those brief flashes when I knew where I was. He came along to meet me and try to talk me down, get me to pull up. He was the voice of rationality, but he could also understand what was going on with me.

SUSPENDED

There were wrenching, emotional meetings taking place between Mum, Dad and various other family members and close friends such as Mainy and Bill Mitchell. Dad was worried that the footy club had cut me loose at a time when being free was what I was taking advantage of. More havoc, more damage: I was really spreading it around.

He decided to make a public statement. He consulted me, and I was dead against it. He and Mainy came over mid-session, and eventually convinced me. With my angry head, I told them not to let it get emotional. 'I don't want people thinking this is getting to us,' I said. The old man thought that was blackly funny: imagine anyone thinking that the public disintegration of a man's son was worth getting emotional about.

On the night the statement was to go to air, I was in the house of a girl I knew. It was one of the rare times I'd been able to get my hands on crack cocaine. Anyone who's taken that drug knows that it's the one thing that can remove you from the room, body and soul. Mainy was with me, watching over my safety, too much of a real mate to use with me. The news came on. Through the hazy euphoria and relief of the crack, I watched Dad front up to the cameras with incredible bravery.

He talked about how our problem was something that affected many other Australian families. He made a plea for privacy.

'Ben,' he said, 'you are not alone with this challenge. Your family, your friends, your fans, your footy club want you to overcome this issue and win, in the same manner in which you have done throughout your whole career.'

It was surreal and sad, smoking crack while my father was pleading for me, and to me. For a drug addict, though, this is exactly the time when you do use. In retrospect, I shake my head at the contradiction in this. But that's how it was. Sometimes the thing that makes least sense is the only thing that makes sense.

Mainy was shaking his head beside me, muttering: 'Fucking hell.'

After Dad's statement, a reporter asked him and Mum some questions. When she came on, I felt the tears well up.

MAINY'S WIFE, Rani, persuaded me to come to their place for a couple of drinks. She wanted to take a close look at me. When I got there, she tried to persuade me to come and stay with them rather than remain on the run. But I was not in a fit state to listen.

I went back to Northbridge, the endless round of strip club, sound studio, house of someone I didn't know. By then I was just running because I couldn't stop. Running from daylight. Running from the people who were important to me, towards those who didn't know me. I was enjoying myself, or thought I was. That was maybe the most telling sign of how far I'd fallen. I found this life amusing. Briefly.

For a moment I thought I'd get out of Australia. A mate was going to Thailand. Great idea! I'd go with him, do some kickboxing on the beach, train, get fresh. Then another great idea came along. Then another.

TWO DAYS later, I had nothing left. I was sick and coming down and busted up, and could hardly talk. Unable to use my phone, I got a mate to call my old man.

'He's not that good, is he?' Dad said.

'No,' my mate said. 'He's not.'

When Dad and Mainy finally caught up with me, I was back in the East Perth apartment with Tracey. They'd been told to brace themselves, but when they arrived I was even worse than they'd feared, totally wasted, lying on a couch.

'Mate, I want you to come home.'

'I can't.'

Dad spent a couple of hours with me. I didn't want to leave, but something inside me, some memory of love or conscience, won through. They scooped me up and took me to Mainy's place.

While I was there, getting fed and cleaned up, it was decided that I had to be smuggled out of Perth, away from the media, to take stock. Our family friend Ken James offered his beach house at Mandurah, an hour south of Perth, and Mainy and my brother Matthew drove me down.

Three days later, I had a meeting there with Mainy and Matt, the West Coast board member Mark Barnaba, Trevor Nisbett, Rod Moore and an addiction specialist, Alan Quigley. I'd slept, eaten, and even had a run with Mainy. I'm amazed and shocked and ashamed, looking back, at how detached I was from the feelings of others. In time, I'd carry the burden of how much I'd put Dad and Mainy through. I was still sticking, deludedly, to the idea that I was only hurting myself.

The meeting made it clear that if I ever wanted to play football again, I had to go to rehab.

I didn't want to. I didn't think I needed to. I thought: *Here we go again, I'm being told what to do.*

But in the end, there was no argument. Rehab was not negotiable.

27

MAKE ME GO TO REHAB

After a few days in Mandurah, Matt and Mainy had to go back to work. I was ruined, physically and emotionally. I did nothing but eat and sleep. I was exhausted from the chase, from being both the hunter and the quarry.

When Matt and Mainy left, Tracey came down to stay with me, and nursed me back to some sort of health. The place was a hideaway from temptation, and also, in a way, from myself. It was eight days since my suspension, and only now I'd come to a shuddering halt did I begin to address what I'd do next.

The club had ordered rehab, which was for my own benefit, but no-one had really analysed what the concept meant or where I should go. Everyone with a vested interest was having a go at me in the media, and even if they were standing up as being concerned for me, it hit the people around me really hard. I was in the eye of the storm, detached from it all.

MAKE ME GO TO REHAB

The first condition of going into rehab, as far as Rod Moore and the other medical experts were concerned, was getting out of Australia. Rod was a tower of strength to all of us – he's been a superstar in my life – and Rani spent hours researching places on the internet. We looked at some places in Britain, but heard that Summit, in Malibu, had a good reputation. I know going to Malibu sent a signal to some people that I was acting like a rock star, but the experts recommended strongly that if I stayed in Australia the scrutiny would compromise my rehab. Anonymity would be necessary for proper treatment. I was going to America to get away from my notoriety, not to exploit it.

I went for a few runs with Mainy and felt better, though still numb, as if all the drama was happening to someone else and I, like Mainy and Dad and everyone, was on the outside looking in. I was still resisting rehab, but everyone around me was adamant that if I didn't go, I'd never play footy again. At some level, that idea still motivated me.

Dad and I were going to fly to the US together, along with Ian Miller, West Coast's player welfare manager who was Dad's friend. The day before I left, when I was packing my stuff, I decided to go for a hard run. When I got back, I thought impulsively, *Well, if I'm going to go into rehab and quit the gear, I might as well have one last crack here*. For a drug addict, probably the greatest fear is the fear of 'never again'. It's a kind of mourning. I'd grown close to my drug life, and loved it, and was overwhelmed by the idea of saying goodbye to it.

So I went to see some mates and spent the next day smoking like I was never going to smoke again. Just before it was time to go to the airport, I dropped in on Fabian, who was at John Kizon's house in Subiaco. Troy Mercanti, his brother and a few others were there, and I think they were taken aback by the state I was in.

'I'm off to rehab,' I said, obviously wired to the eyeballs.

Fabian looked at me. 'Tonight?'

'Yeah, the plane leaves in two and a half hours.'

They shook their heads in disbelief. I ended up having a last-minute panic about getting my shit together in time for the flight, with Dad continually calling to ask if I was going to make it. Looking back, I'm surprised I did.

I got to my place for my luggage, where Mum and my brother and sisters were waiting. They could see my condition. I gave them all a hug and kissed Mum. I could feel the emotion, but pushed forward to a place where I didn't have to deal with it. I couldn't even look at myself in the mirror. My last words to Mum were to ask her to send photos of the family that I could put up in my room.

When we got to the airport, there was a melee of journalists, photographers and cameramen, to whom the disgraced Brownlow Medallist was fodder for that day's news. I smiled away, thinking, *Fuck you all*. I was off my head. I had handfuls of prescription drugs that kept falling out of my pockets.

Amazingly, I wasn't searched before I got on the plane. I had more pharmaceuticals on me than you could shake a stick at. Whenever I sat down, another Xanax would fall out of a hole in my pocket. I'd look at it numbly and think: *That's strange. Where did that come from?*

I left at midnight, in business class with Dad and Ian. During the flight, not even a lot of alcohol or tranquillisers could get me anywhere near sleep.

When we landed, it was a Friday, and I was due to check in to Summit on the Monday. We went to the Shutters hotel right on Santa Monica beach, and had a meeting with Summit's doctor and chief executive.

I knew that the Eagles were playing the Swans, a grand final replay, as the AFL season opener that weekend. The game would be shown at 2 am on cable TV in LA. I had a few mates there, so

I made some calls, thinking we could round up a party and stay up late in a pub to watch the footy. Dad, Ian and I cruised down to Venice Beach, a few hundred metres from the hotel, and went in and out of the shops down there. I love Los Angeles, particularly that area, but Dad and Ian were picking up on the vibe that I was not at all straight and might be thinking of doing a runner. They followed me like a pair of private detectives, waiting outside every shop to make sure I didn't disappear.

When we went back to our hotel, I wanted to go for a swim in the ocean, but Dad sprang a surprise on me.

'There's been a change of plan; we're going in today.'

'No we're fucking not.'

I'd convinced myself that I needed a few days in LA prior to rehab. On reflection, I know what I was angling at, but it never seems like a lie if you believe it yourself. We had a serious blue, but at the end I gave in. At 5 pm we drove up to Summit. I was still numb, tired and slightly high, not really engaging with the significance of the moment. Dad, on the other hand, was going through a whirl of emotions, from disappointment at my state to trepidation about what I was about to enter.

We shook hands goodbye. I remember saying it would be okay. He started crying. In the car, he told Ian he felt like a father leaving his five-year-old in a hospital and flying out of the country. A doctor at rehab had told him that my arriving off my face was pretty typical. It didn't make Dad feel any better.

I was taken into a room and searched by a couple of staff members. One of them, Chris, told me he was twenty-two years old and had been to rehab thirteen times by the time he was nineteen. He'd been clean now for three years. My idea of rehab was that some people who'd never taken drugs would sit you down and say, 'Don't take drugs, they're bad for you.' It was an eye-opener to see, in Chris, that I was going to be faced with something completely different: addicts helping addicts, people who weren't going to ram some doctrine down your throat, people who'd walked in your shoes. They didn't lock you up. They just said, 'Here's a different way of living if you want it.'

During the search, though, I was pretty flippant about the pills that kept falling out of my clothes and other gear. I told Chris some of my story, and immediately felt small. Six years younger than me, he'd been through ten times more.

THE FIRST few days were mainly about sleeping and eating. They gave me Valium to help, and while I was awake I wandered around or sat in the sun meeting patients and staff. Sometimes I met them for the second or third time without realising it.

I stayed up the first night, following the Eagles–Swans game on the internet. I felt calm but weird. It was incredible to think that only twelve days ago, I'd been best on ground in a pre-season match against the Bulldogs. It felt like a lifetime ago.

To show how little I understood, I was still trying to get Frankie J. For the first few days I worked the phone. I tried a few people I knew in LA. Luckily anyone who knew about me had been told to steer clear. If I'd been caught and kicked out, it would have been another massive fuck-up. Hard to believe I even contemplated it.

For the first two weeks I remained numb, both from the sedatives and from the strangeness of this experience. It was all clean and pleasant, but surreal. I could train and get fit and live in a bubble, but I was like a robot, following the schedule the staff had laid out for me. I went to yoga and meetings and came across 'the big book' and 'Reflections', the texts people discussed in the meetings. The weather was beautiful, the views over the hills sublime, and I'd spend a lot of my time just gazing out, wondering how I'd got here. It seemed almost comically unreal. And then, in the middle of a meeting, I'd drop off to sleep.

We had weekly excursions to Venice, where, one day, an Australian guy recognised me in a shop and asked me what I was doing. I was also allowed to leave, with a staff member, to go and train on a Malibu athletics track and in a gym. The guy loved his cars, and got a buzz out of speeding away from the Australian paparazzi, who were camped outside Summit. One day a helicopter followed us.

I'd chosen this rehab program partly because it was tailored to the individual's needs. To keep my anxiety at bay, I trained like an animal. It was good to slip back into that familiar pain. I don't think I'd ever spent a month running harder than when I was at Summit. In the biggest crisis of my life, I was acting true to form: one extreme after another. This is what I was dealing with, and how I was dealing with it.

At first I was resistant to the education process. I said, 'I'm not here to get off drugs. What I am interested in is learning how to stay off drugs when I need to, for the rest of the 2007 season. I want to get through a footy season without drugs, then reward myself with a trip to South America where I'm going to absolutely crunch it. I love a bender, that's the way I am, and I'm not going to walk away from it.'

They just nodded as if they'd heard it all before and said, 'See if you still think like that as you go through the month.'

The program consisted of twelve steps, like AA or Narcotics Anonymous, to break down your thinking and show you a different way. I did the whole thing of 'Hi, I'm Ben and I'm an addict.' My inbuilt problem, I learnt, was that I'm a person of extremes, an addictive personality. There was no such thing as one line of coke. The first one meant going out to the limit. They'd seen a lot of these types, but counsellors told me I was as extreme a personality as they'd ever seen.

It took a week for me to feel comfortable and clean, to sleep okay and to rediscover some optimism about life outside. By the end of two weeks I'd lost the anxiety and vulnerability. I was doing a lot of thinking about my life, and no longer felt tormented by the idea of not using drugs. A lot of this I owed to the friends I made there. Normally I'd never open up to people I hardly knew, but at Summit we were all in the same boat, no matter what our background, and hearing others' stories gave me some understanding of my own. When I spoke, people would shake their heads and say, 'Fuck, bro, you need to be here.'

I was no looser than anyone else there. I was a madman in the outside world, but here I was just another person. The friendships I formed were the best part of that month. Another highlight was a day trip to Malibu beach, where the surf was surprisingly big. For LA, it was as good as surf ever got: they called it a 'double-black' day. I wanted to grab a board and wetsuit and get out there, but the staff weren't too rapt with the idea of one of their rehab clients drowning on a day trip. It took me two hours to convince them that I could handle the double-overhead waves, but eventually I did, and enjoyed an hour and a half of great surf. It was the best type of therapy, and reminded me that surfing was the nearest I could get to the synthetic buzz of being off my head. I remember sitting on my board thinking, *How surreal is this – I'm in rehab and getting out in the world's most famous longboard waves.*

As I worked my way through the month, I began to get antsy about going home and cleaning up the mess I'd made. Getting fit again at Summit was great, but I knew it wasn't the real world, only a retreat from it. My problems were all still waiting for me. I rang Sam one night, and it was difficult. I wanted us to try again, but couldn't give her the answers she wanted about my commitment to doing things right. She said things that hurt me. What hurt even more was that she was dead right.

Halfway through the month, Mum and Dad came to visit. I hadn't been missing my mates from home, but when I saw my parents I realised how much I'd been missing them. I told them stories about the other patients, and we had some good laughs. We watched the West Coast–Fremantle game on cable TV and tried to explain the game to the American patients, with some humorous results. Mum and Dad seemed pleased to see me in a much better state than when I'd arrived, but we also knew that the task I faced back home would be overwhelming. Rehab was the easy part: all I had to do was sleep, eat, study and train. It was a bubble. But outside, the dread of real life was looming. When Chris told us that the stats on people remaining sober for a year after their first rehab were about 6 or 7 per cent, it brought us down with a thud.

It was an incredibly positive month for me. Unlike in Australia, there was no shame about rehab in the US, and everyone was congratulating me for making this investment in my future. But towards the end of the month, as my anxiety about going home began to simmer again, I made arrangements for Chris to travel home with me and stay for a while. I needed a sober companion, and he'd done this before. He was keen to come back, help me settle into new routines, and take a look at the country. I was telling him how I'd take him down south, show him the great beaches in the Margaret River region. I wasn't sure if Summit would allow it, but we sorted it out. One of the main things I needed him for was to help me maintain the positive feelings I'd picked up during rehab, and to integrate them into real life. He'd also help me get on with my readjustment without feeling that everyone was looking over my shoulder.

In the last few days, I was tested for pre-existing psychiatric conditions. It was important to know if my drug use had been a form of self-medication for something which had gone undiagnosed. The psych tests eventually showed that I had ADHD,

Attention Deficit Hyperactivity Disorder. Aha! That might have explained why, as far back as I could remember, I could never sit still in class or meetings. But I didn't want to rely on it too much. Having a condition to blame for my stupid decisions seemed a bit of a cop-out. But it did add to the picture, and helped me understand myself better.

When the twenty-eighth day arrived, I couldn't believe I'd completed the course I'd been set. Considering the shape I'd been in when I arrived, it felt like a major achievement. Looking back, I felt proud. Looking forward, I felt nothing but trepidation. I harboured huge resentment towards the media and the club for the way they'd hung me out to dry. Leaving Summit, I was already bracing myself for a media pack waiting at the airport – at LA and in Australia – and for the sanctimonious lectures I'd get from the likes of Dalton Gooding, who'd been in the press sounding holier than thou. I knew I had to harness this resentment, and let it go, but it weighed more than any of the other baggage I was carrying.

28

FIFTY DAYS

Chris and I flew into Perth on 30 April, a month and a day after I'd left. Naively, I'd hoped the public's attitude might be, 'He's gone into rehab, so let's leave him alone.' Instead there was a scrum of cameras and microphones and questions being shouted at me from every angle. I put on my smirk. I could see how that got under people's skin. My smile might have indicated I was loving the limelight, when the reality was the opposite. There has always been a huge disconnection between the face I put on and who I really was. That smile was my way of saying *Fuck off, fuck you, fuck off*. It was my armour. It was my way of showing the media they hadn't got to me.

I kept silent, but couldn't resist when someone asked if thirty days was long enough to fix me up.

'I hope so,' I said.

We walked straight past them to Dad. I wasn't going to make a statement. My thoughts about what I'd been through, and what I was headed for, weren't going to come out in bite-sized chunks. I hadn't even worked it out for myself.

The first thing I needed was a quiet place to live. For lots of reasons, not least media intrusion, I couldn't get that at my parents' place, so Dad found me a serviced apartment in Mounts Bay Road, South Perth, through friends of his, the Tognolinis, who were the building managers. Warm and friendly people, they treated me like a son, bringing meals and making sure I was okay.

Chris's presence set the family's minds at ease. For two weeks he accompanied me to restaurants, helped me train, and let me do things I wanted to do without everybody fearing that I'd go off the rails. I'd needed one sober friend, rather than dozens who were checking up on me.

Dr Alan Quigley, the addiction specialist who'd been involved with my move into rehab, wanted to introduce me to Carol Daws, who was an alcohol/drug counsellor and psychologist. She was also the CEO of Cyrenian House which is one of Perth's largest alcohol and drug treatment centres. When Dad told me, I shook my head.

'I can't talk about what I've done on drugs to a woman!'

But Chris and I agreed to meet her at a café and chat about my options. She knew of me from the media, but came with an open mind. She said things are rarely as bad as the media make them out to be, but sometimes they can be worse.

Carol and I got on well from the start, and soon we were catching up every week or so. What I liked about her was that she never sugar-coated anything, and she focused on going forward rather than stewing over things that had happened. She said you can't change the past and you'll be overwhelmed if you think too long-term. Rather than say, 'I'll never take drugs as long as I live', you had to set small, achievable goals day by day.

One thing had already changed. I'd dropped the idea of going to South America after the season. Staying clean, now that I'd done it for five weeks, had a real appeal. Choosing life over the turbulence of addiction. That may be an obvious choice for some people, but for somebody with my disposition, it was a mind-blowing discovery.

MEANWHILE, DAD, the club, my doctors and my lawyer, David Grace, who would become a close friend, were weighing up the pros and cons of me making a televised apology for my indiscretions.

I was dead against it. I wasn't accountable to others for the way I lived my life, and didn't see why this was demanded of me. I wanted to say, *Fuck off*. But from everyone else, there was immense pressure to go out and appear contrite, as if I needed the public's forgiveness. It was a strange concept. Why should I apologise for having an addiction? I felt like I was being used as a scapegoat, serving a lot of other people's interests. Making myself the centre of attention also felt counter to what I was achieving with my rehabilitation.

I didn't mean that I didn't have to apologise to the people who mattered, such as my family and Sam and others I'd hurt. I did that, privately, and would keep doing it. But I was angry at the club and the AFL for wanting me to put on a public performance.

'Are we going to fold like cheap tents here?' I raged to Dad. 'This is fucking bullshit. I'm not apologising to them, I put myself in rehab, I did what they asked, I don't owe them this as well. They don't give a fuck about me. I worked my guts out for that club, and ended up in rehab. I've copped my fair whack.'

Part of the reason I'd survived all of this was that I'm a proud person. I saw the apology as an attempt to strip my pride away, to reduce me. The media, who had been onto me like the Spanish Inquisition, wanted the apology, of course, so they could pick over it for days. I knew they had a job to do, but why should I appease them, reward them for the pressure they'd put on me? My whole attitude was *Fuck them*.

As usual, Dad heard me out quietly, letting the storm blow over. Then he said: 'We've got to play the game, mate. There's no point winning the battle if you're going to lose the war. Do you want to get back to playing footy? That's the main thing. Do you want to turn your life around?'

'No, not if I have to do those things,' I ranted. 'I don't want to play footy if this is what they're going to make me do.'

But football remained the club's and the league's leverage over me. They made it absolutely clear that apologising to the public was a condition of my being able to play again. Right till the last moment I was considering refusing, but now that I was sober I desperately wanted to play, and that desperation was bigger than my resentment.

The AFL and West Coast scripted the apology. When I read it, I nearly vomited. My last act of independence was to change a lot of the wording. It had been written by people with no idea of what I was going through as an addict.

Changing the wording wasn't quite my last act of independence. I was losing control of this whole thing. So I chose a loose white V-neck top, very low-slung, what Fab would later describe as a 'Mike Tyson kind of poncho'. It was deliberately casual, the type of clothes that said, 'I'm speaking these words but I don't believe them.'

On 4 May, five days out of rehab, I went into a TV studio and read the words.

'As you are aware, I have been in an overseas rehabilitation centre for the past month undergoing treatment for a number of personal issues, including illness as the result of substance abuse.

I apologise to the West Coast Eagles Football Club, sponsors, the AFL and the community for my actions. I know that in order to play football again I will have to be accepted back by the players and staff of the West Coast Eagles and the AFL and I'm willing to fulfil any obligations imposed on me. At the present time I don't know when I will play again. My priority is to regain my health, my life and my standing.'

Job done, but as I left the studio I felt extremely uneasy. I didn't consider myself to be a bad person, and never thought I was hurting anybody other than myself. This big apology to the powers that be, to people who'd only gained from me, compromised my rehabilitation by bringing up all my anger and resentment. I was inherently rebellious, and once again was walking the fine line. I'd always been a person who, if forced to do one thing, would automatically fight against it. I never felt I had a responsibility to be a role model in all my actions. I happened to play a reasonable game of football. That never meant that I was in a better position than any other twenty-eight-year-old to lead a well-balanced life. Chris Judd, who had none of the scandals or personal problems that I dealt with, was in complete agreement with me on this, and he said so publicly. Being a footballer did not make you perfect. But it was impossible to get this message through without being perceived as surly or big-headed.

My way of getting my message through was the patent insincerity of my delivery, and wearing that top. Later, people got in my face and asked why I hadn't at least worn a shirt. I said, 'I may be a drug addict but I'm not a complete fucken idiot. I do have a shirt. It was a strategic thing, to tell them to go and get fucked.'

IF I'D had to make the apology six weeks earlier, my first action would have been to go out and get on, massively, to burn all the resentment away. But now I had those weeks of sobriety under my belt, I wasn't going to let them break me. This was a new feeling: using some public controversy as motivation not to get bent, but to stay straight.

I went on a surf trip with some mates to Gnaraloo, thirteen hours north of Perth, organised by our good family friend Bill Mitchell. We camped, and had some amazing surf. Phil Read, the former West Coast player, was with me. One day we were at a break called Centres. He caught a wave, leaving me in the line-up for twenty minutes. I sat and looked at the sky – really looked at it. I'd heard in rehab about perceptions getting clearer and colours brighter as you became more sober, and now I got it. I started to smile, a true smile, on my own. Fuck, I felt happy. It was another affirmation that I was on the right track.

At Gnaraloo, I got through my fiftieth day sober. It was a strange way of life for me, to be counting days. Normally I didn't pay much attention to time, let alone stack the days up like savings in a piggy-bank. But my whole attitude was changing. In the old times, on a trip like that, I'd either be doing some gear or plotting to. Now the last thing I wanted was to corrupt the purity of this place.

And I enjoyed that surfing trip in the knowledge that, having done the dirty deed of apologising, I had a chance to come back and play again.

29

COMEBACK

Since January, when we'd agreed to separate, Sam and I had still been talking; for my part, I was trying to talk my way back into the relationship. She was everything to me. We'd had years of great times, and some bad times, mostly my fault.

I was trying to hang onto her, but looking back, it was clear that she didn't deserve to be stuck with some of the things she had to cop because of me. Media would follow her around and ask her questions about me and drugs, or me and other women. It was in her face all the time and she was embarrassed by it. Friends of mine would use her as a conduit to find out how I was going, and this placed even greater pressure on her. Being with Sam had always been a sanctuary for me, but now, when I saw her, she was obligated to ask me all sorts of questions people wanted answered, so I felt like I was being interrogated.

As I got better, she felt, rightly, that she was being neglected. All the people around us were focusing on me, and in so doing they underestimated her importance. *My* life was on the line. *My* career was at risk. Everyone's energy was channelled towards me. When I think of it, it was a miracle she stayed as long as she did. She had enormous dignity throughout it all, but we got to the point where me acknowledging her strength only aggravated her. I guess that was the point where we knew it was over.

I was renegotiating a lot of my relationships. With mates I'd done drugs with, I had to set new boundaries. Characteristically, I'd been the one who revved everyone up for a session, put pressure on blokes to stay with me when they had other things to do. I'd been the one to push on through. But now, I had to make sure I wasn't around them when they were going out. Those friendships were always based on humour. I could see how quickly it could get dangerous for me. I'd get together with them for some innocent reason, we'd start laughing about something, and before I knew it I'd be gone.

Before I could commence training and playing, I had to satisfy the club and the AFL that I was in a proper state to do so. I'd returned from Summit supremely fit, yet not game-ready. I rang Glenn Stewart to ask him to tailor a program for me, just like we did in the old days. He had me doing sprint sessions at public ovals away from the club, and endurance work on the grass athletics track at McGillivray Oval, running against the clock, fine-tuning. I contacted Murray Cooper, a former teammate of Dad's and one of the best kicks of all time. He was renowned as a kicking coach, and I had sessions with him three or four times a week. I enjoyed doing this work on my own, outside the club, even to the point where instead of doing my weights sessions at the club gym I went to Fitness First at Innaloo, working alongside regular punters, a lot of them female, which made another nice change from the Eagles' gym.

I was liking this independence. As fanatical a trainer as I always was, I never liked the one-size-fits-all regimentation of a club. Being in a team is important, of course, in countless ways, but when it came to fitness work I enjoyed the freedom to get myself right and train in ways, and at times, that were most beneficial to me. Getting that outside the club kept my internal pressure levels down. There weren't many players who'd do better when left to their own devices, but I was one of them. I wasn't feeling stressed by having to do things I didn't want to do, and consequently I wasn't feeling any temptation to bust out and do drugs.

IN MID-JUNE I went to the club and spoke to the players. I told them where I was at with my training, what my hopes were, and how much being part of the team, playing footy with those blokes, meant to me. I couldn't just presume I belonged in the playing group. I had to show them and the match committee that I was worthy of it. But I looked fresh and fit, I was speaking sensibly, and after my talk the blokes came up and chatted with me. It felt great to get reacquainted and start to earn their trust again. We'd been through footballing wars together. None of us could forget that.

On 29 June David Grace and I met with officials from the AFL, the AFL Players' Association and West Coast in Melbourne. I spoke about the training I had been undertaking by myself, my mental and physical improvement and my desire to play and train again with the club. At the end of the meeting, it was agreed that I could re-commence training and playing with West Coast, but that my contract would be varied and I would be 'subject to a program pursuant to the AFL Illicit Drugs Policy'. My income would be reduced and I had to agree to regular drug-testing, to stay away from 'undesirable figures' and to re-pay the cost of my rehabilitation at Summit. There was always a chance of relapse, and they understood that. But footy meant too much to me not to agree to all of the new conditions.

At the football club, I enjoyed being back in training but there was an awkwardness between my teammates and me. A lot of the boys didn't know what they could and couldn't ask me about. I didn't want to talk about rehab, or tell drug stories, so I stood a little bit aloof, just so the club could be a nice place where I didn't have to talk about myself.

But it was impossible to escape, especially as my comeback approached. After several discussions, Woosher and I agreed that my comeback game would be against the Western Bulldogs on 14 July. I'd just been through a hundred days sober. There was predictable media interest, the whole narrative of the prodigal son. Then, at the last training session at Subiaco before the game, my hamstring twinged and we agreed that I'd postpone my return by a week.

The anticipation had been so huge, there was a big sense of anticlimax when I pulled out of the game. I went through all of the stimulation and adrenaline rush of preparing, but hadn't had the game itself to bring me down again. It was a risk-filled moment. I was angry and frustrated, and had one of those times when I just screamed in exasperation at being a fucking addict.

I didn't let this show to the public. On my way out of that last training session, I commented: 'Such is life.'

It was deliberate. Over the past few weeks I'd been doing something I'd always wanted, which was to get a tattoo. I'd always admired Ned Kelly, for his rebellion against authority and his corresponding staunch loyalty to family and friends. He lived on a high wire, disregarding the strife he might get himself into. His final laconic words, as he faced the hangman, had resonated for me ever since I'd first read them as a kid.

So I'd been having a tattoo done, over a few weeks, by a mate of mine called Mikey in Perth. I'd always wanted one big tattoo across my abdomen, and I wanted the words in Old

COMEBACK

English script. After everything I'd been through, it summed me up: SUCH IS LIFE in a big arc across my stomach. Punters would tell me I'd regret it when I was older. My response was, *I fucken hope so*. If I got to old age regretting my tattoo, that would be a better outcome than any of the alternatives I could see. Better than sitting in maximum security wondering how I could get over the wall.

As IT happened, the week after the Bulldogs game we were playing the Swans at Subiaco. The build-up and let-down the previous week had been so intense, to let it all come out without the punctuation of a game had actually turned out quite well for me, like a dry run. Now, when the Swans game approached, I was much calmer.

The Eagles had started the season well, winning the grand final replay in round one by a point and having a perfect record after six games. They'd lost a few mid-season, but had never been out of the top four. Sydney were in the same kind of shape as in their two grand final seasons. I couldn't think of a better stage to come back on. If a game against Sydney couldn't remind you of what was good about footy, nothing could.

On the Thursday before the game, I met Dad for a coffee. I felt the time had come to fully acknowledge my gratitude to him. I'd put him through hell.

He knew by now that the problem wasn't anyone else's: it was all mine. So this day, with my impending comeback feeling like the real turning point, I just wanted Dad to know that I appreciated how loyal he and the family had been. I don't know anyone who's had a better upbringing than I had, or had a better network of family support. I'd sure tested it though.

We started by talking about football. It wasn't everything to us anymore, but it was a good place to start.

'Listen, mate,' Dad said, 'whatever happens happens. Relax. It's not a huge drama. Don't get yourself too worked up, just go with it.'

I told Dad that the one thing I could be sure of was that I couldn't have done more to prepare myself for that match.

'It doesn't matter if I don't get the footy once,' I said. 'I'm happy that I've done all I could. In fact, if anything, I should have done less.'

As always, I had that foundation of hard work to rely on. That was where I got my professional self-esteem. The game might go my way or it might not, but I was never going to dwell on whether I hadn't prepared myself well enough.

Our relationship was so close that sometimes the things that needed to be said were overlooked; they seemed obvious. But this time I wanted to say them.

'I want to thank you for being so supportive,' I said, feeling the emotions well up. 'I know you despise anything to do with drugs. That makes it all the more important to me, what you've done. You've never wavered.'

'Mate,' Dad said, 'it's been hard for all of us, but it hasn't changed what I think of you. You don't have to apologise for being who you are.'

That night, I was watching TV and couldn't believe what I was seeing. I rang Dad.

'Are you watching telly? Turn it on.'

The rugby league player Andrew Johns was on, announcing how he'd been a drug user. He said it was his way to get away from the game. He just wanted time to relax, and drugs took him into a space where he was free of the stress and pressure. It was an echo of what I'd been telling Dad just a few hours before. Uncanny. For what it's worth, I got to know Andrew and rate him highly as a bloke.

On the Friday night, I went to my mate Kim Hunter's place.

Kim was a professional punter, a larrikin with a huge laugh, who I'd visit every Friday night if I wasn't playing or interstate, and with another great mate, Geoff, who was an amazing cook, we'd watch the football over a bowl of pasta. I always looked forward to these nights. That night we knocked up a bowl of pasta Matriciana, which the others were lucky enough to enjoy with a few glasses of red, and I said: 'I feel dangerous. I might get forty possessions.'

I was taking the piss out of myself, and we all had a laugh.

WAKING UP on game day felt almost like a grand final day. I was feeling good, but knew to conserve my nervous energy. I reminded myself that I'd played big games before. It was a night game, and by the time I got to the club I was ready, maybe a little jumpy, but managing this was what I'd learnt to be good at. The blokes gave me plenty of quiet pats of encouragement. I just wanted to get on with it.

Running onto Subiaco Oval was a reminder of everything that motivated me. I was dog-hungry, and knowing what I'd been through, having a point to prove, only motivated me more. I actually loved being able to make a statement, through my footy, that I was back. But wrapped up inside that confidence were the questions I was putting to myself: *How am I going to cope? Can I still do it?*

I thought I was in some final battle, but really it was only beginning.

The place was packed, more than 42,000, and I was aware of how much encouragement was coming from the crowd. I'd hear voices shouting, 'Go, Cuz, you're a beauty!' and 'We all love you, Ben!' I'd gone through so many dark nights when I thought the whole world hated me – or more, that *I* hated me – it was shocking and gratifying to hear something different. There was the odd 'You're drug-fucked, Cousins', but I'd have been disappointed if there wasn't a bit of that. They were right! More ammunition for me.

I started on the bench and came on after five minutes in a rotation with Kerry. Tyson Stenglein handballed it to me, and I was away. I had ten touches in the first twenty minutes, and finished the game with thirty-eight possessions. Not that I judge my form by numbers, but I'd played as well as I could have possibly hoped. I was proud of having prepared so well, but football being football, I could just as easily have had a moderate output. You can't dictate these things. I was just relieved to have given myself a chance. We won the game, but my celebrations were reserved. It was ridiculous, like a movie script. This was my first game since winning the grand final. Since then, I'd been dragged through the bush. Now I was back with my teammates, on another premiership charge. I felt my life might have turned a corner.

IT HADN'T. The high of the comeback game was followed by a period of unease. I wasn't taking sleeping pills, I wasn't drinking, I certainly wasn't taking illicit drugs, so I was in uncharted territory. I was trying to deal with the post-game anticlimax without a blow-out to keep me company. My body and mind had been drilled into the habit after a big game of partying and then crashing. It was my way of winding down, and it wasn't available to me now. I had to find a way of letting myself down gently.

I PLAYED six more games that season. We played the Dockers on Father's Day, after which I rang Dad. He'd met a woman from a well-known West Australian family who'd contacted him because she had a female family member battling with drugs. Inspired by my rehabilitation, she wanted to send the young woman to Summit.

COMEBACK

The girl had resisted going, but I calmed her down about it, helped take the pressure off. She got back from America at the time of our Dockers match. As a Father's Day present, I rang Dad to tell him I was taking her to her first Narcotics Anonymous meeting. It meant I'd miss our family get-together that night.

'That is as good a thing as you could be doing,' the old man said. 'Quite frankly, there's nothing that could make me happier.'

AGAINST ESSENDON at Subiaco in the last round, I got to play in the farewell for Kevin Sheedy and James Hird. We got ahead by fifty-one points, but Essendon manufactured an incredible comeback before we squeaked through. The fans waved their jackets around their heads, Sheedy-style, and Hird had had thirty-four touches in a year when he was the club's best and fairest. I felt privileged to be part of it.

We finished third on the ladder, drawing an away qualifying final against Port Adelaide. In the third quarter I pulled my hamstring again. We lost by three points, and I wasn't able to play the next week in the semifinal against Collingwood, which we lost. The final against Port was my 238th game for the Eagles. It was a disappointing way to end the season, but I had been sober now for about six months and felt optimistic. I had no idea how misplaced that optimism was.

30

MAINY

Since he'd retired, Mainy and I had become better and better friends, often going down south together. While reporting on sport for Mix 94.5 FM radio and for Channel Seven, he was always welcome around the club after his transformation from player to media personality. Mainy embodied everything I believed a teammate, or for that matter a mate, should be, on and off the field. He'd kept his amazing rapport with the players, and saw his first loyalty as to the club, so much so that he'd apologise for asking you questions he didn't even need to be apologetic about. He was petrified of being seen to have gone to the other side. When I'd gone to rehab, and Mainy had taken me to Mandurah, Channel Seven, who he had a contract with, were hunting me. He didn't tell them where I was.

MAINY

I'd also been great friends with Rani, and loved going over there to play with their children Madeleine and Zac. Mainy was one of the few people who had some understanding of what it was like to walk in my shoes, because we had such similar personalities. I didn't let too many people into my confidence, but Mainy was one. We had a lot of emotionally searing conversations about my way forward.

On the afternoon of 1 October 2007, three weeks after my season ended, I'd been for a run and was driving along the coast road to my parents' place when, as I was passing through Cottesloe, the suburb where he lived, it occurred to me that I hadn't spoken to Mainy for a week or two. I called him up and asked how he was.

'No, not good.' His voice was flat. 'I'm sort of struggling.'

'Shit, mate, I'm on my way to my folks' place. I'll come over.'

'Yeah, no worries.'

Rani was at her family's farm north-east of Perth. I dropped in to my parents' house for a shower, and coincidentally got a call from her.

'I've just left Chris and he's on his own for the weekend,' Rani said. 'It'd be good if one of his mates could drop in.'

I told her I was already planning to. When I walked in at 2 pm, he was drinking a glass of red. We sat and chatted for three or four hours. He was troubled by a few issues, the sort we all go through from time to time. I hadn't realised how the support he had given me had taken its toll. He had been put in an awkward situation with Seven, and the club for that matter, acting as a go-between. I will probably never know the full extent of the pressure he was under. All I could do was thank him for everything he'd done for me. During the course of the conversation, though, I realised that guilt over me was only one of many problems Mainy was wrestling with. I remembered the bout of depression he'd sunk into when he was injured in the late 1990s, when it was sometimes hard to get a g'day out of him. That wasn't Mainy; the Mainy I knew was the first bloke to be friendly to you.

I had an NA meeting at 6 pm. I told him I'd call him when I was leaving the meeting and, if he wanted, I'd come back to his place.

'I've been in the same situation,' I said, 'and I know that when I feel like I'm going to have a night, nothing will stop me. If you're going to, I couldn't imagine anyone I'd rather have a night with.'

Maybe I was just looking for an excuse. I went to the NA meeting. The irony of what I'd said wasn't lost on me. In fact it really nagged at me, and by the time I left I realised that not only would I be letting myself down after six months of sobriety, but getting on it with Mainy was not the act of a friend. I rang him and said I'd bring some Japanese takeaway over. I picked up Michelle, a girl I'd been seeing, which I thought would make it easier for me to avoid the temptations I thought may occur.

We sat down for an hour or so, ate and talked. Mainy struggled to eat. At 10.30 pm my friend and I got up to leave. Mainy seemed fine now, and I had no concerns about him. He'd had a rough week with different personal problems, but he really seemed to have picked up since earlier in the day. If I'd had the slightest worry about his welfare, I wouldn't have left.

He asked me to sign some football jumpers, which he had in his bedroom. It would have been easy for us to have a night together. All the ingredients were there. But I wanted to be there for the right reasons.

'Listen, mate,' I said. 'When you and Rani got me off to rehab, I bet you never thought I could be strong. So I don't want to let you down.'

I said that I owed it to him, having got to where I was. I had tears in my eyes.

MAINY

Mainy looked straight at me and said, 'I always knew you could do it, mate.'

'You've got radio tomorrow morning?' I said.

'Yeah, yeah.'

'Do you need me to wake you up?'

'No, no, I'm okay.'

I gave him a hug. 'Speak to you tomorrow, mate. I'll leave the phone on tonight if you need to call me.'

We left, and when I got home I texted him: *Mate, I'm home, if you need us give us a call.*

The next morning, my friend's mobile rang. Someone told her that an ex-footballer had been found dead in Cottesloe. I sat up and tried to gather my thoughts. *No, this can't be true.*

Minutes later my phone rang. I saw Dad's name come up.

'It's not true, is it?' were my first words.

'Yeah, mate. Mainy's passed away.'

I was paralysed. *No.* This had not happened. I'd been around people in huge trouble or shocking drug-fucked states, and the man I'd had dinner with the previous night wasn't one of them. It just didn't make sense. I drove to Kim Hunter's and sat there with him, shattered, unable to digest it. I felt grateful that I'd been able to spend five or six incredibly meaningful hours with him, even more meaningful now. And grateful that I'd told him how I felt.

'You are allowed to cry, you know,' Kim said. A tear ran down my face. Yesterday I was with him. I kept reliving the afternoon and evening over and over in my mind.

Apart from being terribly upset, being a mate of Mainy's himself, Dad was very concerned about me. Rod Moore had told him that whatever else he was feeling, Dad had to be at my side. He came to my place to meet me and we talked for an hour, trying to make sense of it. As always, the old man was at his best in a crisis. He asked if I'd used, and I said no. The next day I went to Rod Moore and did a urine test, which proved I'd been clean.

The news was reported widely before Rani had been informed, but thankfully one of her close friends got to her before she switched on a radio or TV. The front pages the next day were full of how I'd been the last person to see Mainy, and there was innuendo about whether or not we'd been using drugs. They seemed to have forgotten that a champion West Australian bloke had died.

When I spoke to Rani, we were in shock. We didn't know what to say. She apologised for the negative attention I'd received for being there. I assured her how lucky I felt to have been able to spend those precious hours with him. I was devastated for her, and their kids.

I got a call from Mainy's sister Wendy, who was very close to him. She asked if I could sit down and chat with her and her brothers Glen and Brett about Chris's last hours. I can only imagine how hard it was for them to try to make sense of what exactly had happened. I walked them through the hours we'd spent together. It was an emotional talk. He obviously meant the world to them.

I found out later that within an hour of our leaving him, Mainy had been seen shouting outside his house and a neighbour had called an ambulance. Mainy had reportedly refused assistance from the ambos, who had placed him in the care of a neighbour. An hour later an ambulance came back to his place. He'd had convulsions and collapsed. A toxicology report said he had a mixture of legal and illegal drugs in his body. He was forty-one.

After meeting Mainy's siblings, I visited Rani. I was knocked flat when I saw her. The kids seemed too young to comprehend, but my heart bled for them. Rani showed incredible strength, particularly for Zac and Maddy, and even had time to stop and ask how I was going.

How I was going was absolutely insignificant.

MAINY

The Mainwaring family asked me to be a pallbearer at his funeral. It was one of the greatest honours of my life. He was a better man than me. Everyone in Perth seemed to have a great story about him. He had a lot of dash but he was never offensive, never insulted people, and had a huge heart. He could never say no. People loved him because of his generosity in volunteering time for junior footy clubs, sick children, people's grandparents on their eightieth or hundredth birthdays. He loved people, and loved using his profile to bring happiness into the lives of others.

I could only think of one consolation for Maddy and Zac, which was that people would forever be coming up to them and saying, 'You're Mainwaring's kids? Jeez, he was a great bloke.' He lived a big, big life.

I was blessed to have Mainy as a friend. I will never get over his loss. I have a deep sense of responsibility to Rani, Maddy and Zac, which I try to live up to. At the time of his funeral, I was falling apart, and it took every ounce of resolve in my body to keep myself in shape to be his pallbearer and be there to console his family. I will always miss him.

But once I got through that terrible day, I unravelled again.

31

SUCH IS LIFE

It was drilled into me at rehab that addiction is a chronic relapse condition. Intellectually, I knew it to be true, but my resolve until now had hidden it. I was about to learn a lot about myself and my illness.

The reason for my relapse in October 2007 doesn't take much explaining. For six months I'd been sober but fragile. Now Mainy's death had ripped apart the tenuous peace I'd made with myself.

I went on a bender. I covered a lot of ground and hung with all types of people. I didn't know it, but the police had me under surveillance, tapping my phone and placing a tracking device in my car. Detectives had interviewed me after Mainy's death, but then some others went to my apartment when I wasn't there. Questions were being asked about where Mainy got the illicit drugs he'd taken before his death, and fingers were pointed at me.

I knew I was innocent on that score, but others didn't.

At the tail-end of that hit-out, I spoke late one night to Rani, who was doing it very tough and was worried about Maddy and Zac going off to their first day at school since Mainy's death. Sam was with her. I went to their place, stayed the night and helped Rani with the kids in the morning. Moments like this, when we shared so much sadness, showed Sam and me that we had a foundation of friendship between us. I felt very emotional seeing her then.

When it was over, I went to Kim Hunter's, picked up Michelle, and met up with Chicky.

The previous night, when I'd been staying at the Mainwarings', someone had thrown a brick through the window of my Volkswagen 4WD, which was outside Kim's place. I was proper fucked when I found it, and didn't call the police. I didn't know who to trust. I didn't even want to touch the car.

I'd borrowed Michelle's sister's car, and needed to return it. Chicky drove it, and I drove his car. Going through Northbridge, I was suddenly surrounded by four unmarked police cars. It was a sting. They were from the gangs task force.

As luck would have it, this was the first time in five days I didn't have a large amount of illicit drugs on me. It was a really hot day, which explains why I was seen on national television, led off by police, without my shirt on. All I was wearing was jeans and my tattoo. It's incredible to think that for many people, that would be their lasting image of Ben Cousins. Such is life.

I felt sorry for Michelle, who was dragged into this. Chicky, who'd been paving a way through traffic for me at West Coast, and was doing me another favour this day, was learning how no good deed goes unpunished. He was pulled up as well. He'd cop a lot of flak through his association with me, but he never complained once and always went beyond the call of duty. He was one of the all-time blokes, and he suffered from a lot more criticism than he deserved.

My jeans had done a lot of ks; they were hanging off me. The police searched me, turning out my pockets, and found Valium. In the car was some Viagra, more Valium, and oxycodone which wasn't mine.

But my luck ran out. As it happened, a couple of days earlier a law had come into force where a person in charge of a car could be drug-tested. I think I was the first person in Western Australia to whom it applied.

'Boys,' I said to the cops, 'I'm happy to be breath-tested.' I hadn't drunk anything for a day, so I knew I'd blow zero. But they weren't interested. They were interested in, first of all, the publicity. They made sure the media were there, and paraded me in the street for what seemed like ages before taking me to the police station. It only penetrated slowly that I was going to be on the news. My first thought was that I didn't want Rani to see it.

I asked the police if I could make one phone call.

'I'd like to call Rani Mainwaring. She's lost her husband and doesn't need to see me on the street with you blokes locking me up.'

Eventually they let me call Sam and tell her what had happened, and that it was all okay. She was still my loyal best friend, and was the first one down at the station with my old man.

David Grace was in New York, so another lawyer, Shane Brennan, came down to represent me. I remember saying to the arresting coppers, 'I've put my hand up and said I had a problem, we all know I've gone to rehab. How is this helping your cause?' I wasn't involved in anything that could interest the gangs squad. My project was nothing more, or less, than the full-scale destruction of myself.

But whatever they thought of me, the gangs squad certainly didn't like some of my mates. I think they did it to clip my wings. They knew I wasn't involved in gangs or drug dealing. In the end I was charged with failure to comply with a police-ordered drug assessment and possession of a prohibited drug, diazepam.

They'd let me charge my phone, I assume so they could listen in to whatever calls I made. My reaction was to take the piss. I rang Michael Gardiner, who was at home in Melbourne watching all of this unfold on TV.

When he saw my name on his phone, Gardy thought, 'He can't be ringing me.'

'Gardy, how ya going? They fucken locked me up. They've only just realised that when they sacked you, they got the wrong bloke. Since you left, the joint's gone to the shithouse and it's taken them two years to get the right bloke.'

While Gardy saw the humour in it, he also realised the enormity of what was happening.

I rang one mate to ask him to book us into Coco's, the fine dining restaurant, and order me grilled fish and a splash of wine at a quiet table down the back. 'I'm going to be a bit late,' I said. 'I'm stuck in traffic.'

I rang a player agent, and asked him to get me a three-year deal with the Waneroo amateurs for a caravan as a sign-on fee and a job for my missus at the tuck shop.

By now, with an audience of laughing cops, I was on a roll. I carried on like this for eight hours. I knew they'd got me. I said to the coppers, 'You've squared up good.' It was payback for a lot of things that had happened previously. I knew how it would look, but was numb to the ramifications. Future gone, career gone, everything gone. Fine. It was too late to care about myself.

Then, when the paperwork had been done, I was released. I walked through the car park to where Dad and Rod Moore were waiting. I smirked at them: 'Do you want me to drive?'

Dad just gave me a blank look.

'Get in the car, Ben. Don't you think it's time to pull your head in?'

32

'HE'S CONSCIOUS BUT HE'S LOSING HIS MIND'

Six months of sobriety had required my full attention. With the football season over, and Mainy's passing, relapse was the predictable result. I was in free-fall, without anything to hold onto.

I don't use any of those triggers as excuses. I was in a shocking state, but in my disordered mind I was reasserting my independence.

Within a day, the club put out a media statement that they'd sacked me. I didn't get as much as a phone call, and I can see why they wouldn't have bothered. Twelve years an Eagle, 238 games, and it was over. The bare facts stood there for me, without any colour or feeling. It was no surprise. I felt disconnected from my own life, swirling with anger about losing my mate, my job and my standing, but these flashes came and went. I didn't have anyone to blame except myself.

My next required appointment would be in November, when I had to front the AFL on a charge of bringing the game into disrepute. Lose that argument, and I could find myself banned from ever playing again.

BACK AROUND mid-year, my doctors, my family and I had all agreed that it would be a good idea for me to spend the off-season back in California. Now, with the media in a frenzy over my sacking, I felt it was imperative.

I wasn't going there, as the media assumed, for a second stint at rehab. I was going so I could avoid the temptations of Perth in the summer, to escape from the feeling of being the most wanted – or least wanted? – outlaw in Australia, and to reconnect with friends. I wanted to see Chris, my sober companion from Summit, and attend some NA meetings. Chicky was over there too, seeing his son and his American ex-partner. My plan was to get sober and get fit, not to go into rehab again, but despite Dad's public statements to that effect the Australian media were still saying I was headed back to the US for that reason.

Nine days after I'd walked out of Subiaco as an Eagle for the last time, I flew to Sydney and holed up for three days. It provided no shelter. The fall-out from my arrest was still in the news. The police had dropped the drugs charge, as Valium in pill form was not prohibited, and Shane Brennan was making moves to get the police to apologise. I just wanted to get out of there, but the media were tipped off about me being in Sydney and started staking out the place where I was staying.

Getting on an international flight gave me some respite, and I slept most of the way to LA.

But when I arrived at LAX it was back on again, a welcoming committee of cameras and microphones. In a daze from the flight, I drifted through the pack until I saw a sign saying 'Angle'. It's the nickname some of my closest friends give me, for Kurt Angle, the professional wrestler. A blonde was holding it, and she said: 'You're with me.'

She and another blonde, both sent by Chicky, bundled me into a black Merc and won themselves the infamy of Australian television coverage. They were amazed and excited by all the cameras. 'What have you done in Australia?' they asked.

'It's a bit of a long story,' I said.

We went to one of the girls' houses in Hermosa Beach. I saw Chicky momentarily, and he did the honours of explaining to the girls what had gone on with me before he headed off to the midwest to see his son. The girls were very hospitable and I was happy to kick back. Susie, one of the girls, was a software sales manager with a three-storey penthouse near the beach, and soon the party was on. I played up to my role as the wild boy from Australia, and before long a lot of people dropped in. I'd arrived in LA with no firm plans, which may well have been my problem. I really felt like I needed a breather, so to let my hair down with these girls was very enticing. I still hadn't faced up to a lot of the stuff that had happened at home. I figured I'd hit it hard and *then* go sober.

The beauty of LA is that everything feels like it's at your disposal. I kicked back, and kept on kicking back. If you were looking for it, you couldn't miss good cocaine in LA. But what I got was exceptionally pure and frighteningly cheap.

Cocaine is a drug where you're constantly heading towards the high or away from it. You need to keep topping up. But you probably don't need to top up as much as I was. My relentlessness mirrored the size of my situation. For five days, I was snorting a line every twenty minutes. Sometimes I'd just swallow it; the rocks were so clean they wouldn't touch your stomach. The

Californian sunshine and the beach were outside, but before long my world had contracted to a coffee table.

For three days I just felt fresher and fresher. The drug kept amazing me by how far it could go; one tiny rock would crush up into eight or ten lines. Then, on day four, I started to get the wobbles, nearly falling over in the kitchen after swallowing a rock. Deceptive little fuckers. I might have swallowed a gram.

I walked out the front, vomited and nearly passed out again. Vomiting made me feel better, but I was pale and sweating profusely.

Susie calmed me down with a cold bath. She wanted to take me to hospital, but I staged another miraculous recovery. Within a short time I was coming good. I got dressed, pushed through, then overheated and had to get into the bath again.

I could barely remember the last time I'd slept. In a way, when I was punching it hard, I was on the run from sleep itself. I was in that old competitive state of not wanting to let go. Of what, I didn't, and don't, know.

By the fifth night, I was in real trouble, suddenly feeling a long way from home. I called Dad, Kim Hunter and David Grace, and might have sounded on top of things, but I definitely was not. At about 2 am on night five I walked to an all-night service station to search for food and alcohol, but I thought a guy in a car was photographing me so I bolted. I ran so far I missed a turn, and soon had no idea where I was. Paranoid, I was convinced the photographer in the car was still following me, and for half an hour kept running through the streets.

I was in no state for this. Who knows what pressure I was putting on my body? I hadn't slept or eaten properly, and had shovelled in a truckload of this and that. Disoriented, I had no idea where I was.

Somehow I found my way back to Susie's, overwhelmed and panicky. To calm down, I snorted a few lines. It made me lucid enough to realise I was having something like a psychotic episode.

'I need help here,' I told Susie. 'I'm fucked.'

I gave Susie my dad's number and asked her to call him. Susie told my dad that I was in a bad way, going out of my mind. Dad told her he would call someone from Summit rehab. It was about 5 am in LA and Dad had the numbers of several of the Summit staff, including their CEO, a lady called Tondra-laya. Tondra was a tall, African-American woman who I had met during my rehab, naturally comforting and caring, with an innate ability to calm you in bad times. One of my fondest memories of rehab is being nurtured by her and another African-American lady named Charity.

While Dad was making arrangements with Tondra to come and get me and take me to Summit, my condition worsened and I pleaded with Susie to get me to hospital.

She called emergency, and tapes of her report on me – 'He's conscious but he's losing his mind' – found their way onto Australian television. I was totally gone. Six paramedics put me into an ambulance. I had a singlet and jeans, but no shoes or phone when they checked me in to the Little Company of Mary Hospital in Torrance. My first instinct, in the observation room, was to run. Always stay on the move. I got up and charged the nearest window, hip-and-shouldered it. I had no idea what floor I was on, and luckily the window was reinforced double glass. I just bounced back off it. Five or six nurses wrestled me to the bed, and a big bloke pinned me. Just to let him know I had a bit of strength left, I kept throwing an arm up at him. He got aggressive and restrained me with even more force. That was my last memory before the sedatives kicked in.

Tondra eventually got hold of Susie and made her way to the hospital. She rang Dad to let him know where I was and said he should get over to LA. This was happening in early morning in

LA, so it was late at night in Perth, and Mum and Dad spent the whole night awake not really knowing how I was. Early the next morning, Dad rang our family doctor Rod Moore who spoke to the doctors at the LA hospital. He confirmed what Tondra had already told Dad, so Dad made urgent arrangement to head off to LA – again.

I woke up with tubes coming out of both arms and a catheter in my cock. If you'd asked me what had happened, I'd probably have burst into tears. Not out of shame, but because I was disoriented and weak and alone, with only the blurriest memory of how I'd ended up here. Where? I didn't know. I was a lost soul.

For two days, I was laid out on a saline drip. I didn't talk to anyone at home. The limit of my communication was asking for food, which the staff resisted for a day. I was so ravenous, on the second day I ate like a man who'd had no food for a week. Which I was.

At home, Dad was being overwhelmed by the ongoing Ben Cousins debate. Everyone had an opinion about whether I was a good person or not, whether I should be allowed to play football again, whether I should ever be employed.

A story had broken publicly that I'd missed rehab and been taken to hospital. Dad filmed a statement denying I'd skipped rehab (since I'd never been going there in the first place), but confirmed that I was in LA and that he knew where I was.

All Dad knew was that I was in intensive care. He drove to the airport, where Mum's brother-in-law Duncan Lewis fronted up and said, 'I'm coming with you.' Duncan had been a Special Air Service commander, would later be the Australian government's national security adviser, was an outstanding bloke and, needless to say, was someone who got things done.

At LAX they were met by the director of Summit, who brought them to the hospital. Tondra told me Dad was on his way. Tears trickled slowly down my cheeks. I was weak, lonely, broken.

I still didn't quite know where I was. The sight of Dad and Duncan walking into my room flooded me with the most profound love and relief and gratitude that I'd ever experienced. Dad had a bit of a smile, a private look we shot each other, and we hugged.

'Fuck mate, it's so good to see you,' I said through tears. Dad would say, later, that of all the times he'd seen me on my knees, this was the worst.

For the next few days, as I recovered, we tried to plan my next move. I had to front the AFL Commission in less than three weeks, and if I wanted to play again, Dad said, I should come home and start preparing. I took a lot of convincing. Australia was the last place I wanted to be, especially now that the latest Cousins fuck-up was making its way into public knowledge.

The compromise we settled on, when I left hospital after four days, was to spend a night at Summit. I was assessed as suffering from a chronic relapse condition. The doctors wrote a report recommending that it served my best interests to stay in the game. Summit also stressed that I'd never missed an appointment there for rehab, which was true. This report was later provided to the AFL Commission.

Back in an LA hotel for a couple of days, Dad and Duncan were fearful that I'd do a runner. I wanted to have a farewell dinner with Susie, and Dad and Duncan made sure they came along. Duncan alerted hotel security that I wasn't to leave the premises alone under any circumstances. Dad checked on me every hour, like I was a sick baby. I was tempted to bolt, again, but knew it would be crazy and disloyal. Without my knowledge, Dad stuck a match into the side of my door so he'd know if it had been opened.

We made our flight to Sydney, and Dad, exhausted from his vigil, took a sleeping pill. It was a big thing for him. Normally he was so anti-drugs that he wouldn't even take an aspirin. This was his approach to life – a fucking good one, I thought, as I sat next to him. But he had his limits. Normally a poor sleeper, he didn't move for the entire flight.

Avoiding the press at Sydney Airport, we drove to Duncan's place in Canberra and began structuring our case for the commission. I wasn't sure if I was up to starting again at a new AFL club, but I sure as hell didn't want the league telling me I couldn't. It was my old rebellious nature coming out. Starting to feel clean and clear-headed again, I took some runs around the army barracks in Canberra. Then someone saw me, the media found out I was in town, and Dad and I chose to leave Canberra. We only had a few days to prepare our case for the AFL hearing and wanted to do it with some degree of privacy.

33

SNAKES AND LADDERS

Ricky Nixon, who'd been in the background as my Melbourne manager for several years, had taken a more active role by now. My misdemeanours were getting too much for Dad to handle, and we'd thought Ricky's experience would be useful in dealing with the AFL. To Ricky's credit, his greatest support for me came when I needed him most, when others had cut me loose.

For my AFL Commission hearing on 19 November, David Grace thought I was on strong ground to plead not guilty to the charge of having brought the game into disrepute. There were eleven points to the charge, and David believed my answers to each were plausible. I always joked with David that 'You're only as good as your lawyer', and I was.

Ricky, on the other hand, thought I should plead guilty and take some time out of the game to clean up. One option he put to the AFL, before the hearing, was for me to go into the draft, hopefully get picked up by an AFL team, but only play in the VFL for the first six weeks, where I'd be drug-tested and kept in the system. The AFL rejected this proposal, so I pleaded not guilty.

In the AFL headquarters at Docklands, I gave evidence for one hour. David Grace made lengthy submissions on my behalf. Evidence was also given to the commission by the AFL doctors, my father and Ricky Nixon. Letters of support were placed before the commission, including from Dr Pippa Grange, psychology services manager for the AFLPA. It was emphasised that reha-bilitation through therapy was preferable to punitive action, due to my precarious and vulnerable state. Then the commissioners deliberated for four hours, before the chairman, Mike Fitzpat-rick, delivered their verdict to me and then to the media. He made some general comments about how much pressure modern players were under, then dropped the bombshell that I'd been de-registered for twelve months. The AFL Resolution was:

1. *The Commision is of the opinion that Mr Cousins has been involved in conduct which was:*
   a) *Unbecoming; and was*
   b) *likely to prejudice the reputation and interests of the AFL and bring the game of football into disrepute.*
2. *The Commission has determined that, subject to the provisions of paragraph 3, Mr Cousins' entitlement to be a player in the AFL Competition, or to be eligible to be drafted onto or included on a Club's List, is suspended for 12 months from this day.*
3. a) *Mr Cousins shall be entitled to apply in writing to the Commis-sion to be eligible to be drafted onto or included on a Club's list in the draft for the 2009 football season.*
   b) *In determining whether Mr Cousins' application is to be granted, the Commission will consider the following:*
   (i) *the extent to which Mr Cousins had consulted and*

cooperated with, and acted in accordance with the advice of, one or more medical experts nominated by the Chief Executive Officer of the AFL for the purpose of this sub-paragraph to advise in relation to a drug rehabilitation program and drug testing protocols that are appropriate for Mr Cousins;

(ii) whether there has been a relapse by Mr Cousins to drug or substance abuse and the likelihood of any such relapse in the future; and

(iii) whether the lifting of the suspension is in the best interests of Mr Cousins and/or the AFL.

c) If the Commission determines to grant the application it may do so without conditions, or on such conditions as in the opinion of the Commission is in the best interests of Mr Cousins and/or the AFL.

d) If the Commission determines not to grant the application Mr Cousins shall not be eligible to play as a player in the AFL Competition or to be eligible to be drafted onto or included on a club's list until one month prior to the draft for the 2010 football season.

4. If and to the extent that this Resolution is inconsistent with any provision of the AFL Player Regulations the provisions of this Resolution shall prevail to the extent of any inconsistency.

I stood up before the media and said: 'I am bitterly disappointed that I cannot continue to play football but that's not to say I have given up hope of doing so in the future. I would like to stress the fact that I am overcoming drug addiction, which is an ongoing process. Contrary to media reports, I am a lot further down the track in my rehabilitation than has been reported.'

I wasn't able to look at my situation with any balance. The argument that the AFL had a duty of care to the rest of the competition, or society for that matter, to set a standard that we all had to live up to, was lost on me. I was still only thinking of myself. One of the first principles of drug rehabilitation is to get the patient back into a work environment, so I was dark at the AFL for taking my work away from me. I thought they were sending me off on the road to relapse.

On the night of the decision, my parents and I ate at Koko at Crown with David Grace, Ricky Nixon and his wife, Robbie Bottazzi, my mate Mark Casey, Gardy and his new fiancée Danielle. Our mood was okay, because we'd pretty much expected the commission to go against me. As we talked about it, I calmed down a bit and understood that the AFL had to set an example. I'd left them with no choice. And to carry on about losing my work routines was to take one very big thing for granted: I had no God-given right to play footy.

In my mind, I knew I had to take responsibility for what I'd done. I had to go back to the beginning and start earning some respect. But that was just a brief moment of clarity. A drug addict's life is rarely about looking at things rationally, making a logical decision, and going from there. In fact, then, as at so many other critical times in those years, my response was, having understood the correct and sensible thing, to charge off and do the exact opposite. While my brain said I had to take responsibility, this other part of me wanted anything but.

There's an expression that an addict in his own company is bad company. Left to my own devices, what was I going to do? Have breakfast – then what? Have lunch – then what? Without any structure, and facing only a temporary ban so that I couldn't just forget football and think about a new career, I was adrift. All I could do was wander aimlessly through the day – or do what I did . . .

I went to the Gold Coast. It was nightclubs, parties, girls coming up to Robbie's oceanfront apartment, where I was staying. Private investigators and media were following me, and someone put out some footage of a bloke snorting coke on the apartment balcony. I thought it looked too grainy to identify me, but when my mates saw it they knew it was me. There's a little dance I did when I approached a table to do a line. A mate called and said, 'We could have denied and refuted everything until you did that dance. There's only one bloke in Australia that could have been.'

For weeks I was lashing out. I went to a mate's place in Sydney. Full of bravado, my response to getting deregistered as an AFL player was to tell my crew that I'd 'hit a witch's hat'. That was our term for something going wrong. We'd all hit a few witch's hats. We put a real witch's hat on the kitchen floor, and when people would ask what it was doing, we'd say, 'Don't worry about why it's there, just don't touch it and don't fucking knock it over.'

We got some exceptionally pure coke. I never stopped to think about the money, except to suck it out of the hole in the wall. It didn't matter. For the time being, I could afford it. I just couldn't afford to stop and think about it.

After a few days, we decided to cook the coke, turn it into crack. The most euphoric and dangerous feeling I know is the one you get from crack cocaine. It took you out to space and set you free, zero-gravity. It never seemed to lose its punch. You could be smoking it on day four of a bender and it felt like the first time.

We were too inept to risk cooking it ourselves, so we got a bloke called the Chef. In two years, the Chef had gone from non-user to full-blown crack addict. He'd lost his money, his assets. His life now revolved around cooking it up for people and smoking it with them. You could ring him at any time of the night or day, and he'd be there in fifteen minutes, without fail. He was remarkable. We called him on day four, and there he was fifteen minutes later, with a couple of suitcases containing his utensils. We provided the cocaine and he sat in the kitchen cooking it for us all.

He spent three days, hardly moving off his stool, in the kitchen. It was like a warped version of MasterChef. He had candles, Bunsen burners and the microwave going. 'It's very pure,' he said. When he cooked an ounce, it reduced from twenty-eight to twenty-two grams: it was 80 per cent pure. Amazing. 'It's the best coke I've ever cooked in Australia,' the Chef declared.

The whole time, he was passing the pipe around and we were smoking it, and he'd get a go too. That was what he lived for. Time stood still. We were out of our heads.

It was a horribly loose period. I was taking GBH, and walking the fine line between enjoying it and keeling over unconscious. More often than not, the latter happened. Once, I passed out on the floor. I was unconscious for an hour, as close as I've ever come to dying. When I woke up I was choking on my own vomit. One of my crew rushed over, turned me onto my side and cleared my mouth. I was spitting out vomit and clutching his leg for dear life. That was GBH. It could have finished me just like that.

I raised myself onto my elbows, still spitting out vomit.

'Just relax, buddy,' he said, stroking my head. 'You'll be all right. You just hit a witch's hat.'

OVER CHRISTMAS, Mum and Dad wanted to take the whole family on a skiing trip to Japan. Clutching at anything that might help me pull up, I agreed enthusiastically. It would get me out of Australia, where bad things happened, and into a safe environment with my parents, Matt, Mel and Sophie around me. We went to Niseko, and my first reaction was excitement at seeing snow for the first time. I was like a little kid. I learned to snowboard and hared down the beautifully-groomed slopes in the sunshine. It was the perfect release, and a privilege to be doing something fun, and clean, with my family around me. At night we'd play darts and go out for a drink. I was just one of the Cousins kids. One night, walking outside after dinner, a bloke called out, 'Hey, Cuzzy, ya fucken lunatic!' and we all looked.

*

AFTER THE ski trip, I went back to Sydney where a mate and I made a bit of a fresh start together. We both ate healthily and avoided bars, and I managed a few runs and swims. Through the Japan trip and that little January stint in Sydney, I started to think more clearly about how I was going to approach my year off.

I'd met Anthony Mundine and his manager Khoder Nasser in Sydney. Khoder suggested a documentary about my life, and introduced me to some guys from the production company Fifty Fifty Films. That gave me some much-needed direction. Back in Perth, I moved into Kim Hunter's place on the Swan River, and loved my time knocking around with his children. Kim and I would eat out or cook at home, and generally look after each other. He asked me to come to his mother's eighty-second birthday party, and I also saw a lot of Rani Mainwaring and Maddy and Zac, doing what I could in a tough time for them. I took Zac to his father–son Auskick match, thrilled and moved to be asked. At the end, Zac, who was six, said, 'Ben, I've got a tight hammy. I need some of those skins that you wear.' I took him and Maddy straight to the sports store.

Playing Wii with Kim's son Olly, or playing tennis with Kim, I could never keep my competitive spirit down. When I lost, I'd say I had a sore hamstring, just to wind them up. I remember Olly once claiming he'd snapped a left-foot goal in his latest footy game, to which I replied, 'Oh, bullshit!'

Kim laughed. 'Cuz, for Christ's sake, he's ten!'

Olly later said to Kim: 'I should have knocked him straight out.'

In April, I did something hugely important with Dad: together we went to the Anzac Day service in Thailand, near where his uncle Jim had died on the Burma Railway. Dad had always taken Anzac Day very seriously. On Anzac Days, I'd always made a point of rallying the footy team to show some respect and solidarity.

With my uncle John Cross leading a small family crew, we flew to Bangkok and then Kanchanaburi, and went out for runs together. It was back to the old days. Then, at night, we'd have some beers and end up singing karaoke. At the service, we met some extraordinary ex-POWs and other servicemen, who were appreciative that a young person was interested in their stories, or Weary Dunlop's, or Jim Thatcher's. Footballers get put on pedestals as heroes. Bullshit, these guys were real heroes. It was a privilege to listen to them. I've never felt more patriotic. The trip was one of the best things I've done in my life, and it wouldn't have been possible without my year off. It was one of the long list of things that would have been good for me to do when I was younger. Singing the national anthem at the dawn service was unforgettably moving. Whenever I hear the anthem, even on TV, I stand up and sing it. Connecting with Dad and these blokes in Thailand reaffirmed all those deep feelings I had about my country.

BUT AMID the flashes of recovery were deep, dark potholes. I became paranoid and convinced myself that the police were following me, and at one point I thought a detail of police cars parked outside the Chinese Embassy near Kim's house was there to spy on me. I dealt with the stress the usual way, bringing bikies, ice dealers and full-on Jack the Rippers back to Kim's place when my friend had just settled down for a quiet night and a DVD. I could be the housemate from hell. I'd say to guests, 'Welcome to the East Perth reptile enclosure, open from 8 pm to 8 am.' If I'd gone out during a bender, Kim would call me late at night and tell me to pull up, come back home. I'd agree, then phone him back and say, 'The badminton's just come on the telly, I've been looking forward to this all week, I've got to watch it. I'll be home tomorrow.'

I was now showing the long-term effects of my habit. I became so convinced that police were watching me from inside the television that I'd say, 'Good morning, gentlemen,' to the screen whenever I walked past it. Once I stopped and shouted at it: 'For fuck's sake, put me out of my misery, I can't handle the suspense.'

Drugs were an escape, but then I'd need to find some escape from them. Feeling the city closing in on me, I left Perth and flew to Melbourne to stay with Gardy and Danielle. Playing at St Kilda now, Gardy was starting to put together the kind of form that had made him the league's best ruckman. I'd really admired the way he'd handled himself since he left Perth. He'd got his very public whack before I did, but showed the resolve and strength to start afresh. Danielle had been a great influence on him, helping him settle down.

When I knocked at their door I'd been up for a week, and had lost my phone. I never intended to be in such a mess when I arrived, but I was just a walking fuck-up.

I looked up to my big mate. Seeing me in that state, right on the edge, Gardy got angry. I got angry back at him, shouting some sort of nonsense to justify myself.

'Shit, mate,' Gardy finally said, 'I might have to give you a flogging.'

That was exactly what I needed, but I backed down.

For the first days when I was with them, Gardy was rightly frustrated with me. One night he told me he was sick of it. He wanted to spend some quality time with me, and I was getting amped up, being a total shithead. After he'd stormed off and left me, I cried myself to sleep, something I didn't do often. Usually I was masterful at distracting my emotions from myself. Such a fuck-up. I thought of what I'd done to Mum and Dad, and now to good friends like Gardy. Keep going this way and I'd have nobody left. Most of all I was missing Sam.

The morning after the fight I woke alone, not knowing where I was. Even when my head cleared I didn't know. I smoked a pipe in bed, then took off, running up the street. I stopped at a service station, still clueless about where I was, and rang Carol Daws, my drug counsellor.

'Carol, I'm fucked, totally fucked. What'll I do?'

Carol guided me back to Gardy's place. She said she'd always be on call, to walk me through my darkest moments.

I crashed, slept a lot over the next week, and started to pull myself together with some training and swimming in St Kilda. For a while Gardy's chihuahua was the only creature in the house who would talk to me, but as I straightened out, Gardy thawed, and we began to have the kind of conversations I'd gone there for, about football, the future, what we still hoped to achieve. We also talked a lot about the past, and I poured out a lot of my grief over Mainy and guilt over Sam. Over time, Gardy, Danielle and Tim Smith, the boxing coach at the Western Bulldogs, rebuilt me. When Gardy and Danielle were out or I was just antsy, Tim, like Carol, was only a call away. I was also forgiven by the chihuahua, which unfortunately I repaid by accidentally dropping on the floor.

Gardy was a big advocate of getting out of Perth; he was clearly showing the benefits. As well as cleaning myself up and getting fit again, and renewing our friendship, this was the most significant result of my stay. Gardy's positive attitude about Melbourne, and playing for a Melbourne club, planted a seed of hope that maybe I could come and develop a similar routine.

WITHOUT MY work, my football, I was always vulnerable. The least setback could send me nose-diving again. In mid-year, I went on a surf trip to Gnaraloo with the doco crew, and we had some great surf and enjoyable evening barbecues with a couple of beers. It was bringing back all the great feelings from my trip there with Phil Read. But four days in, I tore my hip flexor in a bad wipeout. That was it. I couldn't surf. I couldn't run. I couldn't train.

There was one thing I could do. Time on my hands, as always, was my worst enemy.

34

HOME REHAB

When do you say enough's enough? Isn't one definition of insanity to repeat the same futile action, again and again, expecting a different result?

By May I was dragging my suitcase around Perth, looking for action and maybe a couch to rest on. A lot of my old old mates, who'd seen how far I'd fallen, had the good sense to steer clear of me. Even by my standards, my routines and circles were seedy. It's often said that once you've been through rehab the first time, you never really enjoy drugs the same way. It becomes something you have to do, like a task, the euphoria having faded to a grim and grey routine. I told myself I was loving it, the more dirty and dangerous the better, but there were times I couldn't even convince myself. Humour? The only person laughing was me. I still had bursts of elation, but they were more desperate, because all I was really doing was pushing forward to stop myself from thinking.

I didn't even have a place to live. Most of my possessions were in storage. It seemed like I'd been living out of a suitcase forever, like a gypsy. It was wearing me down.

One day I stopped wandering and rang Dad.

'Mate, I'm not sure I want to go on. I'd rather top myself than go on like this.' I was exhausted, and frustrated with the sheer predictability of everything I did. I was barely even a person, more like a host for what the drugs dictated. I was sick and tired of myself.

Dad arranged to come and get me. We sat down and had one of our most frank conversations. I felt like I was slipping down a hill, and every bush I grabbed at came loose in my hands. Nothing could stop me falling. The addiction was bigger than I was. I was run by fear. The fear of coming down without some drug to help me. The fear of inadequacy. The fear of being alone. The fear of fear itself.

Then Dad told me how bad it would be for him, and everybody, if I killed myself. I don't think I have suicidal tendencies, but those words were all I had to let him know how despairing I was. He revealed that he'd been struggling with depression. It came as a bombshell to me. He'd devoted every waking moment to me and my recovery, and I'd just been dragging him down. He was the family representative, the spokesman, the conduit, the bearer of bad news. I could see that I'd broken not only myself, but him too.

Against Mum's urgings, he'd been resisting going on anti-depressants. Here he was, just about having a nervous breakdown, and he refused to take any medication, not even a sleeping pill so he'd have the energy to fight the battle every day. He said he wanted me to see him for real, without camouflage. I got angry at that. It seemed stubborn to the point of self-destructiveness – not dissimilar to me. I threatened him, saying, 'I won't undergo any treatment, I'll let myself go completely, until you get some help.'

We thrashed out a deal. If I got help, he'd get help. If he stopped, I'd stop. He made me promise that if I ever felt suicidal, I would call him. And he undertook to call me, if he ever felt that way. I booked him in to see Rod Moore. We had a pact. It would be the start of Dad's recovery. I can look back on that and feel that at least I salvaged some of my wreckage in those weeks.

AFTER A few conversations with Carol, we agreed that the best thing for me was to try rehab at Mum and Dad's place. To go to a facility meant media exposure and possibly the loss of any remaining hope of getting back into the AFL.

It had to work. This was the true crossroads. Life or death.

Home rehab was my best option, but with all the flexibility it offered, keeping me out of the regimentation of a rehab centre, it also had less chance of success. And if I slipped up and used again, something trained drug counsellors knew was part of the process, to Mum and Dad I'd just look like a liar. How many times had I promised to get off the gear, and been on it again within a day? And then ask myself, How did I get here again? It's not that you're not sincere and honest when you make the promise. It's that you're not strong enough to keep it. I know that to some people those are one and the same, but this is the essence of being a drug addict. You're just not strong enough.

Going back to the family home was a significant moment. It was when I finally accepted that I could no longer manage on my own.

In the first ten days, I went over a lot of the family interviews that had been shot for the documentary. They were really hard for me to watch. Watching Dad, Mum and Mel talking about me was like taking a journey back into all the damage I'd inflicted. Right there in front of me, I saw the pain and hurt I'd put my family through, really good people, the people I loved. Writing this still brings out the guilt and shame.

While I went over the footage in the dead of night, I was using. I couldn't detox completely. I saw the irony in this, but it was how I got through. I didn't use blatantly, in front of anyone, but they weren't stupid. They tolerated it because they saw me making an effort to cut it down. One step at a time.

The important thing for them was that my use didn't escalate into some almighty twister again. So Mum, Dad and Mel set up their shift system through the night of making sure I didn't leave. It was like guard duty, and I quickly came to resent it. No matter that I was smoking ice in my room: in my alternate reality, they were like police, they were oppressing me. During the day they called me, ostensibly to say hello, but really to check I wasn't going out to some dealer's place. In my distorted way, I began to think, *They reckon I'm on, so I may as well be.*

I was just seeking an excuse. The walls were closing in. If I had one thought, I had a hundred. I was losing my mind again. I could deal with it when I used, but of course that made the thoughts clamour even more noisily when I was pulling up. I was slipping, slipping again.

I was beginning to get dangerously low in my supplies. No way did I see coming down as an option, amid what was already going on inside me. I was fighting on too many fronts.

Up until now, I'd agreed with my parents to stay around the house. But as I panicked about having to score, I got dressed, packed a backpack, and headed for the door.

This was the night when Mum intercepted me, and Dad and I nearly had an altercation. I had tunnel vision: I had to go and he couldn't stop me.

So I took him out and left him in the bus shelter while I went and did my business. I'm embarrassed about what I did. I hate myself for it. I'm ashamed by the memory of how selfish I'd become.

LATER THAT day, I talked Rani into taking me to Kim's place. I was back to my scheming self. I spun Mum a complicated yarn about how innocent my outing was going to be, and she rang Dad, who'd gone to work. He was annoyed that I was going to Kim's. 'You're out of control,' he said.

I shrugged it off. I was out of the house. When I was at Kim's, I told him flippantly about what I'd done the night before.

Kim exploded. 'That's a disgrace. If you think there's anything funny about that, you've totally lost the plot.'

I needed a jolt from a friend about what the fuck I was doing. He kept me there until Dad came and met us after work.

'You've hit rock bottom,' Dad said.

In a pathetic attempt at defiance, I said: 'Rock bottom? I'm nowhere near rock bottom.'

Dad and Kim were looking at each other thinking, *If he doesn't think this is rock bottom, what is?*

At times like this it didn't seem we were getting anywhere.

THAT NIGHT I headed home with Dad, and had more conversations with Carol. As it appeared being at home wasn't working, we discussed rehab at length. She let me know that I had to take the whole thing more seriously, or else I'd have wasted another month. If I didn't show some improvement, I'd be looking at going into a rehab centre, with all that entailed.

The next week was hard, as I knuckled down. Something was changing in me, but not quickly. It was two steps forward, one step back. I didn't see anyone for ten days. I only left the house to shuffle around the local streets, attempting a run. Every hour I was fighting a compulsion to use. I thought, *I might go out and see this bloke about something*, but I also heard that other voice saying, *And after I see him I'm going to get on*. So I wouldn't trust myself to go anywhere. It was so humiliating, being where I was, that I was longing for a quick and easy way out.

Always, what pulled me back was that this time I'd really be letting Mum and Dad down worse than ever. So I had to keep on trying. Find distractions. Don't think about drugs. Don't be alone. Keep at it. You can come back. You can play footy again.

My world had shrunk to a series of tiny battles, each of which seemed as big as a grand final. If I had to pay my phone bill, or organise a meeting a week in the future, I'd freak out. Because so many small tasks were insurmountable to me, and presented such stress that the thought of them drove me to want to use, Carol taught me to break up my day into segments. She came around, sat on my bed, listened to what was stressing me, and lowered the demands. So if I had to make ten phone calls, she'd say, 'Here's the important one, ring this bloke, and you can do the rest another day.'

Two days in, I was sure I couldn't last. Ten days in, Carol said I seemed more settled. Dad was going down to Oakford before dawn to train his horses, and I got into the routine of having breakfast with him when he got back. Then Mum walked the dogs. Going with her became part of my day. Mel was staying at home, so I'd watch *The Sopranos* with her. Each little event was an event without drugs. I had to build one on top of the other, like bricks that become a wall.

After two or three weeks, I felt well enough for Kim or Rani to come over to join our family dinner. But that was the extent of my social interaction. It was about family and quiet times. I ran a bit further, a bit harder, and started feeling good when I got out of bed, better about the day ahead.

35

MAZE

Well into my stint at the family home, I had to start thinking about a return to football. The plan was to enter the national draft in November, as long as I jumped through the hoops the AFL would require. Mainly, I needed to pass drug tests, and then I had to hope like hell that the league would re-register me. Throughout 2008, David Grace and I had agreed to whatever conditions the AFL was proposing. There were assessments in June and September by Dr Greg Whelan and Dr Michael McDonough, with drug-testing in between. I tested negative to drugs in urine tests I gave in late June and late July, and Greg Whelan, after the latter test, wrote a report giving me the all-clear while warning that if I 'did not return to playing elite-level football, unemployment and boredom and the associated blow to [my] self-esteem and self-image are likely to be high risk'. I also agreed that random testing would be a condition of any return to the league, with no second chances if I failed.

While Dad, Ricky Nixon and I were making plans, Maylea Tinecheff came into my life.

Maylea was a naturopath I'd met years earlier, when I was sixteen and she was twenty-two. She'd been training at the same beauty school as Sam. Back then, she'd taken my breath away. As an adolescent, I thought she was the best-looking girl I'd ever seen. I'd only run into her once or twice when I was young, and hardly at all as the years went by. Then, in August 2008, I called my mate The Hurricane to see what he was up to.

'I've got a friend here,' he said. 'She wants to say hello.'

It was Maze, and I invited them both to come to Kim's. We had a good night, and a few laughs, and the next day I was still thinking about her. She was free-spirited, great fun and still very attractive. I called her up and asked her over for a drink.

We started to knock around together, and had a lot to talk about. She had two young kids, and had recently separated from their father. In her way, she'd been dealing with crises as big as mine. It was great to be able to share my problems with someone, and I found that I connected with her emotionally more than with anyone since Sam. She soon became a fiercely loyal and protective girlfriend.

Two MONTHS out from the draft, we decided that a training program was what I needed. Despite all the carnage, I never ceased enjoying the feeling of authentic physical fitness, and relished the work it took. I started a regime of long runs, six to ten kilometres, and some weights for my legs. I was determined to play again in 2009, so the aim was to get my body into good shape with a balanced general fitness.

But there was only so much of that grinding work I could do in isolation, so I started thinking about training with a football team. I'd spent too long recently without a ball in my hand. Just kicking balls at practice, moving off a line, wearing boots and doing some skills work seemed very important to me, so I approached Dad's old WAFL club, Perth, at Lathlain Park where my earliest football memories came from. Going back there would be like stepping back in time, to childhood. It had to be good for me.

But on the other hand, my WAFL club had been East Fremantle, and I felt I owed them something. I was an East Fremantle person. If they'd have me, that was.

My old Eagles teammate Chad Morrison was coaching the East Fremantle Colts, and that sounded like a perfect place to start. He encouraged me to come down to train with the young blokes, and Perth were also happy for me to train there. So I got into a routine of Monday, Tuesday and Thursday training with Perth, and Wednesday nights with the East Fremantle Colts. Then, on Friday, Saturday and Sunday I'd flog myself with hard weights and running sessions.

I loved it all. At East Freo, I had the chance to give a bit of advice to the kids and receive the tonic of their enthusiasm. Chad reminded me that I could have a great influence on these kids. I felt the influence was flowing in both directions. At Perth, it was refreshing in a different way. These clubs haven't changed all that much since Dad's time, and to watch guys rocking up after their nine-to-five jobs, and training very hard for nothing like the remuneration I was used to, renewed my respect for the game and the people who play it.

I STILL owned my apartment at Burswood, and moved in there with Mel, who was working in public relations at the casino. We both needed to get out of home, and it was the start of a great little period. Mel and I were always close. I'm also really close with Matt, but during these turbulent times we'd clashed. He stood up to me and refused to tolerate what I was doing. I still respected and loved him for it. He was a great younger brother, who I sort of looked up to, which is an unusual thing for an older brother to say. But we definitely couldn't have lived together at the time. Mel understood me as well as anyone. I'm not the easiest person to live with, but if I could do it with anyone it would be her.

Every night we'd cook excellent meals, and have a few glasses of wine. I'd also regularly go down to Singleton, a beachside town south of Fremantle, where Maylea was staying, and we'd have awesome cook-ups. You know what they say about the fastest way to a man's heart. One night, on a shitty-arsed stove, Maze cooked the most memorable steak meal I've ever eaten. For the next two nights Scotty, one of the doco makers, and I tried to match her with our own meals, but fell just short.

Back in Perth, Mel and I would get together a little party with Maylea, Kim, the doco makers Scott and Paul, and Rick Rifici, a surf cameraman I'd met through Mainy years earlier. In the past, I'd never been able to stop it there. One drink led to a five-day hit-out. But living with Mel and being in a happy relationship with Maylea, I was able to control it, and loved waking up each morning feeling fresh for training.

I volunteered to undergo three urine tests a week with my rehab doctors. I wanted to lay down a dossier of proof of my sobriety leading into the draft, and do it off my own bat, not just because the AFL told me to.

There were signs that I could pull myself out of the cycle. As I trained with the Perth and East Fremantle clubs, I finally learnt an important lesson about myself: that there was such a thing as being too fit, training too hard. At the Eagles I'd never seen any limits to how fit I could get, and had never seen it as just another dimension of my addiction to extremes. But now, after a great little period in my life, in September I broke down again with hamstring strains.

Addiction is a cunning and baffling illness. It hadn't gone away. It was lying in wait for the next moment of weakness. I took my eye off things ever so slightly, and found myself slipping for a couple of days. With so many important events looming, I was lucky to pull myself out. I still needed reminding that the disease never sleeps, but always remains lurking in the shadows.

To make matters worse, these two days would take their toll on Mel, who'd had, so far, an incident-free roommate at Burswood.

Suspecting the worst one night, she rang and told me to come home.

'I'll be home in half an hour,' I said.

I wouldn't have convinced anyone.

'No,' she said, 'right now.'

When I didn't come, she called again. Hours later I walked in with a friend, and started putting stuff in a bag.

'What's in there?' Mel demanded, walking into my room.

She'd seen me wrapping an ice pipe into a T-shirt. She snatched it and ran out, screaming that she was going to smash it.

'Don't smash it,' I shouted after her. 'It's not mine!'

Mel stopped and glared at me, total disappointment and betrayal in her face.

'Just have it,' she said. 'If it means that much to you, there's nothing more I can do.'

I took the pipe, put it in my bag, and left. I couldn't help it. But luckily, this time I was able to pull up fairly quickly.

Part of me felt, as it always did, that I was undoing all my good work. It was a bad time to be fragile again, with clubs starting to look at me for the national draft. Just how close they were looking, I was soon to find out.

36

TAKE THE PACE OFF IT

As far as we knew, there were a number of clubs interested in me: Brisbane, North Melbourne, St Kilda, Essendon and Collingwood. Ricky was conducting the negotiations, but first I had to be re-registered by the AFL. My months off hadn't diminished the resentment I was still nursing. I'd been banned for twelve months. Wasn't that punishment enough?

In August, David Grace and Ricky Nixon met with Andrew Demetriou to discuss my plans, my rehabilitation and my desire to play again. Otherwise I was left to my own devices, which, in 2008, had been like placing a box of matches in a pyromaniac's hands. When I flew into Melbourne, the league did nothing to protect me from the media pack. In my angry moments, I felt that they wanted me to fail; it would make things simpler for Brand AFL.

Through September, I was eased back into the football scene. Garry Lyon flew to Perth to interview me for *The Footy Show*, and it went pretty well. Mum came with me to Melbourne for the Brownlow presentation and grand final day. I gave a couple of interviews and appeared on a panel at a public function. It was all a bit overwhelming, so much so suddenly, but once I broke it down into one task at a time, I coped.

At the official grand final function, attended by the AFL commissioners, Lyon interviewed me again in front of a crowd of 1500. It was nerve-racking, but I felt I got my point across. I told Lyon: 'I have an addictive personality. It's the very thing that has made me single-minded. It's made me train better than the next bloke, or harder than the next bloke. With that came the extremity of the way I balanced that out, and that's what got me into the predicament that I'm in now.'

The West Coast chairman, Mark Barnaba, was interviewed about me. He said that while I was a champion of the club and had done myself and my family credit at the lunch, they were not interested in having me back as a player.

Alan Quigley and Greg Whelan, the two addiction specialists who were associated with the league, both gave me great feedback. They strongly supported my re-registration and knew how counterproductive banning me had been. But they also knew the restraints the AFL was acting under. It was a game I had to play. Jump through hoops, do the right thing, and I'd be able to put all this behind me. I had to draw on all my reserves, because it was about to get a whole lot tougher.

IN MELBOURNE, I met with Mick Malthouse and Collingwood's football manager, Greg Walsh. I'd have loved to play under Mick again, no question. They wanted me to do some fitness tests on my hamstrings, but having tweaked them I wasn't able, and asked if I could put it off a couple of weeks until my next trip to Melbourne.

I thought things were going well with Collingwood. In joining a big club with fanatical supporters, there would be echoes of joining West Coast thirteen years earlier. But then, the story broke that they'd had a private investigator following me around Perth, and had discussed the investigator's report with Victoria's police commissioner, Christine Nixon. On 16 October, they told Ricky they'd gone cold on me. I felt disappointed, and never found out what was true or who'd been in on it.

During these weeks of discussions with prospective clubs, I was knocked back by one after the other. Whether it was private investigators, police involvement or sponsors' objections, I found it hard to know where I stood. Was there anything I could do? I didn't know. Soon, the process of rejection took its toll. I was experienced enough not to believe every last rumour I read in the media, but I was frustrated with how uncertain it all was. Nothing was what it seemed.

ONE OF the conditions of my re-registration was passing a number of tests for drugs in October and November. Urine or blood tests were not enough. About six weeks out from my hearing, out of nowhere the AFL announced I was required to do a hair test. This was a complete shock to me and came like a death-knock. I felt it was an unfair attempt to trip me up. I didn't know the rules we were playing by.

They wanted to check my hair to see how far back I'd been clean. Wearing a hat, I sat in Alan Quigley's waiting room with Ricky Nixon. When I whipped the hat off, Ricky burst out: 'What have you done?'

My head wasn't completely shaved. Alan had told me that the minimum length of hair they needed was half a centimetre. I'd intentionally had my hair cut at one centimetre's length. I couldn't shave it completely – I knew I had to submit to the testing – but I was really worried about what a positive hair test result would mean. I know how it looked, lobbing with a partially shaved head. It sat very well with the perception of me as a smart-arse, showing no contrition, doing what I pleased. But I can tell you, this six-week lead-up was one of the most stressful and Consuming times of my life. No question, I was concerned about my hair if it went too far back. I had no faith in the AFL Commission interpreting and comprehending a failed hair test during my year off. My chief fear was that a positive hair test would lead to a black-and-white interpretation. Instead of showing the truth, which was that I was in the fight of my life to overcome this thing, but had still relapsed from time to time, I was afraid that the AFL would look at a positive test and just shake their heads, refuse to re-register me.

Greg Whelan, the independent AFL doctor, was sympathetic, and was adamant that a hair test would be a better tool to monitor me once I'd returned to the workforce, rather than one to determine whether I should be re-registered or not. On the day, they decided not to do the test.

I waited in trepidation for the public spray I'd get for almost shaving myself. The press loved it, and reported that I'd turned up without a hair on my body, as if I was giving the finger to the whole process. But I'd undergone three urine tests a week and offered hair that tracked back six weeks. I had independent doctors' reports, supporting letters from other medical people, a letter from Carol, another from Rod Moore, all supporting my re-registration. I wasn't giving the AFL the finger, but all that was reported was my so-called hairlessness and bad attitude.

The hair tests, if I'd had them, would have shown I'd been drug-free for at least eight weeks. My urine tests showed no drugs in my system.

ON 12 November, Ricky Nixon, after discussions with David Grace and me, wrote to the AFL Commission saying he had no doubt I was ready physically and mentally to take the field for a number of years, and that it would be a vital part of my rehabilitation.

He outlined a detailed rehabilitation program, with me living in a quiet part of Melbourne, away from bars and nightclubs, and being monitored by a small group including Carol, former player Gerard Healy, Ricky's colleague Carlie Merenda (sister of the former Tigers and Eagles player Mark), drug counsellor David O'Halloran and Ricky himself. He spoke of everyone in my 'pyramid' of support: family and close friends who had been most hurt by my drug problems and would do everything to keep me on track 'to ensure this young man's life is remembered for the right reasons'.

I was incredibly fortunate to have that pyramid. Countless people who've been sucked into drug addiction have a lot less, and their lives are literally lost. I'd lost one of my closest mates, and knew of plenty of others. Drug addicts live on a fault line. It's so easy to slip through. In late 2008, I felt I was right on that fault line and could be facing the end of my life any day. Only a huge amount of family support and personal resolve could save me.

LIFE IS short. I didn't need much reminding of that, but the reminder came all the same when I went back to Melbourne for a re-scheduled hair test in mid-November.

One of my closest mates in Melbourne was a guy called Johnny Giannarelli, or Johnny G. He was ten years older than me, and had lived the life. I think he saw a lot of himself in me. He now lived a much quieter existence and our friendship was based on this, not late nights or letting our hair down. He was not only a great friend, but also became a telling influence on me. When I'd been in Melbourne at times, he'd helped me with exit strategies from nights that looked like they could get away from me. Johnny was a big-hearted, genuine bloke. And now he had mesothelioma.

As a kid, Johnny had made a cubby house with his uncle, which involved removing some asbestos. He believed that was his only exposure to the stuff.

His illness was something he kept private, only letting in a few close friends. He'd seemed to go into remission, but lately had told me he wasn't doing well. Still, he put on a confident front, and I fell for it. I'd spoken to him a few times recently, but got sucked back into worrying about my upcoming hair test.

I arrived in Melbourne attempting to stay under the radar, hoping to get in and out of town without the media circus. This was near-impossible, but was all the more important now that I was getting around with a closely shaved head. I wore a hat in public and snuck into the airport, where Ricky picked me up and took me to his holiday house in the Bellarine Peninsula town of Port Lonsdale. It was the perfect hideaway.

Leading up to the hair test, I had a meeting with St Kilda's board and coach Ross Lyon. I was placing a lot of hopes in St Kilda now. Paranoid after the Collingwood experience, I avoided calling my usual Melbourne mates. But something deep inside me urged me to see Johnny. I finally got hold of him by phone, as Ricky and I headed to Melbourne for the hair test. Reluctantly, Johnny agreed to let me pop through and see him in the Epworth Hospital. Nothing could prepare me for what I was walking into.

When I entered his hospital room, I saw the remnants of my dear friend. He was a six-foot-one, handsome, strongly-built Italian stallion – I called him Horse – but now he was all bones, and a bad grey colour. He looked like he'd been dead for two weeks. His mother was with him. When she left us alone, I became uncontrollably emotional. I cried like a little boy. Johnny, being the strong one, demanded I stop it. He didn't want to see me so upset. I was crying out of shame. I'd been worrying about a fucking hair test, and here was my mate looking down the barrel. He hadn't spoken about his illness, and I hadn't paid it enough attention. Now, to see him like this, I was shattered.

I had a great hour sitting by his bed, hugging him and telling him how much I loved him. I told him how guilty I felt about my self-absorption. The hair test now seemed so insignificant. I felt ashamed to have missed the warnings of how grave his illness was.

He'd always been one to give me advice. Knowing how he'd be reflecting on life at this moment, I asked what was inside his head, what he was actually feeling.

'Mate,' he looked straight at me, 'we're playing it wrong. We're moving way too fast.'

His voice was weak, but his words were unforgettable.

'We're focusing on all the wrong things. Always moving too fast, chasing the excitement. You've got to step back, take the pace off it.'

It was a message that stuck with me. I'd been going too fast. By trying to taste everything in life, I'd almost skated over the top of experience and tasted nothing. Because they came from Johnny, I knew I'd keep thinking about these words for a long time. I felt unworthy, that I hadn't deserved our friendship. I left the hospital a broken man, a mess, and headed for the hair test.

A FEW weeks before my reinstatement hearing, the AFL's medical office made contact. They required me to come to Melbourne for a face-to-face interview on the process I'd been through, to give them feedback so everyone could learn from it.

Having been through twelve months of huge frustration and mixed messages about what I needed to do for my recovery, I was feeling dejected and confused when I sat down with them.

'Is there any comment you'd like to make about this process?'

Did they really want to know? I took a deep breath to calm myself down.

'To be honest, you guys, as the AFL medical officers, I thought that aside from the process and aside from whether I get reinstated or not, I might have warranted a phone call or a face-to-face visit, not to say, 'Are you going to come back and play footy?' but just a 'How are you? Anything we can do? Are you in a good frame of mind?' For all you knew, I could be ready to string myself up. I'm under more scrutiny than anyone in the country, I'm going through something that no-one in our game has ever gone through, and it seems like you're sitting down to pass judgment two weeks before working out whether I'm fit to play.'

As time went by, I would learn a lot more about what had gone on behind the scenes. When I did understand that, I was ready to commend the AFL and their medical officers for their drugs policy. It's one that I believe in now. But at the time, I was operating under too much stress and fear to be able to stand back and see what they were doing for me. Torn apart by my visit to Johnny G, I needed to blow off steam.

MY HAIR test, when I finally gave it, came up fine. Two weeks later the AFL re-registered me subject to stringent conditions, and Johnny G died. I was numb to the first bit of news and in tears over the second. Knowing how vulnerable I was at this moment, I called Carol at six in the morning. I knew it could be as catastrophic as when Mainy had died. She and my family helped me through this time. I made it.

Johnny's family asked me to be a pallbearer at his funeral, and I was honoured. I also knew it was a risk, because of what might happen afterwards, so I asked Dad to come with me. Johnny was the second close mate I'd lost in a short period, and the second for whom I was acting as a pallbearer. Like Mainy, he was a better man than I'd ever be.

We flew on the red-eye, and some photographer snapped me looking tired at the airport, so the next day there was the obligatory 'Is this bloke ready to be let back into the AFL?' headline. If they'd used any of the other photos that would have shown me looking quite fine, the story would have been 'Cousins back on track' or some such. But this was the norm. I was too sad about Johnny to even notice it.

Likewise with the stories criticising me for being at his funeral. Johnny had had some brushes with the law earlier in life, including convictions, and a colourful crowd was attending. Another pallbearer was my good friend Mick 'The Plumber' Hamill, better known for belting Sam Newman after Sam had been mixed up with Mick's wife. It only added to the intrigue. People looking in from the outside had no idea of the quality of bloke Johnny was. All they saw was the potential harm I was doing to my chances of playing footy again. But attending the funeral was non-negotiable. I only had to think of what Johnny would have done if our positions were reversed. Would he have said, 'I'm leading a quiet, honourable life; I'm not going to be associated with the funeral of that drug addict Cousins'? The thought was absurd. We were good mates, and that was all that had to be said.

Johnny had a big Carlton funeral. The wake would involve a big drink and other temptations, so I didn't go. Dad and I got on the next flight back to Perth. On the plane, I reflected on my good mate. Selfishly, I thought about how much help he could have given me now, as I tried to rebuild my life. I felt sorry for myself that he was gone. But he'd left me with priceless friendship, and some advice I'd try to live by every day. Just take the pace off it.

37

LAST CHANCE SALOON

Over the next two months, I needed every bit of that steel that Johnny had left me with. Brisbane, St Kilda and North Melbourne lost interest in me for the national draft.

It was St Kilda's knockback on the eve of the draft that really rocked me. I'd had regular contact with them throughout 2008, and the thought of getting the old firm back together with Gardy really appealed to me. Getting on the end of his ruck work would make me look a better player than I was, for a start! He'd planted the seed for me at St Kilda, introducing me to Matthew Drain, the football manager, earlier in the year, and talks had progressed from there. To give an indication of how far talks progressed, Ross Lyon, Drain and Fraser Gehrig, my old West Coast teammate now at St Kilda, had presented me with a St Kilda number nine guernsey. But just before the draft, when my hopes were sky-high, they informed Ricky that they wouldn't pick me up.

The draft was shown on television, but I didn't watch it. My chances were next to nothing. I'd been disappointed over the Collingwood matter, but now, when I wasn't picked up in the draft, I was beyond anger. I just surrendered. I couldn't get out of bed for five or six days. I talked to no-one. The thought of getting food from the fridge was too much for me. I could barely feed myself. This final rejection had beaten me. The whole process of getting back to footy had been too much. It was so humbling. While I was well aware of the trouble I'd caused, a part of me still felt like the successful footballer I'd been in the past. To be passed over, behind eighty kids who'd never played an AFL game, humiliated me.

Of all the downs over the years, that was the worst. If you designed a process to bring a bloke down, you couldn't have done better than that.

I eventually dusted myself off and went for a jog around the river. It wasn't dissimilar to trying to get moving for a pre-season. The first few steps were terrible, but I gradually pulled it together. That first run is always significant for me, symbolic of a change within.

I was weighing up my options. I had a minute chance of being picked up in the pre-season draft, the last-chance saloon. Essendon loomed as a possibility for a while, which gave rise to a situation that was funny in a grim kind of way.

My old adversary Stuart 'Knackers' Cormack had announced he was leaving the West Coast to go to Essendon. I got a couple of texts from Dean Cox and Andrew Embley, saying how funny it'd be if I ended up at Essendon under Knackers. But I was so desperate, scrambling for the pre-season draft, I'd do anything for a game. Ricky Nixon told me that Essendon wanted me to call Stuart Cormack to have a yarn about my footy and the prospect of coming to Essendon. I thought this was unusual, to have a fitness coordinator as my first port of call.

I've had to do some hard things in my time, but few have been harder than that. It shows how desperate I was. All I wanted was to tell this guy who I'd banged heads with at West Coast to fuck off. This time, if I ended up under him, I'd have my tail between my legs. All my bravado and ammo was gone, and it made me feel crook just to think about phoning him. I put it off for a day or two, then called.

'Mate,' I said, 'we've had our differences.'

He said, 'The first thing I want to say is that I personally want to see you do well and if I can speak to our coach and help you, I'll do it.'

I had to credit him for handling himself so well. We talked about what I'd been doing and how keen I was to play. It was fine. Nothing came of it, and I never heard back from them. It was a hundred-to-one pop anyway.

I GAVE myself little hope of getting picked in the pre-season draft, but wanted to explore every last possibility. Dad said he thought the best bloke to ring was Kevin Sheedy. As it happened, Sheedy was in Perth. On the phone, he said he wouldn't help until he'd seen me eyeball to eyeball, probably having heard as many rumours about me as the next person.

We met at his hotel for coffee, and I told him in no uncertain terms how desperate I was to play. He, more than anyone else to this point, seemed really keen to help. There were so many reasons reported in the media why I shouldn't get picked up. He was the first person to publicly turn the tables and focus on the reasons why I should. He's an influential man in football, and when he speaks people listen.

Someone else who then stepped in and matched Sheedy's amazing support was even less likely. Gerard Healy had been very critical in public of my indiscretions. But he, like Sheedy, saw that I still had something to offer. Between the two of them, they began a campaign to get me to Richmond. Very quickly it generated huge support from the average football follower. On top of this, Healy's continual advice would become increasingly valuable to me in the months and years that followed.

Even so, I didn't think I'd be chosen in the pre-season draft. If I wasn't picked up, part of me was saying I'd never play again, but another part was thinking about playing in the WAFL. I didn't want to walk away from the game the way I had in 2007. Tearing my hamstring against Port Adelaide, then Mainy's death and my arrest, shouldn't be my sign-off from the game. It wasn't right. I owed myself more.

I thought I might play the first five or six rounds of the WAFL season. I wasn't too big to play WAFL. I could still go back and enjoy footy at that level, with Perth or East Fremantle. It would be football in its purest form. One more great season in the AFL wasn't going to complete me as a person. I didn't need it. Playing a handful of games in the WAFL would allow me a last chance to savour the game I still loved. I didn't want to retire. 'Never again' is a long time. Now was the first time the reality of those words set in.

So BY the time the pre-season draft came around, I didn't have the same anxiety and fear as in the national draft. I'd done my mourning. I was more fatalistic now. If it didn't happen, it didn't happen.

I didn't watch the draft or follow it on the internet. When the call came, it was hard to credit. I'd been the very last player chosen, in the last draft: that was indicative of my year. I was now a Tiger.

My immediate reaction was: *Be careful what you wish for!* Without any stability in my life, unable to look too far ahead, in a precarious, vulnerable, depressed state, I was terrified. The fear of getting on a plane, leaving my life behind, leaving my mates behind, leaving my family behind, everyone scrutinising every single thing I did, was hellish. I'd had the confidence knocked out of me by the national draft. I'd been questioning whether I was a good person. Was I malicious? I had to question so many things, because the world was telling me I was no good. When I was seventeen, I'd been relieved at not crossing the country to play for the team I loved, the Cats. Now, at thirty, I was crossing the country to be a Tiger. And I was nervous as a kitten.

The day after the draft, I flew to Melbourne. I owed Richmond a huge debt. When all fifteen other clubs had spurned me, they'd had the compassion to give me a second chance.

From the moment I arrived, I felt I was adding to my debt. When I got to Tullamarine and went to my first session at Punt Road the day after, it was like I'd brought the circus to town. There were media everywhere, experts commenting on how my presence would help or hurt the Tigers, and everyone from the Victorian premier John Brumby down voicing an opinion about me.

It wasn't the best circumstance in which to be meeting young players. The coach, Terry Wallace, came over with the three senior guys, Matthew Richardson, Nathan Brown and Joel Bowden, to say g'day and help me through the first few minutes. I went into the rooms and grabbed a number 32 training jersey – it was the last number left – and jogged out for the 9 am training session. Two thousand people were there, and every time I kicked the ball they cheered. I couldn't have been more nervous, yet these people wanted to show me that they would take me into their hearts, no questions asked.

My first training session coincided with a press conference and a media pack the size of which only I was accustomed to. I was open to questions, and answered freely, flanked by the newly-appointed captain, Chris Newman, and vice-captain Nathan 'Axel' Foley, who must have been wondering what they'd got themselves into. I would later find out that Chris and the playing group had taken a significant role in getting me to Richmond.

I stayed for three or four days to train before Christmas. It felt strange to be in new colours, and even though I wasn't the average recruit rocking up for his first session, I felt as shy as a debutant. I'm a shy person anyway, and went through those first sessions concentrating on kicking, catching and hand-passing as fiercely as when I'd entered Subiaco to train with the Eagles as a teenager.

While I went through the drills, I was hyper-conscious of how the other players were taking it all. As a young squad, it would have been hard for them to know what to say to me. I didn't know what to say to them. I couldn't slip into the relaxed state I'd been in during my best years at the Eagles, so I just kept my head down and focused on trying to rebuild my footy game from the ground up. I didn't want to hear the sound of my own voice, I didn't want to step in and impose my ideas on the club, I didn't want to lead. I just wanted to earn their respect. I was worried that the Richmond boys would think I was being aloof, but there was nothing I could do about it, not straightaway in any case.

The situation, so far out of my comfort zone, brought home to me how severely I'd knocked myself around in the last few years.

After those initial sessions, I flew back to Perth for Christmas and New Year. Even that was tough. I wanted to run away from everything. My fall from grace was really hitting me now. It took every ounce of determination to get back on the plane in January and start my new life. While the year I'd had off was supposed to heal me, it had left me feeling more vulnerable than ever. Which might have been the only way to really teach me my lesson.

From mid-January, random hair and urine tests started. That was okay by me. I knew I was one slip-up from the end, but I also knew how susceptible I was to temptation. The thought of drugs was never far away. But as I couldn't entertain any plans about beating a random drug-testing system, I was able to keep those thoughts at arm's length. So much of my drug-using life had been about planning, that to take that aspect of it away from me was one of the best deterrents.

But because it was hard, I started to feel it was good for me. Everything about this experience that unsettled me – new routines, new people, new club – I attacked as a new obstacle in life's commando course.

One area in which I had to restrain myself was in dealing with the media. I felt I was able to accept responsibility for what I'd done, but the press went for the man. What I saw in the papers wasn't a balanced view of a young guy that got mixed up with drugs; a lot of it missed the point, and often got quite personal.

There were times when I got agitated and angry, especially when I was talking with Dad. I'd say things out of anger, almost to get a response.

I had reason to explode, but Dad played me cleverly, reminding me that that was exactly what they wanted. It wasn't dissimilar to the way he'd taught me about temperament in a game, and not falling into the trap of overreacting to what a heavy opposition tag was trying to do.

Having lost faith in the media, I chose to play footy, and not speak, hoping that one day my story would be about footy again. I suppose that let them make their own interpretation of why I did things.

On reflection, I think this approach to the media made my life more difficult. By not making myself accessible, and appearing aloof, I only added to the intrigue and mystique, which fuelled further scrutiny. My issues weren't being humanised.

In those first weeks, I was desperate for the attention to move away from me. But it lingered. The news was either good – Richmond's membership numbers rose steeply after my recruitment – or it was bad – Tommy Hafey said I didn't deserve another chance – but either way, too much of it was about me. I spoke a lot with Wallace about integrating myself within the group, finding strength in the team, hanging out with the boys. As always, I identified most with the young kids. I wanted to know who had come from the country, who was just out of school, who needed a bit of a friendly word from an older bloke. I just wanted to lose myself in the group.

Gradually I unwound a little bit, making jokes about myself being drug-fucked. I wasn't glorifying my mistakes, but wanted the young blokes to feel comfortable around me. I've always been able to laugh at myself, and thought this might help break down barriers. But it didn't hit the right note with everybody. Wayne Campbell, the former top-line Richmond midfielder who was now an assistant coach, took me aside and said, 'I love the humour in it, it's great, but sometimes people might not know how to take it. It's all right making jokes about it with Richo or the older guys, but the young blokes may not know how to take it.'

I saw what he meant, but told him I was trying to put an end to the feeling that everyone was walking on eggshells. When I put it like that, he agreed.

What we all needed was for the footy to start. I had my first game for Richmond in the pre-season cup on 26 February 2009, against Collingwood. Sophie and Carol came over to watch. I felt good on the ground, moving well and getting a few touches. It was strange but gratifying when the instincts kicked in. Just as I was getting comfortable, though, just before three-quarter time I banged my head on the ground and was taken off.

A little later, I was sent back on but didn't know what position to go to. A runner came out and took me off again. I was vomiting and disoriented.

'You all right, mate?' Nathan Brown said.

'Is this my first game for Richmond?'

'Yeah.'

During the last quarter I asked him that question fifteen times. I didn't know how I'd ended up at Richmond. I didn't know I'd been to rehab. I didn't know I was a drug addict. I was swimming in confusion. During the car trip back to my place after the game, I kept repeating the same questions over and over, unable to remember from one minute to the next. When we got home, I was asking why Maylea wasn't there. I'd forgotten she was in Perth. Then I'd ask again where she was.

'You know you've just come back to football after a year off,' Carol said.

'What?'

'You know, a year off football, you've been to rehab. You're a drug addict.'

'A drug addict!'

I couldn't remember a thing.

'You remember, Ben, it was a tough year. Remember Mainy died?'

That was like a hand grenade. I was distraught, like I'd never heard this terrible news until now.

'Mainy died?' I was overwhelmed with grief. 'How did he die? Was I there?'

They told me what had happened.

'Poor Rarn,' I kept saying. 'Poor Rarn.'

Carol felt guilty, afterwards, that she'd brought that up. At 3 am they took me to Epworth Hospital for a CAT scan, and I was hazy for several more days from the concussion. There are so many ways you can damage yourself, I thought in a moment of clarity, it's really not worth adding to them by taking drugs.

Melbourne held constant reminders of the loss of my mate Johnny G, and how much I'd have loved him around. Here I was, in the hospital where he'd passed away. Since then, I'd got up and moved to Melbourne. He'd got up and moved to a better place. I lay in the hospital and thought: *God bless my friend.*

38

TIGERLAND

A warm Thursday night in autumn, nearly 90,000 in the MCG. Outside of grand finals, it was the biggest football crowd of my life. Richmond versus Carlton, traditional rivals, the country watching. I'm playing for Richmond and Juddy has moved from West Coast to Carlton. If I stopped to think of how surreal this was, I'd go mad.

I can't begin to describe my emotions about playing again. Most of all, I was just trying to tighten the screws and keep them tight: contribute to the game plan, observe the basics, enjoy it as much as possible. Shut out what a massive test of nerve and character this would be.

Round one of the 2009 season was the night I became an AFL football player again. But I'd had a short pre-season, due to being drafted late, and knew I wasn't anywhere near 100 per cent. Juddy was on fire for Carlton, and we were seven goals down by half time, ten by three-quarter time. We were looking at a blow-out.

The bottled-up emotions started to escape in the last quarter. My right hamstring had felt tight earlier in the game, but I was soldiering on until I turned sharply and felt a flash of pain. There's no mistaking a torn hamstring. You're gone. I hobbled off, wondering if I wasn't just gone, but *gone*. Was this it? After all that effort, was it going to end like this? I knew life didn't work like in fairytales, but I deserved more than this. Or maybe not. Maybe I deserved less.

It was immediately clear that I'd be out for several weeks. I got home, lay on the couch, dosed myself with too many painkillers, and iced my leg.

This hamstring injury was a huge setback and challenge. But it would prove to be the best thing that could have happened. I had no choice but to dust myself off and commit to my recovery at the club. Everyone knew the scrutiny I was under, and by not dropping my head and feeling sorry for myself I'd show people at Richmond that it was about more than just me. A certain pressure lifted as I worked my way through my rehab. I played one game at Coburg, a VFL affiliate side, with several young players. This was not only good for my preparation but also to get together with the up-and-coming brigade, and show I wasn't above it.

Most of the Richmond list had had no prior contact with me, and only went on what they read in the papers. This hamstring was a frustration, but it gave me the opportunity to earn the players' respect and remind myself that how I would assess this year would not be about how many kicks or hand passes I had or how many good games, but rather how I would overcome adversity.

The ups and downs have always been extreme. That has many negatives, but the positive is that after a heavy crash I've been able to bounce back off the rocky bottom I've hit. The injury was an opportunity to fine-tune my training, concentrate on core stability, see a chiropractor for my back, treat my body as a thirty-year-old's, not a twenty-year-old's.

Finally, I was learning to listen.

This was the kind of setback that could have pitched me into the self-recriminations that only lead to one place; but I managed to cope. I went to my appointments and did my exercises and kept my mind occupied. I talked a lot with Carol and with Gardy, and Maylea came over from Perth to stay, sometimes with her two children, and I got through those crucial weeks without mishap.

I played proudly for Coburg, in ten-minute bursts, and made it back into the Richmond seniors for round seven against Brisbane. I got through that, but the following week, against Port Adelaide, in the first minute of the game I felt a crunch in my left hand. No doubt, it was bad. On the plane home I growled, 'I wouldn't care if this fucking plane fell out of the sky.'

'Cuz, you can't say that,' someone said, reminding me, again, that the world didn't revolve around me. It was just that when my pain and frustration were this acute, I couldn't see beyond myself.

X-rays in Melbourne showed I had a broken bone – six weeks out. Yet again, my closest friends such as Maze, Carol, Gardy and Tim Smith were worried about the kinds of thoughts it might set in motion. But I had an operation two days later and a plate was inserted, and amazingly I was only going to miss one game.

It was tough playing in a losing side, and Terry Wallace stepped down that week after nearly five years with the club. He'd put his soul into Richmond, and I owed him a massive personal debt. Without his faith, I wouldn't have had a chance to earn back some of the respect and credibility I'd thrown away.

Being new at Punt Road, I didn't understand the politics at the club, and was thankful that my hand operation that week kept me away. I followed developments on TV like the rest of the public.

From the outside, it looked like it was getting messy. I felt so indebted to Terry that seeing his troubles made me feel awkward.

We couldn't lift ourselves enough for him in his last game, against the Bulldogs, the previous team he'd coached, and went down by eleven goals. Later, I made a point of going up to him and thanking him personally.

One of his assistants, Jade Rawlings, stepped into the breach as caretaker coach for the rest of the season. As luck had it, our first game under Rawlings was at Docklands against West Coast. I was more anxious before that than I was for most games. Luckily, it wasn't in Perth. My feelings during the game, I can tell you, were strange. My confusion was evident in the fact that once, when I was asked to take a break, I ran off to the Eagles' bench. There were more familiar faces there than in my own club. When one of the West Coast trainers ran out with a water bottle, I asked him for a drink.

'Fuck me, I did enough for you when I was there, didn't I?' I said with a cheeky grin, to see his reaction.

'Yeah, I'll give you a drink,' he smiled.

FOR THE rest of that season, I was re-learning how to be a footballer and a functional human being. As a footballer, I was coming to grips with a different role. I wasn't one of the best players at Richmond, so for the first time since 1997 I wasn't being tagged. That gave me the chance to impart some knowledge I'd learnt at West Coast. I paid a lot more attention to blocking, bringing other blokes into the game and taking the selfless option to free up the team's spearheads. Nathan Foley and Brett Deledio, who were being tagged heavily, needed help from support players like me. I began to assert myself in team meetings, saying that we had to make a statement to our opponents about how we protected and got the ball to the Foleys and Deledios, how we'd make life tough for their taggers. Steadily the blokes began to understand who I really was. I wasn't a rock star. I wasn't any kind of star. I was a bloke who loved playing in a team, and I didn't care what role I took, I simply loved the way a team can come together for a common goal. That's what had always driven me in football. The rest is bullshit.

On the subject of bullshit, no season would be complete without a bit of it. When we played Fremantle in Perth, my first game back in my hometown, I flipped the bird at a camera in the changing room, thinking it was a private joke between me and whatever bloke was in the outside broadcast van. Instead it went on national television and I copped the usual. People jumped to the conclusion that I chose the Perth match to do it, and somehow directed the gesture as a *Fuck-off* to West Australians, or the Eagles. It was cheeky and careless, but nothing more. I thought I'd had an audience of one. But I received a $10,000 fine and made an apology. It was another instance of me acting without thinking, yet another reminder that I wasn't a carefree kid anymore.

Perth wasn't an easy place to be. When I went out to eat with the family, they noticed me shrinking into my seat to avoid attention. It also brought home to me how hard everything had been on Mum and Dad's marriage. As I learned about that, I had to take on the burden of guilt and somehow make reparations.

Still, they were most concerned about me. When we were in Perth, Dad reminded me of the advice Johnny G had given me on his deathbed.

'You've got to learn to stop and smell the roses,' he said. 'You go too fast. You're always moving around, always on that bloody mobile. Put it down. Watch a movie. Go for a walk, go for a coffee, turn your phone off. You're like a cat on a hot tin roof.'

'I feel like I'm a rabbit caught in the headlights,' I said.

'Mate, that's right, but you're 50 per cent responsible for it yourself.'

No-one's ever known me as well as my family, and I needed them over in Melbourne as much as was feasible. Mel came over to stay with me on my birthday, but when I dropped her at the airport, she looked back at me with a tear in her eye. She said I looked so sad. She didn't want me to go back to my house on my own. Later, she called to make sure I was all right, that I had friends to get me through these spaces of sadness. It showed, for the millionth time, what a loyal and thoughtful sister she is.

IN MANY ways 2009 was as tough a season as the Ken Judge years at West Coast, with our team at the bottom of the ladder and instability around the coaching. But something else was growing. I found that I loved confronting the struggle. Losing football was my new foe. I began to seek the positives and magnify them. I told players how much I thrived on their best qualities: Daniel Jackson's tirelessness, Chris Newman's leadership, Nathan Foley's courage and skill. I walked as tall with them beside me as I did with the bigger names at West Coast, and with my mates at Wesley College. Once they understood that, I began to feel part of this team.

Living in Melbourne also brought its rewards. I rented a house in a quiet bayside suburb and relished the anonymity. Perth had become a fishbowl. In Melbourne, even if people recognised me they had the good grace to leave me in peace a bit more. I had good people around me. Whether I was cooking at home with Maze, meeting Gardy at a café for lunch, or heading into the city for Vietnamese noodles with Tim Smith, I felt safe there.

The drug testing was also an easy thing to get through, because my days of cat and mouse were over. When I went to the testers, I said cheerfully, 'Test me tomorrow, test me the day after, hair test me as often as you like, I've got nothing to hide.' What freedom that was. It was only six months of being drug-free, but after twelve years of using, it was a big, big thing.

That freedom even brought back the humour. One smart-arse opponent sledged me about it, saying: 'You've ruined it for the rest of us. Now we can't get on.'

I chirped back: 'Mate, don't believe everything you hear. I'm on the gear more than I've ever been.'

Another time, in our last game before the mid-season break, an opponent said: 'Dangerous time for you this weekend, Cuz. You gunna go off?'

'Mate,' I said, 'I'm gunna crunch it harder this weekend than ever.'

If it was from over the fence, rival cheer squads having a go at me, I'd give as good as I got.

'Guys,' I'd tell them, 'I'll make any line disappear. I'll make the fifty-metre line disappear. I'm having a ball.'

Having a laugh about it was my return to normality. It did get me in hot water when, after I was ironed out by Hawthorn's Lance Franklin, I told my friends at Nova FM, Kate Langbroek and Dave Hughes, 'It used to cost me $5000 to get in a headspace like that.'

I was an easy target, but nobody laughed at me more than myself and my mates did. People could say to me: 'Cousins, you're a drug addict.' Well that's right, I am a drug addict. I'm also a drug addict who played fourteen years of good footy and won a premiership. I'm a drug addict who has a great family. I'm a drug addict who has a great circle of friends. Yeah, I am a drug addict.

You can't be oversensitive in this game.

AT THE end of the season, Richmond appointed Damien 'Dimma' Hardwick as head coach. He had been one of Mark Williams' assistants at Port, where he had finished his playing career.

I was on a one-year contract, and wanted to play on, so I was hoping like hell that Dimma would recommend I be signed up again. He and I hadn't had much to do with each other over the years, aside from that tribunal hearing when he'd generously confessed to taking a dive, but I knew him as an honest, uncompromising bloke who'd be unafraid to turn the place upside-down.

My more immediate challenge, however, was coping with the end of the season. Richmond's last game was in Perth, against the Eagles, an emotional game for me but also a risky one. My Mad Monday had traditionally turned into a Mad Three Months, and we were all nervous about what I'd do in the aftermath.

Carol was onto it. 'You need backstops here,' she said. 'You're a football player. What do footballers do at the end of the year? They go on a bender. It's a natural thing to do, but for you, Ben, it's dangerous.'

I knew what would happen. So to avoid it, I stayed in Perth and set up in advance a series of media and speaking commitments. I did a charity speaking engagement, auctioned my 2006 premiership jumper and did an interview. I spoke with radio and filled my days. And I made it through.

39

'I WANT TO LEAVE WITH SOME MATES'

Despite the hamstring, the broken hand and the concussions, my 2009 season had panned out well enough. I'd played fifteen games and was in the club's top five in the best-and-fairest. More importantly, I found that the game hadn't passed me by. I still had something to give. I revelled in the club environment, the mix of personalities and emotions, the competition. Some significant senior blokes were retiring, such as Matthew Richardson, Nathan Brown and the former captain Kane Johnson, and I hoped Richmond would appreciate a bit of experience around the place.

Fortunately, Hardwick saw it the same way, and I was offered a new one-year contract. I was dead-keen to get a more solid pre-season preparation under my belt than I had in 2009.

Just prior to Christmas I needed a couple of minor ops on my shoulder and a ligament in my hand. Afterwards, I returned to Perth to recuperate. This became a really tough period, where for one of the first times in my life I struggled to get myself up. I had some very low days and nights. Coming back in 2009 had been a big year, and now it was catching up with me. Hardwick, having inherited me from the Terry Wallace days, must have been wondering what he'd got himself into. I had frank discussions with Wayne Campbell about my footy, when he put his finger on the problem. I had to prove myself all over again for a new coach. That's hard for any footballer, but at my age, having gone through all that I had, it seemed like a bridge too far. But once Wayne put it out there, as a new challenge, it got me motivated again. Always, with me, once I could put the challenge into words and see it in front of me, I relished taking it on. What had been tough was feeling down without quite knowing why.

Hardwick had taken a chance with me, and I wanted to repay that. It became paramount to earn his respect. But then, in the lead-up to the season, I was hospitalised twice in one week with a stomach complaint. We would never find out exactly what the problem was, but I had a history of stomach ulcers from years of taking anti-inflammatories at West Coast.

So at the beginning of the 2010 season I was again behind the eight-ball, less fit than I wanted to be and a bit frustrated. Our young team could not win a game, and plenty of critics were suggesting we'd go through the whole year winless. Dimma set out his blueprint of how he wanted Richmond to play. For someone who had been around footy a long time, I was surprised at how different it was from anything I'd been part of. For as long as I could remember, football had always been about how you made decisions when you were attacking. But now, team defence – techniques of how to cohere as a team when the opposition had the ball – was where the game was evolving. Dimma could only introduce this mindset incrementally, and we would have to appear to go backwards before we went forwards. Most kids coming through the draft had got into the AFL due to what they did with the ball; Dimma was teaching them what to do when they didn't have it. To his credit, he never wavered in his belief in what he was implementing, and the players bought into it.

I broke my ribs in one of the early matches, and missed a couple of weeks. I returned in the match against the Swans in Sydney, and we were flogged again.

I was arriving at another crossroads. In my first year at Richmond, I'd never have been described as being very social among the players. I enjoyed their company, but I'd had the confidence knocked out of me socially. More than that, I didn't want to be involved in anything that could be seen as not respecting the footy club. So I generally steered clear of any socialising. The players might have seen it differently, though. They had no idea what I'd been through, and I wouldn't have been surprised if they saw me as stand-offish.

Early in the 2010 season, Hardwick took me aside and said: 'You've got this rock star appeal, the kids at the club look up to you. So what do you want to take out of your time with Richmond?'

I said, 'I want to leave with some mates. That's what I'd like.'

I really didn't want to be the guy nobody quite understood. So as the year developed, I let my guard down and spent a heap of time with the younger guys, of whom there were a lot at the club. One was Daniel Connors, a good bloke with a bit of dash, but who could get a bit out of hand when he was on the drink. I saw a lot in common between us – his problems were one of the reasons I liked him.

After the match in Sydney, I was in the bar at the Intercontinental having a glass of red wine with an old friend of mine. Late in the night, Dan Connors and some other players came past, and sat down with us. Until 2.30 am, we were sitting quietly talking. But when we went up to our rooms Dan, who'd taken some painkillers during the game, became a bit wild from the effects of the medication mixing with the drinks he'd had. A few of us tried to calm him down, Dan was mouthing off, we exchanged words, and I ended up whacking him. Just a tap on his chin. Then he calmed down and we all went to bed.

The next morning, he thanked me for slowing him down, and we didn't think anything of it. But by the time we were at training back in Melbourne, it had become a huge deal, and I was called into a circle meeting. As Gardy and I always said, anything with a circle is bad news.

There had been a number of incidents with Dan. We went around the room and people were not backward in coming forward. He got an eight-week suspension, which shocked me, and later that afternoon I was called in with Dean Polo and Luke McGuane and given a one-week suspension for my part. I was dirty, but wasn't going to moan about it. Then I started thinking about it, and got more and more agitated.

I went to Craig Cameron, the football manager, who asked if I was all right. I said there had been so much innuendo about me, this one-week ban was going to light another fire about me and drink and drugs. I'd been trying for a year and a half to renew my standing in the community and build a platform for my life after footy, and this ban was undermining it.

'Go and speak to the match committee,' Craig said.

I knocked on the door and spoke to them about my fear that this would be seen as an alcohol-fuelled incident about me. Which it wasn't. They heard me out but didn't change their decision. I was still suspended for a match.

At that point, I sat down and reset myself for the rest of the season. I spoke to Dan Connors several times that week. I'd been where he was, and told him he could use this as a tool to come back better.

'This gives you a wonderful opportunity to show some character,' I said. 'You've copped a fair whack and then some. People will call you and say, 'Eight weeks, that's a bit harsh!' The club wants to see how you react, if you give in to the unfairness of it or screw your guts up and fight hard. Let me tell you, mate, in these eight weeks with Coburg, everyone will be watching you, wondering how you're going to react. What a great chance to show some resolve and then come back strong.'

As the eight weeks went past, I spoke to him regularly about using these tough times to motivate himself. I counselled him to avoid giving media interviews, which would lure him into one-liners about being a changed person. 'That's all bullshit,' I said. 'You've got a chance to set yourself up to play ten years of good footy, so don't start talking about what you've achieved in two weeks. Show the coaches you're fair dinkum. You've almost got an advantage over everyone, because you've got no choice.'

I could tell he listened to everything I said, and as the season went on he really did prove himself. I got enormous satisfaction out of helping blokes in this way. As for the punch, there wasn't a hell of a lot in it. A whack on the mouth was a whack on the mouth, just a normal part of growing up. Dan Connors was like me at that teenage party at Cottesloe all those years ago, giving lip and discovering that you're not untouchable. It's a good lesson, and although it caused us some grief at the time, it was worthwhile for both of us.

40

ONE BAD GAME AWAY

By May 2010, I had to confront the possibility that I wasn't going to make it through the season. The broken ribs were bothering me, I wasn't playing well, and incidents like the one in Sydney were prompting people to ask questions about whether I was now drinking in the way I used to take drugs.

Wayne Campbell, who'd become a confidant for me at Richmond, called me into the club and wrote on a whiteboard the numbers one to seventeen.

'What does that mean to you?' he said.

I understood. 'Seventeen rounds to go.'

'Yeah, probably seventeen rounds in your career,' he said.

'You're probably right.'

'Well, instead of doing what you're doing, which is cruising along and just trying to last out those seventeen rounds, why not try something different? You've been one of the great all-time players. Why not go out as a great player? James Hird won Essendon's best-and-fairest in his last year, when his team didn't make the finals. Why don't you try and do the same? If you're drinking piss after games, it might mean you do a hamstring and don't get up for the next game. It might make a real difference to the rest of your career.'

I went home and thought about it, then texted him: *Fuck ya, I won't drink for a month.*

I stuck with it, making a statement by not drinking, for more than just the next month. Having some beers and a laugh after a game would be fine, but I found that I'd rather wake up fresh and give myself a good chance. Every match was precious now, each one might be my last, and I had to treat them all with due respect.

But at thirty-one, it was a real battle. By the middle of May I was worried that my nightmare scenario was coming true. Still feeling my ribs, I came back against Essendon and played poorly in another loss, Richmond's thirteenth in a row. After the match, while I was driving home I texted Cambo.

These are the times, I wrote, *when I'd love the company of a bottle of vodka.*

I was only referring to his challenge. I had no intention of faltering. In fact the feeling of being sharper, more alert, was steadily coming back to me and I was enjoying it. I was just frustratingly unable to show the benefits on the field.

Concerned that I was actually going to fall off the wagon, Cambo called me straight away.

'Fucking shithouse,' I said, without needing to be asked what I thought of my game.

'Yes, you were.' I always appreciated his frankness. Then he paused and said: 'Have you weakened yet?'

'No, but I want to have a bottle of vodka and when it's finished smash it over my head and then have another one.'

'I know how you feel,' he said.

'But I'm not going to,' I said. 'I'm not going to.'

I owed Richmond more than that. Finally, after all these years, my own compulsions were being balanced out by the debts I owed to others. Richmond had given me so much, and there were only a certain number of ways I could pay them back. One was to get myself right on the field and play some good footy. Another was to contribute whatever experience I could to the development of their young team. But more than those, I felt that my biggest obligation was to save them from the public pressure to drop me.

I'd been around long enough to know how it went: the murmurs start after a few off games, the questions get asked, and before you're really aware you have a problem your club is suffering a whole lot of angst about whether they should force your retirement or not. That very week, we were going to Adelaide where Tyson Edwards, the Crows' 320-game stalwart, and his club were under this very kind of pressure. Edwards was a guy I admired a lot for the way he'd played. He was about to retire, and it was messier than it should have been. It almost always is. On top of that, Troy Simmonds was retiring from Richmond and preparing himself to play his last game. Two long, distinguished careers – gone, just like that.

Was I next? The game was moving so fast, I didn't want to wake up one day and realise it had already flown past me.

In the days after that Essendon game, a lot of thoughts were chasing each other around inside my head. Sure, I wanted to leave football on my own terms, especially after everything that had happened. But I had no God-given right to expect that. Just as I hadn't had the right to dictate what club I'd go to in 2009, I couldn't dictate my terms of retirement. That was another privilege I'd blown. Very few people in sport get to go out on their own terms. Why should I?

I just desperately wanted to avoid putting a burden on the footy club. I was thinking, *If they drop me I'm not going to take it too personally. I'll just accept things. Richmond has been worth its weight in gold to me. So I'll keep my ears open and make sure I retire before I become a liability.*

Early in the week, Cambo called me into his office. I sat down, and he said: 'Match committee this afternoon. What do you reckon?'

Christ, I thought. *This is it.*

I sort of laughed. 'What do you mean, what do I reckon?'

Cambo shrugged and said: 'The consensus is, we might give you a couple of games to see if you gradually get better.'

I didn't know how I felt, having it laid out on the table like that. Relief – *They're not going to drop me today* – competed with anxiety: *Can I get it together in two weeks?*

'Well, that sounds better than the other option,' I said.

'Anyway, that's what I think the committee will come up with,' he said.

I took it as a heads-up, a compassionate warning. I was on two weeks' notice. It was 1997 when I had last been this close to being dropped, on form, from a football team. Back then my place at West Coast had only been saved because Andy Lovell was at the end of a career and I was at the beginning. There was a certain irony in the memory: was I now keeping some promising youngster out of the team? Was I clogging up the works?

In the middle of the week, as we trained for the match against Port and prepared to fly to Adelaide, I kept mulling it over. At least now, after all the negative things that had happened to me, I could accept being dropped. It didn't seem such a huge thing by comparison with the rest of the strife I'd been in. And to be honest, one of the ways in which I'd driven myself during my best years was to put myself in a permanent state of insecurity, almost telling myself that I was no better than my last game.

But in my West Coast years it was a manufactured mindset, all part of the squirrel-wheel I'd been in, caught in the contradictions between my two lives. This time it was real – for the first time in twelve years.

I rang the old man, who was a little more upbeat than I was.

'I'm really under the pump,' I said.

Dad was quiet for a while before saying: 'You can fight your way out of this. You've had your back against the wall before . . .'

And had always fought back. Had I? I felt that I had. This was another bad situation for me, but as always, there was a part of me that ate it up. The worse the odds were, the harder I could pit myself against them. Dad was right. All I could do was play football, compete my best, and fight like I always had.

'I've always backed you in these situations,' he said calmly, like I was a horse he'd had some good luck on and was worth sticking with.

In training, I committed myself to extra work. I paired off with Andrew Collins, a young country boy trying to make his way at the Tigers. He was an absolute trier, a guy who'd do everything he could for a chance at an AFL career. I'd always loved blokes like that, whether they make it or not, and got as much joy playing with them as I had with superstars like a Peter Matera or a Chris Mainwaring. Guys like Andy Collins, in their way, have fewer chinks in their armour than I have. They're strong right through to the core, and I love that strength. I could draw something from it, and I wanted to give something to him, some kind of benefit of my experience, whatever it might be. Only in the last few months had I been realising how much young guys like Andy looked up to me for leadership. I just hoped I hadn't left it too late.

As we kicked the ball to each other, I could see the symmetries. He'd been out of the side the week before, and I was on the ropes. We were both one bad game away from playing in the suburbs, or not playing at all. At the opposite ends of our careers, you might have thought we had less in common than any two footballers; but we were both in the same predicament, going into the Port Adelaide game with the same hunger. I didn't put it to him in as many words, but we both knew where we were at. There was no need to say anything.

ONE OF the things I did before we left for Adelaide was to check the weather forecast. My iPhone told me Adelaide was going to be dry on the weekend, so I packed two pairs of moulded boots and no long-stops.

Sure enough, there was an absolute deluge when we arrived. By the time we were doing our warm-ups at AAMI Stadium, the place was half underwater. It didn't look muddy, and it wasn't muddy as such: there was just a 5-centimetre sheet of water coating the entire ground. The ball wouldn't bounce, it just splashed and skidded. On top of that, an icy wind started blowing. It was just about the worst conditions I'd experienced in 250-plus games – and it could be my last. Great. I hate playing in the rain, *hate* it. But I'd never been able to say that, for all the obvious reasons. So I was trying to pretend, again, that I was relishing it.

Inside, though, I was starting to panic. I did the warm-up in my sneakers, and it was that wet I could barely break out of a walk. I began looking around at the other blokes, and went through the team, as casually as I could manage, asking if they were wearing long-stops or moulds.

'You wearing moulds, mate?'

'No way.'

'You wearing moulds?'

Someone looked at me funny, as if only a lunatic would think of wearing anything but long-stops. The ghost of Malthouse came back. *You wear moulds, that's your choice, but the moment you slip I'll be on you like a curse.* In my first game, fourteen years before, I'd broken a Malthouse commandment and concealed an injury. Now, in what could be my last, I was breaking another.

Soon I gave up trying to find strength in numbers. Richard Tambling said he was wearing moulds, but he was the only one. He did it because his feet hated long-stops, couldn't handle them. I was wearing moulds through sheer lack of professionalism. And in what might be my most crucial game, the last game of all. Damn. Fourteen seasons as a professional footballer, and I was making a mistake you wouldn't expect from a first-gamer.

When we went back into the rooms, Troy Simmonds got up and spoke. He wasn't playing that day, but would make his farewell the following week, against St Kilda in Melbourne.

'The thing I'll miss most,' he said, 'is that half-hour after the siren goes, when you've won. That feeling . . . *that's* why you play the game.'

I knew what he meant, but looking around the rooms, I could see half a dozen kids who didn't. Guys who had yet to taste that pure joy he was talking about.

We charged onto the field knowing at least one factor was in our favour. Shocking conditions, heavy surface water and wind have a levelling effect. Such conditions maximise the effect of pure will and the basic, fundamental, gut desire to win. These we had, maybe more than any of the sixteen teams in the competition.

The rain and wind did a parallel thing for me personally. As much as I hate wet weather, I knew that it would be the best thing for me. Without any false modesty, I thought I was a good wet-weather player, particularly at this stage of my career. This day I would be assessed on my commitment. Would I give it a red-hot go?

I did, and we did. We got ahead early and kept up our intensity long after the Port players looked like they just wanted a hot shower. We ended up getting away with a forty-point win, and I handled the ball as well as anybody. The moulds didn't affect me. As it turned out, the water was so deep it wouldn't have mattered if you were in thongs. No boots could get any grip. You just skidded in there and made yourself hard at the contest. Old-fashioned, traditional football.

We belted out the 'Tigerland' song as if we'd won the flag. A ring of blokes linked arms in the centre of the circle, the guys who'd never sung the song before. I couldn't remember being so happy after a win. I was rapt for the team who'd worked so hard for it, rapt for Hardwick – his first win as an AFL coach – and rapt for the captain, Newman, who'd been carrying so much pain when we'd lost. It was a symbolic moment for this group, and for me.

Hardwick got up after the song and said: 'Now. We've got a six-day break. Nobody have a drink in that time. We can play good footy against St Kilda next week and build on what we've done here.'

For all my emotion about the symbolism of the moment, the larrikin couldn't stay in his cage for long. I leapt to my feet and cried out: 'Fuck that! Let's get our passports and head for the airport! Pointy end of the plane, head to Bali, let's celebrate properly!'

I got shut down pretty quickly, and I hoped they knew I was joking. I did get away with emptying a bottle of Powerade over the coach's head – from behind, of course.

But jokes aside, that week was a turning point in my second AFL career. I thought back to what Troy Simmonds had said before the match, and he was spot-on. There's no better feeling than that half-hour after the siren when you've won, and I still wanted it. I'd been under a lot of pressure that week, from myself most of all, and I was celebrating the release you only get in victory. People mightn't have thought I'd care that much. I'm with a struggling club, I'm at the end of my career. Why would I care? But I did, I really did.

And I'd bought myself another week.

41

MY LAST GAME AGAINST WEST COAST

After beating Port, a few more bricks went into that wall of self-belief. We lost to St Kilda but played reasonably well against one of the main premiership chances, and then had West Coast in Melbourne.

I was thinking this could be my last game against them. It still felt strange to be on the field against West Coast, even though they'd had such a huge turnover since I'd left that my only remaining ex-teammates were Dean Cox, Andrew Embley, Darren Glass and a small handful of others. A big part of me was still very West Coast.

As good a person as I ever knew there was Rod Moore, who'd played such an instrumental role in helping me when the shit hit the fan. The night before the West Coast game, I scooped him up from their hotel – we didn't want any awkward moments –

and took him to Pelicans, a tapas place at St Kilda, one of my favourite joints. I canvassed my possible retirement at the end of the year, and we talked about what I wanted to do, Rod making observations from the perspective of what would be good for my health. Then I slipped in a question about Adam Selwood, who'd been in and out of the West Coast team during the week.

'Good effort getting him right,' I said, fishing for information.

'Yeah,' Rod said. I was looking at him for signals. If we were playing cards he would have had me cold. I left the meeting believing Selwood was playing.

'I'll speak to you after the game, but only if we win,' I said.

'So will I,' Rod said.

We were old friends but competitors. That's the way I like it.

Before the match, Chris Newman asked me to address the group. I wasn't sure at first. I'd never enjoyed the profile of captaincy, and at Richmond I was very concerned not to step on anyone's toes. I hadn't achieved anything of note at this club, so I couldn't bring that authority to bear. If ever I did want to speak to the group, I asked Chris's permission. Now he was asking me, and finally I said yes, I'd speak to the boys when we put our jumpers on.

The Richmond group revolved very much around Chris, who I admired enormously. In warm-ups, when we stood in twos to kick the footy, I usually did it with Chris. In having little chats with him, I felt I could contribute. One of Chris's themes for the year was our jumper – to revere it, not let it fall on the ground, not let it get stepped on. Chris told us what an honour it was to wear it. It was our suit of armour. On game day, the jumper couldn't be allowed to touch the ground before the game, and we all put them on at the same time. I loved that; it tapped into the raw passion that fuelled me.

We were favourites for the game, which was amazing given the year we'd had.

'We've been giving ourselves pats on the back each time we've improved,' I said, 'but now we're in a game we're expected to win. That's often where you stumble, when you're expected to win. It's an exciting week, a big test to see if we can win when we are expected to. The odds will be against us, because when you're favourites you let yourself get happy – that's when it all crashes, so watch out.'

I was quite conscious that I could have been talking about my own life, not just this team's challenge for the day. At the end of my talk, I referred back to our jumper.

'Any side can get up on any given day,' I said, 'but the hardest thing is being consistent, rocking up and playing a hungry, consistent brand of footy, and that's what this jumper means.'

I started on the bench, as I usually did. It took a little bit of the edge off things. It's different these days. When I started, you were on the bench because you were the twenty-first or twenty-second bloke picked. Now it's about providing different options in the midfield. Often you can get on and have an impact before your opposition is aware of you; you can get under their guard. That worked well for me.

So I came on at the four-minute mark and enjoyed the game. It was soon evident that we were on top. I'd have a bit of a wink when an old teammate clashed with me, and it was good to know we were still friends.

Jack Riewoldt kicked ten goals that day. Earlier in the year, in the pre-season, I'd had a go at Jack after he'd kicked a great goal from the boundary against Geelong in Rye, and celebrated with the people over the boundary line. He's an exuberant bloke, and has a swagger when he's playing poorly, let alone well. I've always prided myself on never carrying on with individual celebrations. So at Rye I pulled him aside and said, 'That's not what we're about. We embarrassed ourselves last year, finished bottom of the ladder, we're playing half a side, so if you're going to do this save it for a grand final and even then be careful. You're going to be on the end of a lot of good work up the ground, so you want those blokes to know you appreciate and respect it.'

He took it on board, and through the year he was averaging six goals a game. His ten against West Coast took him a long way towards his Coleman Medal, but what pleased me more was that he remembered, with each goal, to thank the blokes up the ground who'd delivered him the ball.

After the West Coast match I went up to him and said, 'It goes without saying, awesome game, but you're also handling yourself really well, which is important in a team sport so keep it up.'

It was great to have a first home win for the season. The Richmond faithful had been amazing in their support for me. They'd suffered too. We had a bit in common.

At the end of the game, I made sure I said hello to Glenn Stewart, and had a special hug with David Jones, who'd been the head trainer's assistant at West Coast since I'd started in 1996. He got sick in 2008, but was looking better now. We both got a bit flustered with the emotion.

I saw Rod Moore after the game. Selwood hadn't played, and I shot Rod a smirk, to say: 'You got me.'

Later, I texted him: *That's one for the good guys.*

He didn't reply.

42

END OF SEASON

We went on a good run for the rest of the season, ending up with wins over Sydney – by four points after being down by thirty-three – Adelaide, Brisbane and Fremantle. We suffered some tight defeats, but when we lost, we didn't go into a downward spiral. Everyone at the club wanted to keep on getting better, and it was special to be part of that.

When the team started showing signs of improvement, few would have thought we could win five out of six. Many had predicted two winless years for us. Because we were under no illusions about where we were at, this period of the season was as enjoyable as any I have been involved in. To see the improvement in blokes around me and their enjoyment in winning games was infectious and a little magical. I've played with a lot of great leaders and footballers over the journey, and Chris Newman rates up with the best of them. He carried the burden of the team's defeats, and to captain a struggling side is no easy task. I knew that personally. However, his commitment and strength of character were respected by all, and I have no doubt he will leave a long and valuable legacy over the next five years.

But there's always a twist.

After the Sydney win, we had a six-day break before our next match. I was pretty sure by now that I'd be retiring at the end of the year, so each game was like gold. I went home on Sunday evening, watched some UFC and then the Tour de France on television. I spoke with a few friends on the phone but just had my usual wind-down, a couple of glasses of wine and a sleeping tablet before bed.

In rehab, I'd been taught not to take too much caffeine during games, because it could set me onto a cycle of over-stimulation, followed by the over-use of downers to counteract their effects, and then I could be on the gear before I knew it.

But the sleeping pills I'd been using weren't really working. There was another one I'd tried in rehab, but it gave me a terrible hangover. It was too effective, so I'd stopped using it until now, when I got a prescription to replace the usual sleepers. When I'd taken these pills in rehab in America, they'd come in a 50-milligram size and I'd taken four. This prescription, however, came in 200-milligram tablets. Automatically, I took four. So instead of taking 200 mg of the drug, I'd taken about 800 mg. It knocked me out.

The next morning, Maylea found me asleep on the couch. I'd pissed myself and was still unconscious. Unable to wake me, she called an ambulance.

Next I knew, it was 7 am and I was in hospital. I woke up in quite a good mood, almost buoyant. Apparently I'd been a bit hard to handle in intensive care, but I didn't remember that.

The hospital staff said there were a lot of people trying to get in to see me.

'Who should we let in?'

'Only the club doctor and Maylea,' I said. 'Oh, also Mickey Gardiner, he's got recovery on Mondays and it's his birthday. He might pop through, so let him in.' I didn't know it was actually Tuesday.

There wasn't anything more sinister to it than that. When I left the hospital the next day, I rang the AFL drug doctors and said I wanted to be tested. I went to Maylea's place and gave a sample. It didn't stop the rumours, of course, but I knew I'd done nothing wrong. What annoyed me most was that I couldn't play the next weekend.

When Richmond had decided to draft me, everyone knew that it was more than just a football decision. They were also taking on the media circus that had surrounded me. As tough as it was for me, it was equally hard for the club. I have to recognise the football manager, Craig Cameron, not only for his friendship but for his wrangling of that circus. I hate to think of the man-hours this required. What it also did was help me realise how easy it had been for other sides to pass on me during the draft. I'd thought they were rejecting me for my football, or my personality, when in fact they just didn't want all the distractions I brought with me.

For the rest of the season, I achieved what I'd wanted when Cambo had put up the numbers one to seventeen. I played my part in an improving team, and got a huge buzz out of seeing how good these Tigers were becoming.

I ANNOUNCED my retirement two weeks out from the end of the regular season. The decision had come to me a few weeks before, when I'd been struggling with my form and had had to face the prospect of being dropped. I'd played well since then, but in 2011 I would be a rising thirty-three-year-old, and there was every chance that injuries or the speed of the game would overtake me, and I'd be putting Richmond through a lot of grief they didn't deserve. So it was good to finish my career of my own volition.

I'd discussed my decision with Dimma, Craig Cameron and Cambo. They and the club would support whichever way I chose to go. I could have played on, but, as they pointed out, my age and the threat of injuries were among many potential issues that might lie ahead. In the end, I think it was the right decision for both the club and me.

One of the toughest tasks for any long-term player is to say goodbye to your teammates and the club's extended football support staff. I'd witnessed countless retirement speeches, and nearly always they included the words, 'Make the most of your footy career, because it goes so quickly'. Well, I can tell you they are dead right – it goes way too quickly.

I spoke to my teammates and the support staff, who I felt were my mates as well. I spoke of how when I'd arrived at Richmond, I'd brought the circus. Now, I joked, I was leaving with one as well. Opening up my emotions, I told them I was pretty banged up when I'd arrived, and it had taken a while for the guys to get used to having me around, but since then I'd fallen in love with the club. 'I'm amazed at the rapport I've been able to develop with you guys in such a short time,' I said. 'It's been an honour and a privilege to play with you guys and with this club.'

Footy is an emotional game, and that's the way I played it, but, I said, 'The thing I'll miss most is arriving on game day in anticipation of the contest, running up the race and looking over my shoulder and walking taller because of the guy next to me. This is what team spirit is all about.'

If I'd tried to squeeze out another year at thirty-three, it would probably have been for selfish reasons. I wanted to enjoy some of the success and good times I believed were headed in Richmond's direction. But my fate would be to have played my last year while the club was really building something. 'Hopefully,' I concluded, 'something special is to come.'

Dad had brought one of his horses to Melbourne for the Breeders Crown harness racing series, so he was staying with me for the last four weeks of my playing career. After everything we'd been through, I felt proud that I could share these good last days with him. It was always when I was at my lowest with my addiction and facing major crises that Dad was best with me – always calm, always balanced, always trying to look for a positive way forward. Meanwhile, when I was going well in my recovery, he became almost a nightmare, as he wanted my recovery to continue non-stop, whereas I needed to take a breather before I moved on to the next stage. But those four weeks were just great. My career could have ended on much worse terms, and the fact that I'd recovered and gone out in good style was due to the support I'd received from those closest to me, particularly when I didn't do much to deserve it. I hope that Dad, Mum and the others saw, in my retirement, the tribute I was paying them for all they had invested in me.

I know life doesn't always work out like a fairytale, but to me that was what my retirement felt like, considering where I had come from.

I was flattered by the praise I received in the media upon my retirement, but wasn't getting carried away with it. I knew better than anyone how the media tended to go to extremes. Just as I'd never been as bad a person as they'd painted me in 2007 or 2008, I wasn't as good a person as they were painting me now.

BACK IN 2007, when I'd been de-registered by the AFL, my documentary project had started out as something for me to focus on during my year off. It was a survival tool, and I hadn't known what would come of it. I invested my own money in it, paying everyone who worked on it and purchasing all my own cameras and filming gear. Khoder Nasser, Anthony Mundine's manager, had introduced me to Paul and Scott of Fifty Fifty Films, having worked with them before.

Back then, I'd thought nobody really understood what I was going through. I still feel today that it's impossible to know what a drug addict is enduring unless you've experienced it yourself. For me, I wanted to find a way of expressing it, and I'd also found that by stepping outside my self-absorption and looking at it from an external point of view, it had become something of a cathartic experience.

Making the documentary wasn't all joy for me – in fact most of it was the opposite. It was a real uphill battle to get it into a shape in which it might be of interest and benefit to people. I just wanted to tell an honest story about addiction, commit to a project outside of football, and follow it through to the end, no matter what. I wasn't naive about how it might polarise viewers and set off a new controversy, but I never doubted that it was worth doing.

After we'd been working on it for some time, I was introduced to Michael Gudinski, the entertainment businessman. Coincidentally, he had been a boyhood friend of David Grace. We discussed my documentary and where I wanted it to go, and I came away from our first meeting feeling that he was prepared to take it on. I felt he was my type of bloke. He wanted to put together a team who could turn the documentary into a finished commercial product. While I regretted that I couldn't make it that far with Scotty and Paul, it needed a Michael Gudinski's polish, not only to complete the film but to deal with a whole lot of other issues, not least making it acceptable to Richmond, the AFL and other interested parties.

Through this process, I developed a genuine friendship with Michael and his team and was staggered by the personal interest they showed in me, particularly Paul Goldman and Dean McLachlan, who became good friends.

After three years in which nothing ever seemed to go smoothly, in August 2010 it all came together. Channel Seven scheduled the documentary over two nights in the week leading up to my last game for Richmond.

I was glad for the timing, but expected it would be criticised and acknowledged in equal measure for its frankness. I always wanted it to be open and honest. If it wasn't, I was only fooling myself, and it wouldn't produce the benefits for some viewers that I was hoping for.

The documentary achieved far higher than expected ratings. After the second part, Channel Seven arranged for a panel to review and discuss it. Probably the best feeling I got through all of the time I had spent on the doco was the feedback from two panellists who were involved in drug and alcohol addiction. John Rogerson, from the Australian Drug Foundation, and Dr Michael Carr-Gregg spoke of the tremendous potential benefits the documentary would bring to them and their work. John told Dad that, following the documentary, the foundation had a 500 per cent increase in hits on their website. He felt it had brought the issue of addiction to a level of discussion and understanding that they had been trying to achieve for at least five years.

For me, that was what the documentary was all about – that and an opportunity to publicly thank my family, Carol Daws, Rod Moore and the many others who helped pull me back from where I'd gone. I nearly broke them, and that knowledge is a burden I'm going to have to carry for the rest of my life.

AFTER ANNOUNCING my retirement, my overriding emotion was relief. I'd been able to do it with dignity and, a week later, I knew I'd done the right thing for both Richmond and myself.

But there was one final hurdle. In the second last game of the season, against St Kilda, I felt like I'd done my hammy. Had I already played my last game? In the days immediately following, however, I could do a lot of the stretching and isometric exercises that would at least confirm whether or not I'd torn it.

On the Monday after the St Kilda game, I had a scan, which gave me good and bad news. I had a grade one tear, which was bad. But the good news was, the tear was in a part of the hamstring that needn't stop me from running altogether. Early in the week, I really didn't think I would get up for the game, and rang quite a few of my friends and family in Perth who'd been planning to come over for the last round, and suggested that perhaps they shouldn't bother.

It was a closing of the circle, in a way. I thought back to my first game for West Coast, when I'd been worrying all week about my strained ankle. Here I was back where I started, asking the same question: 'Will I get up for Sunday's game?'

No matter how bad the situation, though, I've always been a person to seek out the positive. I'd had a fair bit of practice. I saw that dealing with the injury could take a lot of the emotion out of the week, which was a good thing. I focused on getting my leg right, which distracted me from thinking about the enormity of my career ending. If it was any other game, I certainly wouldn't have played, but I did want to play one last game with my mates and I wanted to sing the great Richmond song one more time with the boys, with the passion we'd sung it during our wins in the second half of the season. Making it easier was that the club really wanted me to play. Dimma was at his supportive and encouraging best.

Richmond had a great medical staff, but I couldn't help ringing the two people who knew me and my body the best. Rod Moore and Bill Sutherland both gave me that extra bit of hope that I needed. Perhaps they knew how my brain worked even better than they knew how my legs worked.

The week leading up to that game really humbled me. I'd only been at Richmond for two years, but the 'Richmond Faithful' gave me a great feeling of being part of a fantastic football club. I just hoped my leg would hold up for them.

END OF SEASON

When you're a young team like us, who'd built momentum late in the season, winning the last game could give us some real impetus. We'd be playing Port Adelaide, and were slight favourites in front of a very large crowd. Port, under their new coach Matthew Primus, hammered us in the first half, and were eight goals ahead at half-time. No fairytale ending here. I played off the bench, at less than full pace, but did my best. In the third quarter we started to claw our way back, and the Richmond army of supporters gave us a huge boost. We kept chipping away at their lead, and with minutes to go we hit the front. Or not quite. We scored a goal which would have put us in the lead, only to hear the umpire's whistle indicating a free kick to Port. Our goal was disallowed, Port steadied, and my career came to an end in a close defeat.

If I'd felt humble before the game, it went to another level afterwards. The Richmond supporters gave me an extraordinary acknowledgment. As I walked off the ground with my mates, I felt so much a part of the club. I really hope I get to watch my mates play finals footy over the next few years.

43

REMORSE

I'm still working out what to do with myself next. I have been lucky to be presented with a number of opportunities, most of which are outside of football. I think I've got something to offer in the coaching department, but there's a lot of homework required, and that might get to me. But I would love to be able to mentor young players in some capacity. I think I can contribute to the development of young guys in the AFL, both from a footballing perspective and in how they deal with adversity off the field. It's just a matter of finding a role that I can perform successfully, and that doesn't put me back into the regimented structure that I've always rebelled against. My future is about permanent vigilance: how I watch out for signs of danger, and how I counteract them.

How I'm going to harness my need for adrenaline is the main thing. I want to get into running and boxing. I'd like to tackle a marathon at some stage – Dad did it in his fiftieth year, so I can't see why not. I don't want to be a guy who can't run anymore because his knees are buggered.

Beyond that, there will always be the spectre of relapse. I'm a drug addict. It's never behind you. But the most lasting benefit from my trouble has been the self-knowledge that came with it. It was hard-earned, but I do understand myself better than I would have if I'd never come down so hard. I missed the end of childhood and the start of adulthood. I was in a fishbowl town and was crying out for anonymity. But all the little perks that came with the fame, I didn't want to give them up either. They came at a huge price. I paid it.

For all those years, I was rarely able to get into the habit of doing absolutely nothing, just being. To be: that's the hardest thing for me to learn. I didn't understand that until everything fell apart, and even now I'm still working towards it. It's still hard to hang on, but it's getting a little easier. I don't know if I could get into that obsessive state again: the two obsessions, the double lives. I hope not. Maybe that's the best part of getting older, losing that obsessive streak.

I'm often asked how much remorse I feel for what I did. It's a complicated question. When I think about how my actions affected my parents, my family, my closest friends, and West Coast and its supporters, I don't think remorse is a strong enough word. Guilt, shame, embarrassment, regret, sorrow – I feel all of those emotions, and always will. The rest of my life will, at some level, be an apology to those I loved and hurt.

Towards the great game of Australian football, I feel like we've been through a rough ride together, but we're at peace with each other now. West Coast was a great club for me, and although I underwent a period of feeling very angry towards the hierarchy at the club – never the players or the coaching staff – I can see now that my actions were a rude awakening for the Eagles and I can now understand much better their reaction to my behaviour and the perceived need for them to act as they did. We were moving into a new world, that nobody knew how to deal with, so of course there were going to be bumps. Similarly with the AFL. In 2008 there were times when I hated the league and felt that it just wanted to be rid of me. As with so many other things, though, time has proved the cure. With time, I've been able to figure out that there was some plan in there, some way to help a young man's struggle towards health, some path forward. I hope that dealing with me has left the AFL with a greater knowledge of the illness of drug addiction.

Of course, I'd never have been able to redeem myself as a footballer without the Richmond Football Club and the great people who work for it on and off the field. I owe Richmond for life. When Richmond picked me up, I was busted up in every way. I might have survived, but I wouldn't have had two seasons of being able to rebuild my name as a footballer. I had no right to that. Richmond gifted it to me.

Remorse? Not only is it too simple a word, but I am not one to walk around wringing my hands and moaning that everything I did was wrong. I know how much was wrong, but I can't disown all the good that was mixed in with the bad. As is probably obvious by now, I love people. Those people don't include just my family, my staunch friends and the great players, coaches and staff I've known through football, but also a lot of the people I used drugs with. I can't run away from the fact that there were true and lasting friendships that were forged in some part with the help of chemicals. If I look back on some of my drug-using days with fondness, it's because of those mates. The drugs themselves lost interest for me. Life became too busy, and the drug experiences became boring and repetitive, not to mention destructive. I have no nostalgia for drugs. The friends, however, remain my friends, and the memories remain my memories.

So remorse is too one-dimensional a word. It's also too familiar to the drug addict, who feels remorse continually. Remorse is as much a part of the cycle as everything else. Life is too complicated for me to just say I'm remorseful without all the other things I also have to say that go with it. Remorse only goes so far without actions to back it up.

Our good family friend Bill Mitchell once said that, having received so much, I needed to understand the joys of giving. As a retired footballer, that's what I want to develop. I received more than I ever expected from the game of football. From family and friends, from West Coast, Richmond, loyal football supporters and the public at large, I received more love and support than so many others have. I was lucky. From here, I want to give back, and keep on remembering the words of Johnny G: take the pace off things. If there's to be one benefit from all I've experienced, it's to learn something from it and use what I've learnt to help someone else, maybe to help them avoid making the same mistakes, maybe to inspire them to do good, or maybe just to show them that there's someone else in this world who's been through it all too.